The Private Passions of
BONNIE PRINCE
CHARLIE

To Wendy Glavis and Clive Burton
with grateful thanks

The Private Passions of
BONNIE PRINCE
CHARLIE

HUGH DOUGLAS

SUTTON PUBLISHING

First published in the United Kingdom in 1995 as *Bonnie Prince
Charlie in Love* by Alan Sutton Publishing Ltd,
an imprint of Sutton Publishing Limited
Phoenix Mill · Thrupp · Stroud · Gloucestershire GL:5 2BU

This revised paperback edition first published in 1998 by
Sutton Publishing Limited

A catalogue record for this book is available from the British Library

ISBN 0 7509 1902 7

 ^{TM} ALAN SUTTON^{TM} and SUTTON^{TM} are the
trade marks of Sutton Publishing Limited

Typeset in 10/14pt Photina.
Typesetting and origination by
Sutton Publishing Limited.
Printed in Great Britain by
The Guernsey Press Company Limited,
Guernsey, Channel Islands.

CONTENTS

LIST OF ILLUSTRATIONS

Between pages 176 & 177

Letters (illustrations Nos 3 and 11) are from the Royal Archives at Windsor Castle and are reproduced by gracious permission of Her Majesty The Queen. Other illustrations have been supplied by and are reproduced by kind permission of the following: National Gallery of Ireland (1, 2), Aberdeen University Library (5), National Galleries of Scotland (6, 8, 14, 15, 16), Derby Museum and Art Gallery (4), Walker Art Gallery, National Museums and Galleries on Merseyside (9), Bibliothèque Nationale, Paris (10, 13), Bastille Archives, Musée de l'Arsenal, Paris (12), Alan Morrison (7).

PREFACE

Ce n'est pas des amis qu'il vous faut, mais des victimes.[1]

Bonnie Prince Charlie's love life stormed across Europe: from Italy, where he was born, to Scotland, France, Flanders, Germany, Spain, Switzerland and back to Italy where he died. And, if one includes those countries where he had brief matrimonial hopes, Poland, Austria and Russia as well. The Prince's amorous progress was neither a Grand Tour nor a Passionate Pilgrimage, but a series of battle campaigns, each of which (like the '45 rising) had its Prestonpans and its Culloden.

The Private Passions of Bonnie Prince Charlie is not a biography, although I have followed the Prince's liaisons with women more or less chronologically. Instead, his relationships with women are set against his personality and dynastic aspirations, demonstrating the influences of both genetic inheritance and environment on his love life. Prince Charlie was descended from two lines of highly sexed bonnie fighters, the Stewarts/Stuarts and the Sobieskis who each had their own triumphs and defeats in bed and on the battlefield. But if genes made Prince Charlie's basic character, environment was the anvil on which his love life was shaped.

The Private Passions of Bonnie Prince Charlie reveals why Charles Edward Stuart was so greatly loved by almost every woman he met, yet was never able to return that love even when his ardour burned white hot and passion overruled every other instinct.

1. Letter from the Princesse de Talmont to Bonnie Prince Charlie. Royal Archives, Windsor Castle, Box 4/Folder 1/56.

ACKNOWLEDGEMENTS

Much of the information on the Prince's relationships with women is contained in letters among the Stuart Papers in the Royal Archives at Windsor Castle, and I am grateful to Her Majesty The Queen for graciously permitting me to quote from those and to publish two of them in the text.

I have had help from many individuals, libraries, archives and museums in a number of countries. Starting nearest to home, I must thank the staff of Peterborough Central Library and the London Library for unfailing help. The British Library, National Library of Scotland, Polish Library, London, Edinburgh Central Library, Mitchell Library, Glasgow, Cambridge University Library, Aberdeen University Library, with its incomparable MacBean Collection of Stuart and Jacobite material, and Inverness, Elgin, Stirling, East Kilbride, Kendal and Barrow-in-Furness Libraries have all been of great assistance. I thank the National Gallery of Ireland for permission to use its glorious Panini painting of the fête in Rome and to single out the detail of James, Charles and Henry Stuart in the crowd. The Scottish National Portrait Gallery, Derby Museum and Art Gallery and the West Highland Museum, Fort William, have also been of assistance.

Abroad I have received the most courteous help from the Archives Nationales, Bibliothèque Nationale and Musée de l'Arsenal in Paris, the Musée d'Evreux, France, the Archivio di Stato, Bologna, Bibliothecha Herzianna, Rome, and the Ossilinskich Biblioteka, Wroclaw. Marian Rosa of Wroclaw Tourist Promotion Agency, Dr Z. Jagodzinski of the Polish Library, London, and Ursula Phillips of the School of Slavonic and East European Studies, University of London, all helped with Polish matters. In France Kristin Parker and Florence Pluvinage tackled research requests with expertise. Maria Diemoz

ACKNOWLEDGEMENTS

made things happen in Italy, and I am grateful for translation assistance from Georgina Beresford, Sonia Millar, Wolf Moser, Tore Tocco, David and Mima Williams and Jane Zolotuhin. My thanks to all of them.

It is not possible to mention everyone, but I must single out June C.F. Barnes, Helen Boyle, Andrew Brown, Pat and James Bruce, Clive Burton, Keeta and John Campbell, Iain Coates, Eithne Douglas, John Douglas, Wendy Glavis, Doris Hermanns, Keith Horrox, John Horsburgh, Bob McClymont, Donald F. MacDonald, Sir Fitzroy Maclean, Alastair MacLeod, Dr Rosalind K. Marshall, Alan Morrison, Joyce Wakenshaw and Frances Robertson.

Of the many books consulted, I must mention two. Frank McLynn's biography, *Charles Edward Stuart, a Tragedy in Many Acts* is by far the best recent biography of the Prince, since it opens up many new lines of thought – which sent me happily down many Stuart byways unrelated to the project in hand, but irresistible! Laurence Bongie's *The Love of a Prince*, the first book ever written on Prince Charlie's little known affair with his cousin, Louise, is clearly the result of much painstaking research among European sources where archival material is often scarce and difficult to track down. It is not easy to find new things to say about Prince Charles Edward, but Professor Bongie has achieved that. I have consulted the letters in the Royal Archives at Windsor on which *The Love of a Prince* is based and, with Professor Bongie's permission, have used his date order for this largely undated correspondence. In the text I have acknowledged where these two works have been of assistance, and express my thanks to both authors.

Lastly, my thanks to anyone I have omitted and to my wife Sheelagh and all my family and friends who have helped in the making of *The Private Passions of Bonnie Prince Charlie*.

HUGH DOUGLAS

CHRONOLOGY

THE LIFE OF CHARLES EDWARD STUART, 1720–88

The reader may find this chronology of Bonnie Prince Charlie's life and loves helpful to follow the amorous progress of the Prince through life:

1720 **Charles Edward Stuart**, son of **James Stuart**, the Old Pretender, and **Clementina Sobieska** was born at the Muti Palace, Rome on the last day of the year. Probably in the same year **Clementine Walkinshaw**, best known of his mistresses and mother of his daughter, **Charlotte, Duchess of Albany**, was born.

1725 On 6 March his brother, **Henry, Duke of York**, was born, but following quarrels with her husband, Clementina left her family and went to live in a convent.

1727 King George I died and James prepared to try to win back his throne.

1728 In April, while James was in France trying to find support, Clementina returned to her sons. She now turned into a religious fanatic, praying and fasting much of the time.

1734 In August Charles had his first experience of war at the siege of Gaeta.

1735 On 18 January Clementina died.

1737 Charles made a highly successful tour of northern Italy, following which first thoughts were given to finding him a wife. His father rejected Charles's cousin, **Louise de la Tour**, daughter of the Duc de Bouillon.

1744 Charles left Rome on 9 January for France to join an invasion of Britain then being mounted on the Channel coast by King Louis XV. He was never to see his father again. In March storms destroyed much of the French fleet and the invasion was abandoned. Charles returned to

xiii

Paris to persuade King Louis to mount a new attack, but he would not.

1745 Charles sailed for Scotland on 2 July (12 July by the French calendar) with only two ships, one of which was damaged in a fight with a British warship, and had to return to France.

On 21 July he reached the Western Isles and two days later landed on Eriskay with only a few supporters, the Seven Men of Moidart. On 19 August he raised his standard at Glenfinnan and after a lightning march captured Edinburgh on 17 September. Four days later he defeated Sir John Cope at Prestonpans.

For the next six weeks he held court at Edinburgh and tried to raise more support. On 1 November he marched south and captured Carlisle. By 5 December he had reached Derby, but turned back to Scotland on the insistence of the clan chiefs and generals. On 20 December they arrived back in Scotland and Charles stayed at Glasgow.

1746 During January, Charles stayed at Bannockburn House, where he met **Clementine Walkinshaw**, who nursed him while he had a cold, and became his mistress. He won the Battle of Falkirk, but on the advice of his generals retreated to Highlands.

On 16 April his army was defeated by the Duke of Cumberland at Culloden. From mid-April until 21 September Charles was hunted in the Western Isles and Highlands and had many narrow escapes. On the night of 28–9 June, **Flora MacDonald** escorted him over the sea to Skye dressed as her maid, **Betty Burke**.

On 21 September he sailed for France, where he was greeted as a great hero in Paris, and was reunited with his brother.

1747 France and Spain refused to support a new rising. In May his brother left secretly for Rome and soon after became a cardinal of the Roman Catholic Church. Charles was furious and refused to return to Rome to see his father.

Through the autumn and winter of 1747–8 he had a wild affair with **Louise, Duchesse de Montbazon**, the cousin who had been rejected as a bride ten years earlier. Her husband, the Duc de Montbazon, was one of his best friends.

1748   He abandoned Louise for the **Princesse de Talmont**, a woman older than his mother. That summer Louise bore him a son, who died. On 10 December he was arrested in Paris and expelled from France.

1748–50 These years were spent wandering around Europe, with de Talmont much of the time.

1750   Charles visited London and stayed a week, plotting with Jacobites. There he was received into the Church of England.

1752   **Clementine Walkinshaw** joined him and from then until 1760 they lived together in Flanders, Switzerland and France.

1753   Clementine bore him a daughter, who was baptized **Charlotte** on 29 October at Liège.

1758–65 Lived mainly at Bouillon, France.

1760   Clementine left him on 22 July, taking Charlotte.

1766   The Old Pretender died. Charles returned to Rome and proclaimed himself King Charles III. The Pope refused to recognize him as king.

1766–74 Lived mainly at Rome.

1772   Married **Louise of Stolberg**.

1774–86 Lived mainly at Florence.

1778   Louise began to have an affair with the poet, Count Alfieri.

1780   Louise left Charles and fled to a convent.

1784   He declared his daughter, legitimate and conferred on her the title **Duchess of Albany**. She came to live with him.

1784–8 Lived mainly at Rome with Charlotte.

1788   Charles Edward Stuart died on 30 January. Charlotte did not claim the crown, but Henry proclaimed himself **Henry IX**.

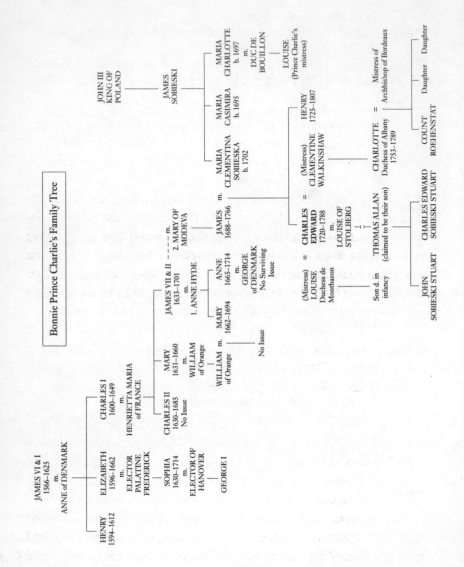

Bonnie Prince Charlie's Family Tree

ONE

YE BONNY PRINCE

Si vous avée etée content de votre nuit mon amour je vous avoue que pour moi j'en ai etée enchantée Je me flatte que nous en passerons encore longtemp de même . . .

How easy it is to imagine the scene: it was already past two in the afternoon and outside, beyond the rich curtains, the winter's day was beginning to fade as the young duchess emerged from her dressing room and sat down at her escritoire to write. In the privacy of her own room, she could savour the joy of what had passed last night within these walls, on that very bed, and anticipate what might be tonight. The moment she put her pen to paper the words began to tumble from it:

If you were happy with your night my love I swear that for my part I was enchanted I tell myself with pleasure that we shall spend many more of the same . . .

Her passion ran so high that she forgot grammar, punctuation and spelling. But what did these matter? For him she had already risked much, and was prepared to risk as much again – her husband's distress, her mother-in-law's anger, her father's sorrow, her own reputation. Nothing mattered – for Louise was in love.

Such a scene might have come straight from the pen of Victor Hugo. Had it done so, readers might have thought it had been inspired by a ghost from this room: for this house, in the fashionable Place Royale in the heart of Paris, was to become Victor Hugo's home a century later. Today it is the Victor Hugo Museum.[1]

In the latter part of 1747, when it was a lovers' tryst, the house was the Hôtel de Guéméné, home of a branch of the powerful Rohan family. The author of the letter was Louise de la Tour d'Auvergne, wife of Jules de Rohan, Duc de Montbazon, and daughter of the Great Chamberlain of France, the Duc de Bouillon. Her lover was none other than Charles Edward Stuart, her own cousin, and the hero of Paris since his return the previous year from his brave but disastrous attempt to win back the crowns of England, Scotland and Ireland for his father, who ruled in exile as James VIII of Scotland and III of England.

Louise and Charles were passionately in love and had been meeting secretly in her bedroom for months. Now the risk was even greater because her husband, one of Prince Charlie's best friends, was an officer in the French army, newly returned from the campaigns in Flanders, which had just ended for the winter.

Louise didn't care about the risk she ran; her letter was urgent if she was to be sure she would see her lover again tonight, so she continued in short breathless sentences:

That will be my only happiness I await your news with impatience Goodbye my love I am very well Until tonight come and spend it in the arms of the one who loves no one in the world but her own dear love.

The letter was unsigned and so secret she had made her lover promise to destroy it, but he didn't – so it is still there for anyone to read as proof of Prince Charlie's broken promise, a piece of bad faith as well as testimony to the remarkable power of the love that existed between them.[2] Every nightly tryst brought the lovers closer to the eye of the storm that discovery would unleash, for ardour and jealousy were making the impetuous Charles take risks even here inside the Rohan house under the noses of Jules and his mother, a tough but wise woman. Louise's mother-in-law, Madame de Guéméné, must have suspected something of this kind might happen because, when she drew up her son's marriage contract, she insisted it should stipulate that the young couple must live at her house in Paris.[3] Charles described the mother-in-law as '*une vieille folle*' (an old lunatic).[4]

At the time of the marriage Madame de Guéméné's son was only sixteen and his bride a year older, but in royal circles, where the more powerful a man was the more he could break the rules, one could not be too careful – after all, if King Louis could flaunt mistresses, Madame de Châteauroux and later Madame de Pompadour at Fontainebleau and Versailles, why should pretty little Louise, with her husband a serving soldier, not fall prey to some lecherous young man at court?

And that was exactly what had happened to Louise in spite of Madame de Guéméné's precautions and the eagle eye under which she kept her daughter-in-law.

Charles Edward was not exactly a young man of the French court, lecherous or otherwise, for no Stuart had been permitted officially to set foot on French territory ever since the Treaty of Utrecht barred them from the country in 1713. However, Charles returned to France after his disastrous defeat at the battle of Culloden, and he was still there in 1747. King Louis would have been delighted to be rid of him and tried hard to coerce him into leaving, but the Prince stayed on, the hero of the people of Paris who admired his daring achievement, which had so nearly come off. Parisians – indeed the whole of Europe – adored him almost as passionately as Louise did. They applauded him in the street and cheered him to the echo whenever he appeared in public at the opera, and they bought pictures of him in warrior's uniform which were on sale all over Paris. Prince Charlie was a never-ending source of gossip, and so powerful that even King Louis XV could not order him out of the country as he certainly wished to do since Prince Charlie was a constant nuisance and critic of the French government. Whether France or Britain liked it or not, Charles Stuart continued to enjoy Parisian life to the full and to mix brazenly among court circles from which he was officially barred. He even attended masked balls at which royalty and government ministers were present.

And now he had fallen head over heels in love with his own cousin, the daughter of his mother's sister and the wife of one of his best friends. It was the first time Prince Charlie, up to now a confirmed bachelor in the eyes of the world, had been known to show deep affection for any woman, but when love struck it did so with all the force of one of the claymores his Highland soldiers had wielded in battle in Scotland. When Charles Stuart fell for Cousin Louise, there was no mistaking that he was in love!

The Jacobite world, or at least those in that small circle close enough to him to be aware of the momentous happening, wondered how this could be. Was this the man who, only a couple of years before in Scotland, had been so cold and offhand with women that both friends and enemies commented on it? His supporter, Lord Elcho, had watched the Prince's awkwardness in female company at Holyrood Palace in Edinburgh, and felt compelled to make excuses.

'He had not been much used to Womens Company, and was always embarrassed while he was with them,' Elcho remarked as he watched the Prince at levées and balls.[5]

During all the time Charles had been holding court in the Scottish capital it had been the same: his coldness could not be hidden, especially whenever fashionable ladies rushed to the palace in droves to kiss his hand, and Elcho was embarrassed to recall that 'his behaviour to them was very cool'.[6]

Coolness towards women, surely born of shyness, was one of the lesser charges which dogged Bonnie Prince Charlie, not merely during his time in Scotland, but all through life and into history. There have been smears that he was undersexed, or at least partially impotent, but these are as ill-founded as are insinuations that he was homosexual like his great-great-grandfather, King James VI and I. His younger brother, Prince Henry, Duke of York, has also been accused of having homosexual relationships, but on much stronger grounds.[7]

During the '45 Rising many slanders were put about, some labelling Charles as homosexual while others accused him of flagrant womanizing – enemy progaganda didn't care how the sexual slanders were slanted or even whether they contained a basis of truth, just so long as they showed the Prince in an unfavourable light and were detrimental to his Cause.

Apart from the many reports of aloofness towards women during the rising, a story circulated that, when asked why he would not dance at one of the Holyrood balls, the Prince beckoned a huge Highlander standing guard at the doorway. Stroking the man's beard, the Prince exclaimed, 'These are the beauties to whom I must now make love, and for a few thousands of whom I would fain dispense with all yonder fair damsels.'[8] The brawny Highlander's response is not recorded, but we must resist the temptation to judge the incident against today's sexual attitudes. If any such thing happened and Charles did make the remark, it was certainly not prompted by any homosexual proclivities, but was merely a joke with a deal of common sense behind it. At that moment Charles Stuart's sole objective was to win back his father's crowns, and the Highlanders were his main supporters in the fight to achieve that.

On the reverse side of the sexual coin the Hanoverians tried to make propaganda of 'affairs' with mistresses in Scotland, especially poor, innocent Jenny Cameron, who did nothing more than bring a group of Cameron men to join his army, but was pilloried by pamphleteers and cartoonists, and Flora MacDonald, who helped him to escape over the sea to Skye disguised as her maidservant. The accusations against both Jenny and Flora were so preposterous they could not have been believed by his most gullible enemy, but nonetheless the country was polluted by them during the '45 and after.

By some strange omission, the anti-Charlie propaganda machine did not pick up the one sexual fling the Prince enjoyed during the '45. Clementine Walkinshaw was almost certainly the Prince's mistress during a brief period in January 1746, but the relationship was never noticed by his enemies, nor made use of by them.

The truth is that Prince Charlie was a late starter when it came to falling in love, but when he did, it was with wild crazed fervour, which set the Jacobite movement buzzing. What's more, his love was usually reciprocated with equal ardour. He may have been late to develop, but was as well endowed with sexual drive as his great-great-great grandmother, Mary Queen of Scots and his great uncle, Charles II, had been. Charles Edward Stuart could love passionately.

Charles Edward Stuart showed little interest in the female sex as a child because, from his birth in Rome in 1720, he was brought up in a largely masculine environment. His parents' marriage was an unhappy one and it was left to his father to arrange most of his education and guide him towards manhood. The upbringing of a prince has always been remote from the world around him, but for Charles and his brother, Henry, born five years later, growing up was a very unnatural experience, cut off from the real world at a court, which was not really royal at all. Their grandfather, James VII and II had lost his throne more than a generation earlier, and their father, James VIII and III, pretended to be a king in Rome, a city remote in distance and outlook from the country he claimed as his.

Women played little part in life at the Pretender's court and the boys grew up with no experience of female company other than as partners at formal balls at the formal little courts they visited in friendly Italian states. They were naïve insofar as making love was concerned.

When Charles discovered love at last, he was past his mid-twenties, and it was unfortunate that he did not marry then for a wife might have brought some degree of stability and point to his life. Instead he 'campaigned' through a series of love affairs in the middle years of his life, which aroused him to white hot passion and resulted in at least two illegitimate children and a succession of fights as heroic as the battles he fought during his 'rash adventure' in Scotland.

But the bonnie prince proved to be a rough and jealous wooer, who flew into wild rages, and insisted on always having his own way with every woman for whom he cared. Louise was the first in a line of liaisons with unhappy endings. Worst of all, he became insanely jealous without reason and abused nearly every woman he ever loved, and he beat his women if they dared to disobey him.

As far as the ordinary supporter of the Cause was concerned this wild and utterly unacceptable social behaviour finally killed off the Jacobite Cause as much as any political or military victories of his enemies. Charles's drinking has been blamed for the destruction of Jacobite hopes, and the Prince's fondness for the bottle certainly did inflict serious injury, but supporters began to leave in disgust when they saw how he treated the women for whom he professed to care. Love always proved another Culloden for Prince Charlie.

Yet, all through life, Charles Edward Stuart exercised a kind of magic power over women, those who met him and those to whom he was no more than a name. He had an ability to retain a mesmeric power even over the women he treated badly and could always cast his spell over those whom he ignored; in Edinburgh they hung from windows and crowded round him in the street just to touch him. Strangers, many not even Jacobite sympathizers, cheered him as he passed by and remembered him long after:

'Ye windows were full of Ladys who threw up their handkerchiefs and clap'd their hands and show'd great loyalty to ye Bonny Prince,' wrote one of them, Magdalen Pringle, as she watched the Prince ride out to review his army at Duddingston, just outside Edinburgh.[9]

Charles paid scant attention to these fawning women who went wild about him, yet they continued to surround him in ever-growing numbers when he ignored them. In spite of his outrageous behaviour towards them, they still called him Bonnie Prince Charlie, swooned at his feet, and urged their menfolk to go out and fight for him. Why? Because he was a princely, charismatic figure, a leader who had in him that ability, which some men possess, to attract women to him in spite of treating them with unfeeling cruelty.

Prince Charlie has much to answer for insofar as the women in his life are concerned, for he showed them no consideration and demanded everything they had to give, while offering little in return. It has to be admitted that the same charges have been levelled at him in regard to his relationships with men: to those who surrounded him and supported him so loyally he showed ingratitude, insensitivity, and meanness of spirit as well as of pocket. A charge of cowardice after his escape from the battlefield of Culloden, does not stand up, but most of the others do.

It was in Scotland in 1745 that the bonnie prince who has survived in historic legend, was born – the darling of almost every woman, the hero of many men until he marched into England, when his rash adventure fell apart at Derby. There he was forced to accept the advice of his generals and retreat to Scotland. He headed north with ill grace and all the way was sullen and withdrawn. The campaign was lost during that retreat, long before Cumberland's deadly gunfire raked the ranks of the Highlanders on the battlefield of Culloden.

Charles has been accused of being ill educated, stupid, a bad leader and without a scrap of political awareness, and it has even been suggested that it might have been better if he had died a hero at Culloden rather than live on to become Europe's wild man. But all that is grossly unfair to him: Charles Stuart was a brave man. He may not have been an intellectual and had little book learning, but from childhood he was a perceptive boy, who took in all that was on offer by way of education at his father's narrow little court at Rome. He may not have learnt much about reading, writing or mathematics, but he absorbed the elements of kingship as it should be practised under the rules of divine right by which his father lived.

Charles's downfall is often blamed on an inability to come to terms with the demise of his Cause after Culloden – disappointment which made him turn more and more to the 'nasty bottle'. This change of character has been attributed to political naïvety and crass ignorance of diplomacy, but the Prince was not inept at all. It is true that he was a poor diplomat who never learnt to negotiate: as a prince of a royal house which believed it had ruled by God's divine right for nearly four centuries, he saw no need to negotiate with anyone. He bade people do what he wanted, and ordered his women about in the same regal manner as he commanded his generals – and usually the women were more obedient than the generals.

Prince Charlie was foolish in his handling of those adherents to the Cause who haunted the court at Rome or the Paris Jacobite circle, and he never trusted them totally: in the light of the shiftiness of some of the professed loyal Jacobite followers around him, this perhaps demonstrated shrewd judgement rather than a lack of it.

The Prince certainly was politically aware: he had been well trained from childhood in the conspiratorial atmosphere of his father's court to follow world events. The only pity is that Jacobite supporters who came to Rome were inclined to tell King James what they thought he would want to hear rather than what he *needed* to know, a charming, but sometimes irritating fault still found in many Irishmen and Scots. Consequently both King and Prince were far less aware than they ought to have been of what was really going on in Britain, France, Spain, the Holy Roman Empire, or even in the Vatican a few hundred yards away from their own court at the Muti Palace.

Prince Charlie was a recalcitrant child, but his rebellion can be attributed largely to that strange upbringing in what was to all intents and purposes a broken home. His parents' marriage was marred from beginning to end by differences that need never have arisen – mainly due to Clementina's jealousy over being cut out of her husband's state business, and this led to accusations of infidelity. Clementina's accusations were groundless, but they cost James Stuart dearly. The Stuarts were far from popular in Rome, but Clementina always managed to maintain her hold over the city. While her husband was ignored or criticized, society remained 'enchanted by her charm, her gaiety, her pretty little accent in Italian and French, and the mixture of sweetness and gravity in her expression'.[10]

She exercised the same hypnotic power over those who met her as did her son. Baron de Pollnitz wrote after meeting her:

Were she mistress of a kingdom, she would certainly make it her rule to discharge the duties of her rank as became it.[11]

Clementina became a recluse, a neurotic and a religious bigot who had to be handled with great care. She and James both loved their sons in their own peculiar way, but it was not the kind of love that could be reciprocated nor could it teach Charles and Henry how to love. As a result, Henry retired into homosexuality and the celibacy of the priesthood, but Charles had neither of these to fall back on – he was heterosexual and not religiously inclined, so he had to cope with love in his own rough and ready way. He was shy and awkward with women, and he loved them, yet he could never give himself totally to them – not even to those with whom he had passionate affairs. The same was true of his relationships with men; he kept everyone – men and women alike – at arm's length because they were mere subjects while he was a man set apart, a prince waiting to become king.

It is interesting that the only people with whom he did build a strong relationship were those among whom he lived during his months as a fugitive following Culloden, especially the MacDonalds. No one denounced him to his enemies for the fortune of £30,000 that the

London government offered to his betrayer, and dozens, if not hundreds, who wore the uniform of his enemies went out of their way to help him.

Prince Charlie actually enjoyed his time with the clansmen, particularly a few idyllic weeks while he was in hiding at Corodale on South Uist during June 1746, and two months later in Cluny's Cage, a concealed mountain shelter where he hunted during the day and spent evenings talking and drinking with his loyal Highlanders. Even at this early stage in his life he could drink all of them under the table. One long-remembered session continued until every man, including MacDonald of Boisdale, one of the greatest drinkers in the whole of Scotland, lay unconscious. The Prince covered the casualties of the night with plaids and sang '*De Profundis*' over them before he left them to sleep it off. One of the party recalled afterwards, 'Never have I seen a punch bowl attacked more freely or frankly.'[12]

Although the voyage over the sea to Skye helped to further the 'bonnie prince' image, his legend does not rest on that alone. In adversity Charlie won respect; the only pity is that after his return to France he degenerated into the wild man of Europe, drinking and living a rumbustious, dissolute life.

Even then women were able to discern a vestige of the handsome young man who came so close to sending the Elector back to Hanover and restoring the Stuarts. Behind the face of Charles Edward in middle age, which friends and enemies alike admitted was heavy, red, pimply and bloated, there still lay nobility.

'He is by no means thin, has a noble person, and a graceful manner . . . upon the whole he has a melancholy mortified appearance,' a Jacobite lady reported.[13]

And so the bonnie prince stormed on through his middle years, into old age, for Charles Stuart never did anything quietly or in moderation. He had mistresses, children and even a wife, but failed to find peace or a lasting relationship with any of them.

Charles and his father both realized that the Stuart crowns could never be won back without France's help, and therein lies the reason why the Prince came running when King Louis XV summoned him to join an abortive French invasion of England in 1744.

When storms in the English Channel and the British fleet wrecked that plan, France abandoned Charles, leaving him stranded at the port of Gravelines. Only then was it brought home to the Prince that, necessary as the French might be, they could never be relied on: they would support the Cause when they wanted to twist the British lion's tail or to tie up the Hanoverian army in England while they achieved their own objectives on the continent, but the moment foreign policy or personalities at Versailles changed, the Cause was abandoned. If Charles Stuart's diplomacy was crude, that of his erstwhile friends was little better. By the middle of 1744 it was clear that the French had other plans, which did not include a Jacobite invasion, so the Prince began to make his own preparations to set out for Scotland on his rash adventure of 1745, alone, without adequate weapons or soldiers.

Charles Stuart did not sail for Scotland in search of glory: he made the journey in 1745 with the sole mission, as he saw it, of rescuing his father's subjects from the usurping Electors of Hanover and restoring their rightful ancient royal house. Personal glory did not enter into it, although he undoubtedly did exalt in those months when he was leader of a victorious army and had his own royal court at Holyrood. As Prince of Wales he genuinely wanted to do what he believed was best for his countrymen, and failure of that destroyed him.

The French could have done more – much more – to help while the Prince was actually in Scotland, but they prevaricated and in the end did little except despatch an envoy to see what was happening, then botch what little support they gathered together to help him. Put crudely, but not inaccurately, France's contribution to the Stuart cause in the '45 rising was little more than to rescue him when it was all over. As a result the Prince who returned to France in the autumn of 1746 at the end of the terrible affair, was a bitter and angry man.

Although in his heart he still did not trust the French and foolishly criticized King Louis openly, he tried hard to persuade them to mount a new expedition, but should have known better, for soon it became clear that the Jacobites had served their purpose and the

French had no intention of backing the Prince then or probably ever again. Spain too refused to help, and Charlie was never able to come to terms with this double blow, which left him feeling betrayed and rebelliously unforgiving.

Worse was to follow. An unbridgeable rift now opened up between the Prince of Wales and his father and brother, and that was probably the greatest tragedy of Bonnie Prince Charlie's life. He had loved both of them very dearly up to the time of the rising, although Charles and Henry were too different in character ever to be soulmates, but now they actually quarrelled. This was a great pity because his family, his father especially, were the only people who could give Charles Edward the support he needed now he saw treachery everywhere around him and he slowly sank into a morass of paranoia.

About this time it became clear to the gloomy old fatalist, which James had become, that the game was up for the Jacobites: there never would be a restoration, return to the Palace of St James could only be a dream, and they would always reign in exile in Rome. James was past caring very much about that, and the Duke of York accepted it too, although not in the same fatalistic way as his father. He had plans of his own.

Then the blow fell: Henry, who had been with Charles in Paris, disappeared without a word to his brother, and soon he was back in Rome with his father. Hard on the heels of that news, came a letter which told the Prince that Henry was to be appointed a cardinal of the Catholic Church – it had all been planned in advance by their father and word was only sent to Charles when it was too late for him to interfere to stop it. This betrayal was the more bitter because it came just at the moment when Charles himself was prepared to abandon the Roman Catholic church in order to make himself acceptable to the British people (and soon afterwards he actually did so), but Henry's promotion within the church of Rome damned his chances for ever.

That was the moment when the Bonnie Prince turned into the Wild Man of Europe. He never forgave his father who pleaded with his son for nineteen years to return to him, but Charles refused.

Although his father deluged him with letters and pleas, he seldom even bothered to reply. Charles Stuart would not be reconciled, and only set out for Rome towards the end of 1765 after he learned that his father was dying: but he had left it too late. He arrived to find his father was already dead and he was Charles III, the King over the Water. But by then not even the Pope would recognize the new Stuart monarch's sovereignty. He was accepted only as Count of Albany.

Charles's last years were spent trying to ensure the succession, an obsession which led him into a dynastic marriage, which failed just as dramatically as that of his own parents had done. There was no love in the match, so it is not surprising that his wife ran off with a poet, leaving Charles an aged cuckold, a pathetic figure, whose health was decaying daily. His mind clouded, his heart threatened to give out, his limbs became swollen, and breathing was difficult.

Why, in spite of all that, has Charles Stuart gone down in history as the charismatic Bonnie Prince, the ill-starred royal heir who broke the hearts of men and women? Historian Andrew Lang offers a romantic explanation:

Charles is loved for his forlorn hope: for his desperate resolve: for the reckless daring, the winning charm that once were his: for bright hair, and brown eyes; above all, as the centre and inspirer of old chivalrous loyalty, as one who would have brought back a lost age, an impossible realm of dreams.[14]

That may all be true, but surely the reason must lie also in the fact that, from the cradle to the grave, two Charles Stuarts existed iin the same body, the gallant prince and the impetuous adventurer, who could not handle relationships with anyone rash enough to commit himself or herself to his Cause. And his tragedy was that these two personae were as unable to co-exist as were Charles and his father or his brother.

From the moment he was born on the last day of the year 1720 until the disputed date of his death at the end of January 1788,[15] people saw in him whichever of these two personalities they wanted to see.

It was like that all through his life: to one he was a weak, sickly child, but kinder eyes saw a fine young prince; some thought him a spoilt brat, while others admired the courtly young man who dressed in silk and fine velvet, wore diamond-set Orders of the Garter and St Andrew, and danced gracefully at ducal courts around Italy. In Scotland he cast spells even over those who were his enemies, but in England he found few friends. Throughout the years he spent on mainland Europe, kinder critics remembered his brief moment of glory that so nearly became an enduring reality. And to the ordinary man or woman in the street he was the greatest hero of the day.

When he died Charles Stuart was mourned only by Charlotte, the daughter his mistress, Clementine Walkinshaw, had given him: of all the women who had admired him, loved him, suffered his tantrums and ill usage, only Charlotte was there to comfort his last days. It was a lonely end for a man who had loved so ardently. But that was Charles Edward Stuart's tragedy: women loved him to distraction and he loved them just as passionately, yet he never really learned how to love.

The seeds of Bonnie Prince Charlie's misfortunes lay in the genetic inheritance passed on from his father's Stuart ancestors and the Polish Sobieskis on his mother's side. Yet it is equally true that Charles Stuart, the man and lover, owed much to the family and political milieu in which he grew up. He never received or was given love at his mother's knee, which is where most good lovers learn their craft. Clementina Sobieska has much to answer for.

Life dealt Charles Edward Stuart a poor hand both in the genes he inherited and in the environment in which he developed. Bonnie Prince Charlie's ill luck as a lover began early and it dogged his footsteps all the way through life.

TWO

A POISONED INHERITANCE

Let every man, who has a tear for the many miseries incident to humanity, feel for a family, illustrious as any in Europe, and unfortunate beyond human precedent; and let every Briton, and particularly every Scotsman, who ever looked with reverential pity on the dotage of a parent, cast a veil over the final mistakes of the Kings of his forefathers.

Letter from Robert Burns to the *Edinburgh Evening Courant* in defence of the Stuarts on the centenary of the Glorious Revolution.[1]

Bonnie Prince Charlie was a Stuart through and through, a 'bonnie fighter' and a highly sexed individual: his mother, Maria Clementina Sobieska, belonged to the great Sobieski family of Poland, who were no mean fighters either, and could boast plenty of sexual adventures of their own. By an ironic twist of history the marriage of James Stuart and Clementina Sobieska brought together two exiled royal lines, since Clementina's father, Prince James Sobieski, was the son of John III, King of Poland, but had not been chosen to succeed him.

Any marriage likely to produce an heir was to be welcomed by supporters of the Jacobite Cause, but Clementina as a bride for James Stuart was a spectacular coup since she would bring a much needed rich dowry to the Cause as well. That on top of a union with one of Europe's great family names was something to cheer Jacobite hearts everywhere. The only pity was that by the time of James and Clementina the blood was diluted, the genes flawed, so that while Charles and his brother, Henry, inherited the strengths of the Stuarts and the Sobieskis, they also fell heir to their weaknesses. To understand the character and sexuality of Bonnie Prince Charlie it is necessary to understand the Stuarts and the Sobieskis.

15

The Stuarts, or Stewarts, to give their name its original form,[2] had proven staying power: by 1720, when Charles was born, the dynasty had already endured for three hundred and fifty years and its direct line was to continue for another eighty-seven. In all, the House of Stewart existed as a living monarchy – *de facto* or *de jure* – for four-and-a-quarter tumultuous centuries against all the odds. Its birth was difficult, from first to last its existence was beset by tragedy and turbulence, and the death of the direct line in lonely exile proved long drawn out and full of pain.

Chateaubriand summed up the Stewart tragedy when he wrote at the death of Cardinal Henry of York in 1807 and the end of the dynasty's direct line:

The Stuart race took 119 years to die out after having lost the throne which it never found again. In exile three pretenders passed on from one to the other the shadow of a crown: they had intelligence and courage, what did they lack? The hand of God.[3]

No one has offered a better explanation for the fate of Scotland's revered but accursed royal house.

The Stewarts' origins lay within two noble families, the ancient hereditary High Stewards of Scotland and the Bruces, both of whom came over with the Normans at the time of the Norman Conquest, and arrived in Scotland after David I became King of Scots in 1124. Robert de Brus, the king's companion-at-arms, was given the lordship of Annandale and his descendant was the Hero-King, Robert I, victor of Bannockburn.

On the Stewart side the family was originally Breton, but they set down strong roots in the south-west of Scotland, where they prospered as Stewards of the royal household, the office of state from which the name Stewart is derived. In the wars against the English which followed the death of King Alexander III of Scotland, James Stewart fought alongside William Wallace, and in due course his son, Walter, was with Robert the Bruce at Bannockburn. Walter's reward for this loyalty was the hand of Bruce's daughter, Marjorie, and this marriage brought the two powerful families together to found the Stewart dynasty.

King Robert the Bruce had no legitimate male heir at the time of Bannockburn, only Marjorie, by his first wife, Isabella of Mar. His second wife, the Earl of Ulster's daughter, Elizabeth, had not yet produced a child, so in order to secure the succession, Parliament decreed that, in the event of the king dying without a male heir, the crown should pass to the male heirs of Walter Stewart and Marjorie.

Queen Elizabeth did give Bruce a son in 1324, who succeeded him as King David II, but David died childless, and that is why Robert the Bruce's grandson, the child of Marjorie and Walter Stewart, was crowned King Robert II in 1370.

Seventeen Stewarts reigned either as acknowledged sovereigns or in exile as Kings over the Water, between 1370 and 1807, and of these two were assassinated, two beheaded, one was killed accidentally by a bursting cannon, another fell in battle with his nobles, and four died in exile. From beginning to end, from the two weak kings who established the dynasty to the last three who ruled in exile, the story of the Stewarts is a sad litany of failure, misfortune, tragedy and disappointment, not just in kingship but in marriage and sexual relationships as well. From generation to generation the crown of Scotland was a poisoned inheritance.

Prince Charlie and his brother tasted the bitterness of failure. Charles saw success snatched from him when he was within an ace of winning back the crown in the '45 rising: Napoleon's conquering sweep across Europe drove his brother, Henry IX, into a second exile from that in which he had already spent the whole of his life. And, as if that were not humiliation enough, poor Henry ended his days on a pension doled out to him by George III, the man whose crown he claimed.

In the light of their family's earlier history they ought not to have expected anything better. Previous generations had suffered even more. Charlie's father, James, the Old Pretender, spent all but six months of his seventy-eight long years on this earth in exile, sixty-four of them as King over the Water, ever hoping that by some miracle, someone – the King of France, the King of Spain, anyone, anywhere – would help him to come into his own again. Prince Charlie's grandfather, James VII and II, was exiled twice (when his father lost the Civil War and his head, and at the Glorious Revolution in 1688) and his great-uncle, Charles II, once. His great-grandfather, Charles I, and great-great-great-grandmother, Mary, Queen of Scots, were both beheaded and his great-great-great-grandfather, Lord Darnley, was murdered in a seedy, far from royal plot involving his queen. Five Jameses reigned before Mary, the first and third of whom were assassinated, while the second was killed accidentally, and the fourth died in battle at Flodden. The fifth died shortly after his army was defeated in battle in 1542 and his wife gave birth to a princess instead of the strong prince Scotland needed. They said he died of a broken heart: the only surprising thing about the Stewarts is that more of them didn't die from the same cause.

All seven monarchs who succeeded between 1406 and 1567 – the six Jameses and Mary, Queen of Scots – were minors at their accession, the oldest, just fifteen, and the youngest, only six days old. Five – Charles II, Mary, Anne, Prince Charlie and his brother, Henry – left no legitimate heir at all.

Such a failure rate in supplying the dynasty with an heir might suggest a sexual failure, but the opposite is true: they had plenty of children who could not succeed because they were born on the wrong side of the blanket, or died prematurely, probably because one of their parents was infected with venereal disease due to their own or a progenitor's promiscuity.

Alongside a strong sexual urge there co-existed among the Stewarts a touching sense of romance, a trait first revealed in the earliest days of the dynasty. James I, who reigned from 1406 until 1437, was captured by pirates on his way to France in the very year he became king and was held in England for eighteen years. There James Stewart found a wife and his voice as a poet in *The Kingis Quhair*, a long poem in which he describes the moment he first set eyes on Lady Joan Beaufort whom he married and took back to Scotland as his queen.

The Kingis Quhair tells how, lying awake in his prison one night, he began to read and to meditate on his ill fortune. To escape the misery in which he was enveloped, James went to the window and there he saw Lady Joan and immediately fell in love:

> And therewith kest I doun myn eye ageyne,
>   Quhare as I sawe, walking under the tour,
> Full secretly new cummyn heir to pleyne,
>   The fairest or the freschest yong floure
>   That ever I sawe, me thoght, before that houre,
> For quhich sodayn abate, anon astert,
> The blude of all my body to my herte.[4]

James married Lady Joan in February 1424 and two months later returned to his kingdom with his bride.

Romance benefited the Stewarts very little: over the years they were as unlucky in love as in kingship. And their sexual lives became so horribly intertwined with sovereignty that, as long as a Stewart sat on the throne or claimed the crown, sexuality ruled, often without restraint, and promising reigns ended in disaster. A sixteenth-century writer compared them to horses from the district of Mar in Aberdeenshire, which 'in youth are good, but in their old age bad'.[5]

The very first of them, Robert II, a bad ruler and a poor soldier, set the pattern for the lack of prudence that was perpetuated in the character of almost every one of his successors: he fathered half a dozen sons and eight daughters by two wives as well as eight or more natural sons. James V had three illegitimate sons before he was twenty, and his final tally (so far as we know) was seven, all by different mothers. The Scottish historian Gordon Donaldson points out in his favour: 'It may be to his credit that he did occasionally contemplate marriage to one of his mistresses, which would at least have secured the succession.'[6]

Fathering so many natural sons was always a sure recipe for producing a nobility packed with virile, ambitious young men who considered that they had claim to the power and honours due to a king's son – even to his crown itself.

James V may not have bequeathed a son to his nation, but he left it a daughter who inherited his sexuality along with the rashness of all the early Stewarts rolled into one. Mary, Queen of Scots made three marriages, all bad: the first fired by ambition, the second by love, and heaven alone knows what motivated the third – it was nothing less than a piece of madness emanating from the heart.

Mary's first marriage was made for her by the French king and the pro-French faction in Scotland. As a child she was betrothed to the Dauphin and in due course became Queen of France as well as of Scotland, making the two kingdoms one, exactly as the French had planned. But the king died and Mary's power in France went into the grave with him, so she returned to Scotland, where she met her kinsman, Henry Stewart, Lord Darnley. It was love at first sight. Mary 'was struck with the dart of love', overwhelmed 'by the comeliness of his sweet behaviour, personage and virtuous qualities'.[7] She was so deeply smitten with Darnley that she did not even wait for the papal dispensation she needed to marry him because they were closely related (they had a common grandmother, Margaret Tudor), but married him – and discovered too late that he was drunken, unstable and so insanely jealous that he murdered one of her favourites, David Rizzio, before her eyes while she was pregnant with Darnley's child. Afterwards he forced her to swear to him that the son she bore him was 'begotten by none but you'.

In emotional turmoil Mary turned to James Hepburn, Earl of Bothwell, and there can be little doubt that both were implicated in the plot by which Darnley was murdered while he lay ill at Kirk o' Field, just outside Edinburgh. Whether they were or not matters not a jot: the point is the Scottish people believed it to be true.

Bothwell, a wild, brash character, carried the queen off to Dunbar, where he raped her so that she would have to marry him. Many believed that Mary went willingly and that her sexual intercourse with Bothwell fell far short of rape: nonetheless, Mary, claiming she feared she might be pregnant, gave permission for Bothwell to divorce his wife, and a week later she married him. Branded the Scottish whore by the Protestant reformer, John Knox, and the Lords of the Congregation, Mary was compelled to abdicate in favour of her infant son, James, and was imprisoned on an island in Loch Leven. By then she had fallen out with Bothwell and he fled to Scandinavia, where he went mad and died in a Danish prison a decade later. Mary escaped from her island prison and tried to raise an army, but was defeated at Langside, near Glasgow, upon which she fled to England and threw herself on Elizabeth's mercy. She was held for eighteen years, but in the end became caught up in a plot to murder Elizabeth, and the English queen signed her death warrant.

Passionate love even more than religion cost Mary Stuart her throne, and at Fotheringhay Castle in Northamptonshire on the morning of 8 February, 1587, it cost her her life as well.

Mary was reckless: all the Stewarts were. A modicum of caution was brought to the dynasty only with James VI, who inherited other character defects which far outweighed the welcome trait of canniness. James was intelligent and learned, even scholarly, yet his nickname 'the wisest fool in Christendom' was well deserved because he lacked judgement. In his favour it must be said that he never had a chance to grow into anything other than a fool, even a wise one, for he was taken from his mother in infancy to be brought up under the aegis of dour, sober, ambitious men, in a world devoid of women, yet dominated by women – his mother, Mary Stuart and Elizabeth of England.

James added a new dimension to the Stewarts' sexuality – he was homosexual, or at least, bi-sexual, which deeply shocked his nobles and shook the dynasty to its foundations. Just as he was growing towards manhood in that environment devoid of female company, a handsome kinsman, Esmé Stuart, arrived at the court, and James was smitten. Esmé was the start of a succession of liaisons with courtiers, which aroused deep feeling both at home and abroad. An English agent wrote home: 'It is thought that this King is too much carried by young men that lie in his chamber and are his minions.'[8] As James's biographer, Otto J. Scott, points out, the agent chose his words precisely – at that time *minion* was used to describe a mistress.[9]

Alongside his homosexuality, James VI managed to maintain a heterosexual relationship in order to perpetuate the dynasty, and in doing so he actually fell deeply in love with his bride, Princess Anne of Denmark. Here he showed that recurring Stewart streak of romanticism; when Anne's arrival in Scotland was delayed he sailed off to Oslo with a little fleet to fetch her himself. Unfortunately, the novelty of romance soon wore off, leaving James and Anne with little in common: he was solemn, she was frivolous, and while he wrote poetry and talked theology, she was shallow, showy, extravagant and adored dancing. For the dynasty the important thing was that they produced sons: Henry, the heir who died, and Charles, who succeeded as Charles I. Their daughter, Elizabeth, married the Elector Palatine, and it was her grandson, George, who finally displaced the Stuarts and established the Hanoverian dynasty in 1714.

James VI believed implicitly in the God-given right of monarchs to reign, and for the benefit of his heir, he set these views down in a book on the craft of kingship, called *Basilikon Doron*. It explained James's strong views on matrimony:

> Remember also that Mariage is one of the greatest actions that a man doth in all his time, especially in taking of his first Wife: and if he Marie firste basely beneath his rank, he will ever be the lesse accounted to there-after And lastly, remember to choose your Wife as I advised you to choose your servants: that she be of a whole & cleane race, not subject to hereditary sicknesses, either of the soul or the body.[10]

He told Henry that marriage existed to stay lust, to procreate children and to provide a monarch with a helpmate. One should therefore choose a wife of one's own religion, a beauty, rich, and offering the dynasty 'a great alliance'. A wife should be treated as if she were 'your own flesh', he told his son, and the 'filthy vice' of adultery was to be avoided. If sleeping with a partner of one's own sex can be called adultery, then James was guilty of the 'filthy vice' which he condemned. But of course James Stuart reigned by divine right and was above the constraints he set for other men. For James VI it was a case of do as I say, not do as I do.

Prince Henry did not live long enough to follow or reject his father's precepts, but James's second son, Charles I, believed implicitly in his own divine right to rule and turned into a devoted husband, who heeded his father's marital advice. Unfortunately he also listened to his wife's urgings on how a monarch should treat parliaments and that cost him his crown: it also lost him his head on the execution block.

After a difficult start, Charles and his French wife, Henrietta Maria, grew to be a more devoted couple than any Stewart before or after. Few queens could say as Henrietta Maria did, 'I was the happiest and most fortunate of queens, for not only had I every pleasure the heart could desire, I had a husband who adored me.'[11]

Their son, who succeeded as Charles II in 1660, grew up within a happy contented family, passing an idyllic childhood which was only shattered by the outbreak of the Civil War, followed by exile, and his father's execution.

Charles II was forced by circumstances to mature early, and is reputed to have become a father for the first time at the age of sixteen, which means his child was born in 1646. Only three years later Lucy Walter, the first mistress of whom we know much, gave him his first son, who grew up to be the rebellious and ill-fated Duke of Monmouth. From then on Charles's life was a succession of mistresses – ladies of the court like Barbara Villiers, Louise de Keroualle, the Duchess of Marazin and others less noble, the actresses Moll Davis and Nell Gwyn among them. While Charles's mistresses presented him with lots of little earls and dukes whose names still adorn the English aristocracy, his wife, Catherine of Braganza, suffered miscarriage after miscarriage and failed to provide a legitimate heir. Charles's sexual partners were ill rewarded: in return for their favours he passed his own venereal disease on to them.

Bonnie Prince Charlie's grandfather differed in character from his brother, Charles II, in almost every way, except perhaps sexuality. He had none of his brother's affability, friendliness or political wisdom, and he set his Roman Catholic religion above all else. James married twice, but kept mistresses, who – like his brother's extra-marital partners – proved more efficient at producing heirs than the wives. His principal mistress, Arabella Churchill, gave birth to four children while his first wife, Anne Hyde, mothered half a dozen babies who failed to survive, as well as two daughters who subsequently reigned as Queen Mary and Queen Anne. His second wife, Mary of Modena, also lost one child after another until all hope of a legitimate male heir faded; it was at that despairing moment that Mary fell pregnant again and gave birth to a child in June 1688 – a son, whose birth confirmed a restoration of a Roman Catholic monarchy, and that of course led to the Glorious Revolution and banishment of James and his heir.

Thanks to the promiscuity of Charles and James, the Stuarts were by now contaminated with syphilis, which may have been the reason why neither Mary nor Anne was able to give the dynasty a surviving heir. Poor Anne's personal tragedy was as great as that suffered by any of the Stuarts: in the first five years of marriage she suffered four miscarriages, then two children died in infancy before she had the fleeting satisfaction of presenting the country with an heir, frail little William, Duke of Gloucester. Six more miscarriages and two children lost almost as soon as they were born might have been enough for any woman to suffer, but then William died just the day after his eleventh birthday. As well as inheriting his mother's frailties he had suffered from hydrocephalus, which ran in his father's family, the royal house of Denmark.

By 1701, when the exiled James VII and II died and Anne had lost her heir, the government in London was unwilling to accept James's son, James Francis Edward as heir because the boy was growing up at Saint-Germain-en-Laye, conveniently close to Versailles, under the dominant Catholic control of his mother and the French. It was decreed therefore that, on Anne's death, the crown should pass through the line of James I's daughter, Elizabeth, to the Electress Sophia or her heir – and that is precisely what happened: when Anne died in 1714, Sophia's son, the Elector of Hanover was offered the British crown as King George I.

This was a great pity, for young James Stuart grew up to be a much abler man than his father and less bigoted. From childhood he looked a Stuart through and through; he was tall, elegant and a Royal Stewart down to the tips of his fine-boned fingers.[12] Although he had also inherited the melancholy countenance of the Stewarts, his deep, dark eyes came from the genes of the Modenas. No wonder they called him 'the Blackbird' at Saint-Germain. In character he was brave, a sensitive boy, intelligent, but with his mother's quick temper, which he learnt to control in time. Many said he would have ruled wisely, and the historian, Peggy Miller, went so far as to suggest:

James Francis Edward had all the makings of a good king, and perhaps of all the Stuarts most deserved to reign.[13]

James was only thirteen when his father died in September 1701 – once again a Stuart succeeded as a minor. Louis XIV did not hesitate to proclaim him King of England, Scotland and Ireland, but wisely omitted France since they were living in France on the bounty of the French king.

James Stuart's greatest misfortune was that he was cursed with the worst of bad luck in almost everything he touched, from choosing men to lead his Cause to timing every attempt he made to win back his crowns. It is easy to say that people make their own fortune, good or bad, but the Pretender's failure went far beyond normal fate, and cannot be dismissed as self-inflicted or due to incompetence. Even the weather favoured King George, destroying or delaying every seaborne invasion and blowing a storm the moment James set sail in a ship in the seas around Britain or even in the Mediterranean. No wonder they called these gales Protestant winds. They blew when James tried to invade in 1708; they delayed him in 1715; they destroyed an invasion fleet in 1719, and they even did their worst when the French organized a fleet to support Prince Charlie in 1744.

Poor health and psychosomatic illness at crucial moments also helped to shape James Stuart's ill fortune. Neither he nor his second son, the Duke of York, was able to eat normally and even on fast days both were allowed meat. Fortunately, Charles did not inherit this delicate constitution, although he had his own health problems, probably handed down from his mother rather than from his father.

James turned into a neurotic, whose health broke under stress, so in this sense he can be said to have created his own ill fortune. At the crucial moment in almost every personal crisis, attempt to win back his throne, or any planned action throughout adult life, he went down with an attack of a type of fever which left him weak and unable to act decisively.[14] This illness, which dogged the Pretender, must surely be one of the principal causes of the indecisiveness and lack of confidence which prevented him from making politically or militarily astute decisions, and inevitably it led to the defeatist attitude and depression which ruined his chances and in the end it destroyed the man himself.

The miracle is that James Stuart lived to be the longest reigning sovereign *de facto* or *de jure* in English or Scottish history – he reigned for more than sixty-four years, beating Queen Victoria's sixty-three years and George III's sixty.

The Old Pretender shaped the Cause for his son to inherit, but it was a poor inheritance. From the very first he made it more difficult for his son to succeed. Un-Midaslike, whatever James Stuart touched turned to dross – and that included love!

An invasion planned in 1708 in the wake of the widely unpopular Union of the Parliaments of Scotland and England the year before was thwarted by those Protestant winds and the British fleet whose efficiency ironically owed much to the reorganization of the Royal Navy by James's father. All James saw of Scotland was a distant view of its capital from the far side of the Firth of Forth.

James had no more luck when Anne died. The 1715 rising was lost almost as soon as it started when command of the Jacobites fell to the Earl of Mar, a Scottish noble, who richly deserved the nickname history put on him – 'Bobbing John'. Mar lacked ability, flair and decisiveness – all bad failings in a leader – but he was also untrustworthy and 'bobbed' from the Jacobite side to the Hanoverians and did James's Cause enormous damage. Mar raised the Stuart standard in Aberdeenshire on 6 September 1715 and marched south to seize Perth, but there 'Bobbing John' dithered and threw away the best opportunity the Stuarts were ever to have of winning back their crowns. Unaware that most of his plans had been betrayed by spies, James landed at Peterhead in the north-east, in December, only to find the '15 had failed and he had no choice but to return home.

But where was home? The French would no longer allow him to stay in France, so the Pretender had to settle first for Avignon, then papal territory, and later in Italy. He went first to his mother's family home at Modena, and there fell head over heels in love with his cousin Benedicta, but Benedicta's father had other ideas: he had no desire for James Stuart as neighbour or son-in-law, so the Pretender was compelled to move on. Pope Clement XI gave him the use of a palace at Urbino and a pension, which suited the London government very nicely since it placed the exiled Stuarts so securely within the Roman church that they would never be accepted by the British people.

Urbino was a glorious ducal palace, standing high above the old town, its towers splendidly majestic against the Apennines and the sky. It was beautiful, and worthy of a king, but too isolated for James Stuart. At Urbino he felt miserable and cut off from the whole world, and he quickly sank into a quicksand of depression and self-pity, which earned him a new sobriquet, Mr Misfortune. He tried hard to persuade Clement to give up his own summer residence at Castelgandolfo which would be much nearer the centre of things, but the Pope drew the line at that and in the end James had to settle for a *palazzo* in Rome.

But by that time his luck had changed.

James's first piece of good fortune was news that Spain was prepared to mount a rising on the Jacobites' behalf and the King over the Water was invited to come to Spain and take part in it. This was not a generous or philanthropic gesture, but simply a piece of opportunism to further Spain's own cause, but James Stuart was grateful and accepted. At the end of 1718 he travelled in great secrecy to join the Spanish fleet at Corunna, but before he left he set another piece of business in train – arrangements to find a bride.

The king's marriage had become a pressing matter for the Jacobites because James was now thirty and without an heir, or prospect of marriage, and his supporters feared there was a very real danger of the Stuart line dying out. The question of the succession had to be faced quickly. Finding a wife for the Pretender would be no easy matter, for most of the suitable brides would be unwilling to accept a king without a throne, and even those who might consider him would be warned off by threats from the British government.

The search for a bride among the friendly courts of Europe would be a delicate matter, but James believed he had just the man to act as his emissary. Charles Wogan was a bold but polished young Irishman, who had already proved his loyalty to the king. Wogan had fought at Preston in the '15, was captured and escaped to make his way to the Jacobite court at Avignon. James took so great a liking to this charming Irishman that when the time came to find someone of unquestionable loyalty to search Europe to find him a bride, he thought of Wogan. The Earl of Mar, who had by now insinuated himself into the office of James's Secretary of State, was instructed to write to the dashing captain on James's behalf with instructions for the delicate mission:

You will be very glad he thinks now very seriously of setting about what all who wish him well so much desire, marriage. There are amongst others two princesses proposed to him, one the Princess of Baden Baden, the late Prince Lewis' daughter, the other a Princess of Saxe, cousin to the King of Poland. It is reasonable he should be well informed of their persons &c. by one he can trust, before he made any advances towards any of them, and you are the person he has pitched upon for going to see them and giving him that information . . . If any other Courts fall in your way through Germany, where there are princesses, it will not be amiss that you endeavour to see them and inform yourself about them . . . in some of them there may be princesses as fine women as any of the two we have been informed of.[15]

As an afterthought James himself added a postscript:

Prince James Sobieski, son of the late King of Poland, has several daughters, who, I believe, are somewhere in Germany. You may inquire about them and endeavour to see them all, if they fall in your way or be not much out of it.[16]

James Stuart could not have realized it at the time, but that postscript was to change his life and the Jacobite Cause.

THREE

JEWEL OF THE SOBIESKIS

Your merit, Madame, can only draw from above new blessings for the righteousness of my cause and give a new ardour to the zeal and devotion of my faithful subjects. May heaven grant that the summit of my personal happiness may be the beginning of that which I shall henceforth share with you, unable as I am to envisage any that is not involved with you.

Letter from James Edward Stuart to Clementina Sobieska, accompanying formal proposal of marriage addressed to her father. 24 June 1718.[1]

The Sobieskis came as an afterthought, a postscript to the letter of instruction to Wogan at the start of his mission in search of a wife for James Stuart. They ought not to have been at the back of the king's mind, for James must have heard of the redoubtable dowager Queen Marysienka Sobieska of Poland while she was living at the Château de Blois, following the death of her husband, John Sobieski, King John III of Poland. Like James Stuart, Marysienka was a pensioner of Louis XIV of France. She had also lived in Rome, where the Sobieskis were held in the highest esteem by the Pope, and it could well have been someone in the Vatican who prompted James to remember the devout Polish family with three eligible daughters.

The Sobieskis derived their name from a place called Sobieszyn, and were as Polish through and through as the Stuarts were Scottish. Mikolaj Sobieski was a man of property around Lublin in 1480, and from then on the family grew quickly in importance, acquiring much wealth through good marriages. Marek Sobieski, was a famous warrior and hero, whose marriage into one of the leading Polish families not only brought him into the front line of the aristocracy but introduced a sensitive, artistic and intellectual strain into the rather dull adventurer character of the earlier Sobieskis.

Marek's son, Jakob or James, was a statesman, general and orator of note, and his studies at the Sorbonne brought the family into contact with the West for the first time. By marrying Theofila, granddaughter of Stanislaw Zolkiewski, Jakob added the blood of 'bonnie fighters' and heroes to the many other talents of the Sobieskis, for Stanislaw was a textbook hero – he defeated the Swedes, conquered Moscow, rode into battle against the Turks and, as an old man, fell at the battle of Tutora.

The son of Jakob and Theofila, Jan, or John, who was elected King John III of Poland, made the name of Sobieski resound throughout Christendom when he led the Christian army against the Turks and drove the invaders back from Vienna in 1683. It was he who tore the crescent down from the pinnacle of St Stephen's spire and replaced it with the cross. John Sobieski went into history as a hero-king, the saviour of Christendom.

Sobieski resembled the Stewarts, as a fine warrior and as a monarch whose reign began with much promise only to end in tatters. His love life bears comparison with the Stuarts too, for it proved as great a battlefield as his public life.

As a wild young man, serving in the French army John experienced as many skirmishes with women as with enemy soldiers. One of these liaisons produced a son, who turned up in Poland some time later, causing an enormous scandal. Next John fell head over heels for a woman his mother considered quite unsuitable, so Theofila, a woman of spirit, hurriedly married the girl off to someone else before her son had time to propose. In the spring of 1652, John was again in trouble when he fought a duel with a Lithuanian aristocrat: he was wounded and as a result missed the battle of Batoh against the Tatars, in which his brother was killed. His mother never forgave him for this.

It is hardly surprising that 'he acquired the well founded reputation [in the words of a German biographer] of a successful *Schürzenjäger* [ladies' man, literally *apron-chaser*] and a not altogether accommodating neighbour'.[2] Perhaps it was from this great-grandfather that Prince Charlie inherited some of the wilder traits that came out in his character.

Among the 'aprons' chased by John Sobieski was a French girl, Maria Casimira de la Grange d'Arquien, usually known in Poland as Marysienka, then only fourteen, but sufficiently mature for John to fall deeply in love with her. While John was away fighting the Swedes, however, Jan Zamoyski, one of the wealthiest men in Poland came along and married Marysienka, much to John's fury. John was a jealous man and was beside himself with rage when he learned that Marysienka's husband, described as 'très débauché pour le sexe et Bacchus',[3] was cruel to her. Marysienka bore her husband two children, the first of whom 'died in its cradle; it had paid for the sins of the father, having been born with an inherited disease'.[4]

Marysienka's sorrow and John's passion brought the two together and, although she was still a married woman, they swore undying love for one another before the altar of Warsaw's Carmelite church, then began to plot to have Marysienka's marriage declared invalid. Old Zamoyski saved them the trouble by considerately dying 'from the disease which has a habit of revenging the sins of youth by premature death'.[5] Zamoyski almost certainly had syphilis, in those days so prevalent among erring aristocracy, and as Marysienka had been married to him for seven years and her first child by him died from the same cause, it may well be that she subsequently passed it on to her son by John Sobieski, who was Clementina's father.

John, by now King of Poland, married Marysienka, and they had three sons, the eldest of whom was called Jakob, or James. While the two younger boys were strapping lads, James was described as small of stature, thin and scrawny, hump-backed and with a high girlish voice – and inclined to sexual deviations. Another who knew him described him as moody, imperious, and with a thin, pinched face. He had to wear a corset and special padding to conceal his deformity.[6]

John was dominated by Marysienka, who was not a woman to be crossed even by Louis XIV of France. When the French king refused to make her father a duke she egged her husband on to annoy him by going to the rescue of the Emperor who had been driven out of Vienna by the Turks.

Then in the middle of the campaign she belaboured poor John with hectoring letters, accusing him of not reading the letters she sent him.

'Can you seriously affirm that I do not read your letters?' he wrote back from the battlefield, 'Can you believe it, while it is a fact that in the midst of all my occupations and cares I read each of them at least three times? the first time when they come; the second when I go to bed – in fact, when I am free; and the third when I set about answering them.'[7]

In spite of Marysienka's incessant demands, John succeeded against the Turks, which made him so great a hero that King Louis of France wooed him and Marysienka to become his ally. But Sobieski's great days were over and he spent the last part of his reign fighting military campaigns in the East, designed more to ensure that his son, Prince James Sobieski, would be elected to succeed him, than to benefit his country. He was a better general than a politician, and all he succeeded in doing was to stir up trouble among envious factions at home and in neighbouring countries. Inevitably, Marysienka who has been described as 'avaricious, despotic and revengeful',[8] made many enemies too, and she tried to dominate her husband and son.

John gradually abandoned his role as king to spend his time studying science, law, astronomy and mathematics. He was a tall man, with staring eyes, who cut his hair in a monk's tonsure: he dressed in a long scarlet robe, lined with silk for summer and fur for winter, and wore a fur hat set with diamonds and other jewels. As a reminder of his glory days against the infidel he carried a scimitar at his side and wore Turkish leather boots whose deep heels were made of silver curved in a half-moon shape. John overate until he grew so gross that he suffered a series of heart attacks between 1691 and April 1696 when one ended his life. The great hero of Christendom had so little hope left by the time of his death that he refused even to draw up a will. 'They don't want to listen to me when I'm alive,' he said, 'so why should they obey my wishes when I'm dead.'[9]

He was right; the Polish monarchy was not hereditary, but kings were elected by a strange mixture of nobles and petty princes in Poland and even as far away as Germany, and his son, James, was not chosen. The great days of Sobieskis were over – the glory of Poland sank with John and the direct line of the family died with James.[10]

Marysienka departed for Rome and then France, where Louis XIV gave her the castle at Blois and a pension, and James left Poland for Silesia to live on estates at Ohlau, which had been given to his father by the Emperor as a reward for his great victory over the Turks.

John and Marysienka wanted their heir to marry well, and at one time there were plans for James to marry the immensely rich Louise Charlotte Radziwill, who owned half of Lithuania. However, the jealous Polish aristocracy, thwarted the scheme by whisking Louise away to Berlin, where she fell in love with the Count Palatinate of Neuberg. It was love at first sight and they were married only four days after they met. Gossip said that no sooner was the wedding ceremony over than she took her husband by the hand and dragged him into an adjoining room where the marriage was consummated forthwith.[11] James Sobieski could certainly never have lived up to that!

James did not do badly for himself in the end: he married Hedwig Elizabeth, a sister of Neuberg, who had stolen the Radziwill girl, and whose sisters were Holy Roman Empress and Queen of Spain. The marriage gave the Sobieskis the most powerful European connections.

It has been said that Marysienka was so displeased with James's marriage that she opposed his succession to the Polish throne[12] on his father's death, but that seems unlikely. More probably what happened was that James, having suffered for years from being a poor misshapen creature dominated by his mother, rebelled. Marysienka ruled her son: even when he went off on military campaigns she made him write down everything he got up to, and she would not allow him to have an opinion on anything even after he was married. All his life she bombarded him with advice on everything – clothes, travel, books, friends – and demanded total obedience. Finally the worm turned and they quarrelled over whether to cultivate relations with Austria, where the Empress was his sister-in-law, or France, which Marysienka, being French, favoured. A united Sobieski family might just have snatched the crown of Poland at John's death, but there was no unity among the family, and rival nobility saw to it that James was not chosen.

James was luckier in his married life than in his relations with his mother, for Hedwig was beautiful and charming, although a rather silly woman without drive and certainly no Marysienka. James and Hedwig held court at Ohlau, and schemed for his future accession to the Polish throne in their own ineffectual way. It was all rather similar to the Stuarts' little court in Rome, for Sobieski was a man without spirit or any real hope. He grew into a dumpy, rather plump middle-aged man, who wore a permanently worried expression on his face and, with no son to succeed him, James soon lost interest in the Polish crown and concentrated on finding suitable husbands for his three daughters.

Here at Ohlau, towards the end of winter in 1718, Prince James received the strange visitor whose outgoing, charming Irish personality brightened the dullness of the court.

Wogan had carried out his king's commission to the letter, even through the worst of the central European winter weather. He travelled over hundreds of miles of frozen and dangerous roads to view eligible girls as instructed, all in the greatest of secrecy because the British, if it came to their ears, would do everything in their power to stop the king's marriage plans. Wogan went first to Baden-Baden, but was greatly disappointed to discover that the princess there was so diminutive that tall, stately James Stuart would have looked ridiculous beside her. On to Saxony he rode only to find the girl there too old, so he continued to Furstenburg where there were two eligible princesses to view, but both turned out to be dull and far from pretty. Having drawn a blank in Bavaria, Westphalia and Swabia, Wogan was left with only the postscript to the king's letter to guide him. He discovered that the Sobieskis were living at Ohlau and set out for Silesia, where, by a stroke of good fortune, he met an old friend, who was able to introduce him to the Sobieski court incognito. Neither Prince James nor his three daughters, Casimira, Charlotte and Maria Clementina, had the slightest inkling as to who their visitor was, or why he was there.

Wogan found the Sobieski family immersed in all the fun of a carnival for, by pure chance, he arrived at Ohlau halfway through Lent, when the family paused briefly from the rigours of fasting and prayer that their strong Roman Catholic faith demanded of them. Poles lived life intensely because their very existence as a nation was under constant threat from enemies on all sides – they could not even choose a king themselves, but had to accept the sovereign elected by a crowd of petty German princes and other outsiders, who didn't care a jot about Poland. Their Roman Catholic religion was lived with deep devotion, too, because it was under constant threat from Orthodox Russians, Protestant Swedes and Muslim Turks. But Wogan did not see that side of the Sobieskis and, as a good Catholic himself, it is unlikely that he would have thought it important if he had been aware of it. His king needed a staunch Catholic at his side and here he was among a faithful family who were enjoying the mid-Lent carnival.

Wogan was delighted with his visit to Ohlau, but kept his counsel as he studied the Prince and Princess Sobieski and their three daughters carefully. Casimira, the eldest, was the least beautiful, and he was told that she could be bad tempered and (like her mother) was inclined to fall short on common sense. Besides, she was already betrothed to James Stuart's cousin, the Duke of Modena.

Charlotte was prettier; tall, red-headed and with many admirers, but she too was promised to a French nobleman.

That left Maria Clementina who, although only sixteen, was the jewel of the Sobieski family; Wogan fell under her spell the moment his eyes lit on her, and the only fault he could find with her was that she was rather small in stature. This tiny slip of a girl with such beautiful brown hair and large, glowing eyes, captivated everyone she met. She had advantages other than her physical attributes to offer an impoverished exiled king; she was the Pope's goddaughter, her aunts were Queen of Spain and Dowager Holy Roman Empress, and she would bring him jewels and money.

When James heard about this little Polish princess who was known in the family as 'our Queen' because she had longed as a child to be Queen of England one day, his heart raced and he wrote at once to Prince James to ask for Clementina's hand in marriage. Like so many of his Stewart ancestors, there was a romantic streak concealed somewhere within that sombre personality, for James accompanied his formal proposal of marriage with a romantic personal letter to Clementina, telling her how much he wanted to marry her:

> May Heaven grant that the summit of my personal happiness may be the beginning of what I shall henceforth share with you, unable as I am to envisage any that is not involved with you.[13]

James's proposal was accepted and, to the annoyance of Charles Wogan, in the early autumn of 1718, Colonel John Hay was sent to escort the bride and her mother to Italy. As always, Stuart secrets were soon known in London, and the strongest possible pressure was brought to bear on the Emperor to kidnap his cousin and aunt, Clementina and her mother, as they travelled through Austria. The Emperor capitulated and ordered that the travellers be held prisoner in the Schloss Ambras at Innsbruck.

The two Jameses, Stuart and Sobieski, protested angrily, but were powerless to persuade the Emperor to defy Britain, so Clementina and her mother spent months in comfortable, but secure confinement while the Emperor did nothing. As luck would have it, that was the very moment when it suited Spain to organize the attack on Britain on the Stuarts' behalf, and James was invited to sail with the invasion. Of course James was desperate to go, but how could he leave his bride a prisoner in Austria?

Wogan again came to the rescue and devised and carried out the plan to spirit Clementina out of the castle in disguise. In the midst of the late winter snow and ice, Clementina was taken over the Alps to Italy and arrived in Bologna on the last day of April 1719, only to find no bridegroom there to meet her. James had been compelled to leave for Spain to join the invasion, and by the time his bride arrived he was in Corunna where he found his journey was wasted; the invasion fleet had been wrecked by another of those Protestant winds and the expedition was abandoned.

Fired by love, James had thought of everything before he set out: he left instructions with James Murray that a proxy marriage ceremony should take place as soon as possible after Clementina arrived. So on the morning of 9 May, Clementina dressed in a simple white gown, set a white ribbon in her glowing dark hair and the fabulous Sobieski pearls around her neck and went to church, accompanied by Mrs Misset, one of the female helpers in the escape. There she confessed, was given communion and was married by proxy. Charles Wogan watched proudly as his little Polish princess replied 'Yes' in a small voice when asked if she consented to marry James Francis Edward Stuart.

For Clementina this moment was a childhood dream come true; she was Queen of England at last, even if at that exact moment she had neither king to cherish nor crown to wear. Clementina's dream did not fade immediately, for the Pope arranged for her to make a state entry into Rome, where the people gave her a rapturous welcome. If only James had been there, Clementina's world would have been perfect.

Wogan was able to reassure his king of the virtues of the woman who was now his wife:

Our admirable, I could almost say adorable, Queen has given my endeavours yt blessing they have mett with, by her firmness her prudence and a constancy in all situations without example. Yr Mty was highly in yr right as to ye judgement you formed of her when you hoped allways so much from her conduct and steadyness. They are indeed beyond anything that can be imagined in her age and sex, and not to be equalled but by her extreme affection for yr person . . . She is in perfect health and safety and suffers only by a continuance of those arguments and obstacles which keep her from you.[14]

Clementina, in her youthful impetuosity, saw no obstacles; she begged to be allowed to join her husband in Spain, but the king would not hear of it: instead, she was compelled to pass another three long months at the Convent of Saint Cecilia in the Via Vittorio in Rome while she awaited his return. At long last on 1 September they were united in the little grey town of Montefiascone in the foothills of the Apennines, between Bolsena and Viterbo. To the onlooker, seeing them together for the first time, they must have looked a strange pair, for James was now thirty-one, tall, dark and with an abstracted look, while his bride was petite, pretty and painfully thin from a lifetime of constant fasting in obedience to the Church's rules, and just a child beside him. After all, she was still only seventeen.

At Montefiascone James and Clementina went through a second marriage ceremony – a much grander affair conducted in the cathedral by the Bishop of Montefiascone and followed by a great banquet. They listened to an oratorio and a play, performed in their honour, and then retired. The Jacobite world waited and hoped. . . .

If history were a fairy tale or even just fair, James and Clementina would have lived happily ever after. But it is not and circumstances proved very different from what the beginnings of their story might have led one to expect.

James and his bride settled into the Muti Palace, a smallish *palazzo* on the Piazza degli Sant' Apostoli, which the Pope had given to James for his marital home. The Muti was far from imposing, a cramped-looking ochre-walled building constructed in 1644 by the Giovan Battista Muti-Papazzuri (now known as the Palazzo Ballestra) and set round a square courtyard with a fountain in the middle, and a sombre staircase which led up to several fine rooms on the main floor, the best feature of the house. Here James Stuart held court. Apart from the Vatican and Quirinale, the Muti was the only building in Rome to be honoured with a papal guard every day. And one essential feature for two people as devout as James Stuart and Clementina Sobieska was that the tiny chapel of La Madonna dell' Archetto, just behind the palace, was kept open all night with a special sentry guarding it so that the royal couple could go there and pray whenever they wished. For good measure the ancient Church of the Sant' Apostoli stood nearby and James and Clementina also worshipped in it regularly.

The royal couple were blissfully happy in those early days, although portraits of Clementina depict an air of uncertainty in her round and rather attractive face. The smile on her lips appears fragile, with a measure of sadness in those large, glowing eyes which captivated Charles Wogan so much when he first looked into them at Ohlau. Clementina's face even in those early days hints at the troubles that were to follow. In Rome at the end of 1719, however, no one saw any shadows of the future: at that moment every Jacobite was as much in love with the new queen as was the king himself. Beauty, sweetness, grace, compassion, were words which flowed from those who met Clementina: piety, too – perhaps rather too much piety.

Clementina was devoutly Roman Catholic, and put her religion before everything – even her health. At the time of her escape from Austria she was fasting, and even in that moment of extreme physical and mental strain when she needed every ounce of energy she could call on, Clementina would not compromise. As she travelled over the Brenner Pass she refused to eat chicken or even to sip some wine because it was a day for fasting and as a result she fainted. Her protectors had great difficulty in persuading her to take a little white wine mixed with water, to give her strength. As supporters of the Cause were soon to find out, Clementina was accustomed to fasting, and as a result she was as thin as a rake. This depriving herself of food was to have a profoundly detrimental effect on her husband and her sons as well as on herself.

At Pentecost, while she was in Rome awaiting the return of her husband, Clementina made the round of seven churches, and at St Peter's took off her shoes and stockings and proposed to walk round the church barefoot, but was stopped by her father confessor. After she returned to Rome with James following their marriage, the couple paid three or four visits a week to the convent at which she had stayed while James was away in Spain. Clementina was too devout for the good of the Cause, for such commitment to the Roman Catholic Church was hardly likely to make the exiled Stuarts acceptable again in Britain.

At first it did not occur to Clementina that there was any likelihood of her husband failing to be restored to his throne; for her it was simply a matter of waiting a short while until matters sorted themselves out and her husband was summoned back in London. She didn't give a thought to how the restoration might come about and it was only slowly that the awful truth dawned – she might be Queen of England, but she would never be Queen *in* England.

From then on she began to realize that her marriage was a cruel mismatch. James was serious, formal, ever aware of his position as king by divine right, and at all times he expected the whole of Rome to bow and scrape before him. He never gave glittering parties or balls at the Muti and, as a result, the local nobility became angry or just laughed at him. As a result, he and Clementina were seldom invited to any except the most public events, and they had no intimate friends.

What a change this all was from the jollity of Ohlau, the adventure of the escape from Innsbruck and the wild dash across the Brenner to be worshipped as a queen. In their drab little *palazzo*, Clementina found herself left alone much of the time while her husband spent interminable hours writing letters and plotting with Jacobites from England, Scotland, France or Spain. He had terrible problems to face, especially the rivalry among some of the people closest to him and the start of a series of moves which were to lead to the defection of Mar to the Hanoverian side. But he did not confide any of this to his wife: she remained cooped up in the cramped palace, bored to tears, while he talked interminably or brooded alone. Apart from occasional excursions into the Roman *campagna*, or visits to Cardinal Aquaviva at Albano, there was nothing for her to do and nowhere to go but the little chapel of the Madonna dell' Archetto behind the Muti, or the Church of the Sant' Apostoli. She disappeared there more and more to pray and pray again until people began to call her 'Regina Apostolorum'.

To escape the burning Roman summer and the claustrophobic stuffiness of the Muti, the Pope gave them the Savelli Palace, at Albano, then set on the edge of the town, but now in the centre and serving as the town hall of Albano. The Savelli was set high and surrounded by olive groves and woods and gardens, with magnificent views across Lake Albano to the Mediterranean. To escape to Albano was bliss, but visits were too infrequent to provide much relief and certainly they were not sufficient to make marriage more bearable for either of them.

A child still and far from friends or familiar surroundings, Clementina's calm began to wear thin and it is hardly to be wondered at that another side to her character manifested itself. The instability of the Sobieskis, that trait of unreliability, became apparent just as it had come out in her parents and grandparents, and the vivacious, pretty little girl suddenly took on the untamed quality of a wild animal. James discovered that his wife could fly into violent tempers, and disagreements between them became a regular feature of Muti life. She and her husband began to bicker over the smallest details of life at the palace and here they found they had one trait in common – pig-headed stubbornness which would not allow either of them to back away from a quarrel, so that the Muti became riven with disputes and raised voices. Sir Charles Petrie's judgement of Clementina is harsh but accurate:

> Frivolous in the early days of matrimony and fanatically superstitious later on, Clementina was quite unfitted to be the wife of such an exile as James and had he been restored to the throne during her lifetime, she must of necessity have become as much his evil genius as Henrietta Maria had been of his grandfather, and more than Mary of Modena had been of his father. As it was, she exercised no influence upon the course of the Jacobite Movement.[15]

Clementina's defects of character might have manifested themselves even more clearly and brought their quarrels to a head earlier, but for the fact that good news swept the Jacobite world during the Spring of 1720 – Clementina was pregnant. For the time being the evil spell was broken and the king and queen were brought together again.

Clementina, little more than a child herself and sadly lacking in knowledge of gynaecological matters, had no idea what pregnancy involved, not even enough to be able to hazard a reasonable guess as to when the child was due. James, no expert himself in sexual matters, was bewildered. 'The Queen returns to you her kind compliments and continues very well,' he wrote to the Duke of Ormonde in Spain on 11 November. 'It is indeed a little singular to have mistaken so much as 3 or 4 months in her reckoning.'[16]

James's half-brother, the Duke of Berwick, was more understanding. He reassured the king:

> I do not wonder at the Queen's being mistaken in her reckoning, it happens often at first being with child, but I hope she will repair the delay, by giving us a prince at the end of this month.[17]

Clementina did not 'repair the delay' until the last day of the year 1720. Soon after five o'clock on the afternoon of that New Year's Eve momentous news burst from the drab little Muti Palace in Rome: it raced across the city to the Vatican, and soon was winging its way to every part of Europe – Clementina Sobieska, wife of James Stuart, King over the Water, had given the Jacobite Cause a son and heir. As the child was born a great storm raged across Germany, laying waste the homelands of the Electors of Hanover, and that night a new and brilliant star shone in the skies over Europe making the birth of the Prince messianic. To Jacobites everywhere the star and the storm were omens: the fortunes of Scotland's ancient royal house had turned and one day this child would wear the crowns which were rightly his.[18]

The boy was healthy and strong and he was truly the child of the Stuart sovereign: there would be no refuting that, no scurrilous insinuations that the baby was a changeling, smuggled into the queen's bedchamber in a warming pan, as had been spread when James himself was born in 1688. James had taken every precaution. The moment Clementina's first hint of labour manifested itself he invited the nobility of Rome and dignitaries of the Roman Catholic Church to be present, and they crowded the queen's room and the ante-rooms of the Muti Palace off and on for the best part of a week while the queen was in labour, so that when the child arrived at last, all could testify to the fact that this was truly Clementina's son and James's heir. There had been much coming and going at the Muti during the five days of the queen's labour, with everyone sent away when it was clear that the birth was not imminent, only to be summoned back almost immediately because it appeared about to happen. The Pope himself became involved in all the furore, visiting at the palace to give Clementina his personal blessing and offering up special prayers. More practically, he sent a supply of linen for the new baby.

When the Prince was born at last, the witnesses who pressed around Clementina's bed included cardinals 'to the number of a hundred',[19] which surely must be an exaggeration. Among them were cardinals representing Scotland, England and Ireland as well as the Vatican, France and Spain, and a host of noblewomen, most of them accompanied by their husbands – Lady Nithsdale, Donna Teresa Albani, the Duchess of Bracciano, the Duchess Salviati, and the widowed Principessa di Piombino with her three daughters, who were also escorted by their husbands. Humble Mrs Misset was rewarded for her part in Clementina's escape from Austria by being present and appointed lady of the bedchamber. James himself knelt at a prieu-dieu close to his wife's bed as his heir was born. It takes very little imagination to appreciate the effect this public spectacle they had created out of a private and intimate personal moment had on this frightened and inexperienced girl. The baby was handed over to nurses, the Pope sent a present of money and holy relics, and the whole of Rome fussed around the newborn Prince. By the time a royal salute echoed across the Tiber from the Castel Sant' Angelo next morning, the exhausted Clementina realized that the child she had borne, *her son*, was not hers at all, but belonged to a great royal dynasty of Europe and to the Jacobite Cause.

The names he was given confirmed this – Charles for his great-grandfather, Edward for England's only royal saint, Louis for the King of France, Philip for the King of Spain, Casimir for the kings of Poland, and the saints' names, Sylvester, to mark his birth on St Sylvester's Day, and Maria. He was rarely called Charles Edward: within the family he was known as Charles, although his parents – with typical inability to agree – used different names; James often called him by the Italian diminutive, Carluccio, while Clementina used the Polish form, Carlusu.

The French called him Edouard, and the name Prince Charlie, which was to come later, was not a pet name but a rendering of the Gaelic *Tearlach* into English.

He was immediately created Prince of Wales.

Reports from Rome told the Jacobite world that the new prince was a fine, strong child, but English spies who had been listening at keyholes for weeks, gave out a different story. One despicable member of the community of British spies, Baron Philip von Stosch, who sent his reports back under the codename John Walton, reported that the child's legs were 'so turned inwards and deformed that one doubts very much whether he will ever be able to learn to walk'.[20] Jacobites hearing this refused to believe it, but in their hearts they may have feared that the child had inherited the misshapen body of his grandfather, Prince James Sobieski, or even that some genes tainted with the venereal disease of his grandfathers.

There was genuine cause for worry, because the baby's legs were not strong and it was feared that he might not be able to walk as Walton claimed. One suggested cause of this is that Charles suffered from rickets, a common enough complaint in those days, and one to which the Prince was exposed due to his mother's fasting and secluded life which may well have deprived her of vitamin D during her pregnancy. James consulted a number of physicians and tried to persuade the Prince's nurse, Mrs Sheldon, to try various remedies and exercises recommended by the doctors, but Mrs Sheldon went her own way and supported the child with reins. Charles was unable to stand steadily until after his third birthday.[21]

In spite of this poor start, Charles grew into a healthy boy and with a strong character, some aspects of it good, but others bad. The Stuarts had contributed the nobility of generations of kings who knew they were chosen to rule by God; the Sobieskis, with a more solid rise to power and brief kingship, should have added a more practical dimension, but this quality was lacking in Prince Charlie just as it was absent in John Sobieski, who never managed to deal with all the recalcitrant and jealous families among the Polish aristocracy. That would have been an invaluable genetic inheritance for the Prince when he came to deal with feuding and unreliable, tittle-tattling leaders of the Jacobite Cause later on. One of the great tragedies of the Jacobite Cause was that neither side of his family passed it on to him – neither really possessed it.

Fortunately Charles inherited bravery from both sides: from an early age the genes which had made the Stewarts fighters over the centuries made their presence evident in this latest heir to the dynasty, and his courage could fairly be compared also to that which drove generations of Sobieskis to become leaders in the fight to drive eastern invaders back from the gates of the West.

If both sides of the family contributed bravery, why was the Prince never able to put it to better use? The reason is that neither side combined generalship with fighting spirit: neither the Stewarts nor the Sobieskis were strong on statesmanship or the strategic ability, which might have won them more battles, or enabled them to make better use of their victories. Certainly a better diplomatic sense would have saved them from some of their worst defeats; it might even have saved their lives.

Charles inherited one valuable quality of leadership from both sides too – that ability to charm, which had so often helped his grandfather, James VII and II, and the quality which won Wogan over the moment he set eyes on Clementina. In Charles it was to gain him his men's loyalty against the greatest odds when he came to Scotland in 1745.

On the debit side, Charles Edward inherited Stuart and Sobieski faults – the wild temper of both parents, his mother's health problems, something of her instability, and his father's inability to come to terms with failure. And as he grew towards boyhood, he soon began to reveal that headstrong stubbornness that lay buried deep in the character of both James and Clementina, a fault which was to dog him and cause him great hurt all through his life.

Charles Edward took after his mother in many ways and inherited some of her constitutional defects although he was fortunate never to suffer from her manic depression.[22] Both suffered from asthma and it has been suggested that they also may have suffered from an allergy condition which displayed itself in different ways in each of them. Clementina had a serious eating problem, which could well have been anorexia nervosa, and Charles's tendency towards alcoholism may also have been triggered by an inherited allergy. Certainly Charles suffered from some kind of allergy while he was skulking in the Western Isles in 1746: John O'Sullivan was alarmed by some persistent form of dysentery or haemorrhagic diarrhoea – he called it 'a bloody flux' – from which the Prince suffered. O'Sullivan believed it was associated with drinking milk and wrote, 'The Prince drank no more milk, lived upon watter and was parfectly well.'[23]

There is a strong statistical connection between allergy and dyslexia[24] and Prince Charlie always had problems with his spelling. It has been suggested that he may have suffered from some degree of dyslexia.[25]

However, it is dangerous to attempt to diagnose at a distance of two hundred years. The question of whether the difficulties of mother and son were caused by a defective gene or an allergy remains a tantalizing one. 'It certainly seems plausible that some biochemical problem undermined the Prince's otherwise splendid constitution, and whether or not one concludes that his difficulties were physical, emotional or psychological, it is likely that his genetic inheritance is an important element in understanding this complex and vulnerable man,' Dr Rosalind K. Marshall concluded.[26]

On the first day of the year 1721, these strengths and faults could not be seen in the newborn prince before whom all of Rome knelt. In their eyes he was a perfect child, a saviour for the Stuarts.

Only a soothsayer could have divined what lay ahead for him.

FOUR

BELOVED, BETRAYED CARLUSU

I shall strive to obey you in all things. I will be very dutifull to Mamma,
and not jump too near her. . . . I long to see you soon and in good health.

Letter from Prince Charles Edward to his father, written when he was
seven years of age.[1]

If heredity created the intrinsic strengths and weaknesses in the
character of Charles Stuart the man and the lover, it was
environment that shaped him into the Jekyll and Hyde personality,
who could be the bonnie Prince or the wild partner in love. His
parents, their relationship with him and – equally important – the
way in which they related, or more often failed to relate to one
another, must bear responsibility for shaping the future prince.

Charles Edward's upbringing did not provide him with the
background against which he could grow into a monarch, nor even
guide him towards stable, relationships with those around him, let
alone help him to mature into a lover to be trusted. The saddest
feature of Charles's childhood and youth was that he loved both of
his parents passionately, and both were devoted to him, yet their
flawed personalities strained the bonds between them and their son.

The gloomy walls of the Muti Palace held only the frailest
happiness – there was no contentment to provide the young Prince
with the security he needed, and from early on he was well aware of
his mother's tantrums and his father's cold withdrawals. Their
quarrels, which were the talk of Rome as well as below stairs gossip
among servants and Jacobite followers, could not be hidden from him
even though sympathizers made great efforts to smooth over the
cracks in the marriage and continued to write and talk of the king

47

and queen with sympathy and tact. Long after they were aware that Clementina was not the innocent child she had been when she first arrived in Rome, they were determined to find good in her just as they saw what they wanted to see in the Prince of Wales.

James needed all the kind words that could be reported back from Rome about himself or any member of his family for at this moment there were stirrings among Jacobite supporters in England. Christopher Layer, a young London barrister, had arrived with news that Britain was in turmoil; discontent was everywhere and Layer believed that James's supporters could seize the Tower of London and clap the Hanoverian royal family in it. James was to travel to Holland to await the call home.

The Atterbury Plot, named after the pro-Jacobite Bishop of Rochester, Francis Atterbury, took up every minute of James's time – there were letters to be read and answered and secret meetings to be held constantly, all of which kept him so busy that he had little time to spend with Clementina. James would trust no one in the widely scattered community of the Cause, not even his wife or those closest to him in the Muti Palace. In spite of all his care the walls of the Muti still had ears; word slipped out and the plot fell apart. The chief conspirators, including Layer, were arrested.

Clementina resented being excluded from state business; up to that time there had been very little Jacobite activity since her marriage, so that the Cause remained nothing more than an ever-present background to court life, and as far as Clementina was concerned, everything revolved around her adored and pampered self. She could not understand why she should suddenly find herself pushed aside now and ignored, and her resentment began to show.

Both she and James displayed their fierce tempers as never before, although the more experienced and mature James was cleverer at controlling his – after all, he was older and had had more practice. But what was especially galling for James was that Rome tended to take his wife's side and point the finger at him as the one who ought to know better. This made it harder for him to bear Clementina's childish outbursts.

The spies and gossipmongers loved it, and used every quarrel, every harsh word or awkward circumstance, to stir up feeling between the king and queen. Von Stosch in particular continued his wicked work: he wrote to his master that several ladies of the royal household who knew about such matters, assured him that Clementina could not have another child because of her poor health. Impulsive as usual, the queen suddenly decided to escape from all the malicious backbiting and gossip by visiting the spa of Lucca, whose waters were renowned for their curative properties. Walton, of course, wrote that the trip was an attempt to help her to conceive.

James and Clementina could not help themselves; they rowed viciously when they were together, yet missed each other and sent touching letters when they were apart. No sooner had his wife reached Lucca than James wrote to her and she replied, 'I am trying now to overcome my bad temper so as to appear to you in the future as the best girl in the world. I am delighted to learn that one no longer thinks about the nasty plan "D" which has deprived me of the satisfaction of being with my Carissimo.' She ended by telling him, 'I shall not know rest or quietude until I am in the arms of my Carissimo.'[2]

Just at this time word arrived from Poland that Clementina's mother was dying, so James, the caring husband, dropped everything and dashed to Lucca at once to be with her and arranged for family correspondence to be intercepted so that he might cushion the blow when news of the Princess Sobieska's death arrived. When mourning for the princess was over, he took Clementina to Bologna to divert her with her favourite occupation of visiting religious houses. There they also watched the *palio* of San Petronio and James revived the ancient royal custom of 'touching' people suffering from the King's Disease, scrofula.

Lucca and Bologna was only a lull: soon the pathetic cycle of quarrelling and making up began all over again, demoralizing those followers who were devoting their lives to the Cause. As early as April 1722 John Hay poured out his soul to Mar, the most unfortunate choice of confidant he could have chosen, since Mar, never reliable, was at that moment on the point of changing sides again, and was reporting everything he could back to his new masters in London. Hay told Mar:

Their tempers are so very different that, although they are never of the same opinion on the smallest trifles, the one will not yield an inch to the other; the dread of being governed and the desire of governing, passion, youth ingrafted by a little mean education, will even afford matter for supporting their differences, which must end in something very dismal, their healths are equally ruined by it, and it is impossible they can hold out so . . .[3]

To Charles, now a lively toddler, growing stronger thanks to the exercises his father insisted upon, these violent quarrels, which ended in his mother storming off and his father sulking for hours on end, were frightening. One minute he was bathed in smothering love, the next his little world was blown apart by an explosion of vicious recrimination and separation, which left him with only his nurses and the gloomy, dark palace around him. He may still have been only two, but he was already coming to realize there was no security, no lasting or sure love. And he was aware that he himself was the source of one of his parents' bitterest disagreements.

Charles adored both his parents, and theirs was the only affection that he was ever able to reciprocate. Yet by undermining their son's love now, James and Clementina must share the blame for Prince Charlie's later difficulty in creating or sustaining a loving relationship with others.

The Prince of Wales's upbringing by Protestant nurses and, later, his education were a running sore in the relationship between the king and queen. That troublemaker, Mar, exacerbated it by proposing that Mrs Sheldon, a Catholic who was the daughter-in-law of the king's representative in Paris, General Arthur Dillon, should become governess to the young prince. James accepted the idea because he knew it would please his wife, but in the long run it proved a terrible mistake. Mrs Sheldon was under Mar's evil influence and the appointment placed her in an ideal position to stir up trouble between the king and queen over the handling of the Prince and over John Hay, who was heartily disliked by many Jacobites, but especially by Mar.

Mrs Sheldon's appointment could not have come at a worse time because she came on the scene when Clementina was at her most vulnerable: still only twenty, she had recently lost her mother and felt lonely, far from home, away from her father and her sisters, the only other women to whom she had been close. Without friends, and with her husband permanently shut away with his mysterious state business, Clementina felt so miserable and deserted that she turned to the insidious Mrs Sheldon. They became as close as conspirators.

This sinister woman worked in devious ways: she was a religious bigot, who resented every Protestant around the royal household, and soon inflamed Clementina into new quarrels with her husband over the education of Prince Charles and, worse still, sowed seeds of the slander that the king was having an affair with John Hay's wife.

This gave the British an excellent opportunity to undermine James's closest supporter, Hay, who posed the greatest threat to them, and in their efforts to discredit Hay, they found excellent allies in Mar, Mrs Sheldon – and (unwittingly) Clementina herself. The Muti Palace was packed with spies to keep Walton and his English masters well informed of the trouble between the king and queen, and at the same time to create yet greater scandal.

Mrs Sheldon was not a woman to guard her tongue, which was the source of most of the mischief around the Muti. Directly and indirectly, she must also have contaminated the child's mind with her own bigotry and poisonous backstairs gossip about wicked Protestant heresy and his father's behaviour.

The adultery rumours were nothing new: they had been blowing along the cold passages of the Muti before the king's marriage was six months old,[4] but Mar now succeeded in reviving them through his mouthpiece, Mrs Sheldon. James certainly did not have the sexual appetite of his uncle, Charles II, or even his father. The only woman he ever loved other than Clementina was his cousin, Beatrice, who had been refused to him, and there is not a shred of evidence that he was ever unfaithful to his wife with Mrs Hay or anyone else. But rumours are insidious things and they preyed on Clementina's mind, just at a time when it was becoming less stable and manic depressive.

Clementina herself was not above gossip. Writing several years after her death, Lady Mary Wortley Montagu repeated the nonsensical anti-Jacobite slander that Pope Clement XII was 'commonly suppos'd' to have been the queen's lover. 'She us'd to go about publickly in his state Coach to the great Scandal of the people,' Lady Mary wrote. 'Her husband's mistrisse spirited him up to resent it so far that he left Rome upon it, and she retir'd to a convent where she destroy'd her selfe.'[5]

Charles responded to this unstable environment by becoming a difficult, disobedient, wilful child who was hard to manage. Even at the age of three he could display winning charm one moment, then dig his determined little heels in the next if he did not want to do as he was told. To the mortification of Catholic Jacobites and the secret amusement of Protestants in Rome, he refused to kneel when he was presented to the Pope Benedict XIII soon after his election towards the end of May 1724.

Alarmed by his son's wilfulness, James decided it was time to take the boy away from the nursemaids who had raised him hitherto and hand him over to male tutors who would supervise his formal education and training for kingship. To provide a religious balance acceptable in Britain, and in one of his more statesmanlike moves, James sent for the Protestant James Murray in August that year, created him Earl of Dunbar, and appointed him governor to the Prince of Wales. The Roman Catholic Sir Thomas Sheridan was made under-governor.

There was a darker side to the appointment of Murray, however: not only was he a Protestant, but he was the brother of Mrs Hay. The appointment affronted Mrs Sheldon, who saw it not merely as a piece of heresy and confirmation of the king's relationship with the Hays, but a slur on her ability as well. She lost no time in making Clementina aware of this new affront, and unfortunately the dispute which ensued came at a time when Clementina had just discovered that she was pregnant again. With memories of the horror of her last confinement, she dreaded losing the only woman in whom she felt she could confide at this time when she so desperately needed a friend to whom she could pour out her heart.

By the time Clementina's second child was born on 6 March 1725, another son to make the Stuart succession doubly secure, Mrs

Sheldon had done her work well and the queen was close to hysteria. The Pope himself came to the Muti to baptize the child Henry Benedict Maria Clement Thomas Francis Xavier, and he was given the traditional title for a second son, Duke of York. Within the family the little duke was generally known as Harry. Again the Jacobite world rejoiced, but this time the joy was muted for relations between the king and queen were at an extremely low ebb.

James made matters worse by choosing the Protestant Lady Nithsdale to take charge of Prince Henry, and then by appointing John Hay, whom he had now created Earl of Inverness, as his Secretary of State in place of Mar who had betrayed him so badly. Stirred up by the poisonous Mrs Sheldon, Clementina's mind, already disturbed by post-puerperal depression, became very unstable and she prayed and brooded by turns. Anger and hysteria engulfed her, and she stormed at James that he must get rid of the Hays, Lady Nithsdale and James Murray. When the king refused, she threatened to leave him.

James knew he dared not yield to Clementina's demands for several reasons: if he dismissed the Protestants around his sons he would destroy any chance of ever being restored; if he sent Hay away he would lose his best adviser and the only man he could trust; above all, if he allowed Clementina to run his personal life, she would soon start to interfere in all official matters – as indeed she was already trying to do over Hay.

The more Rome gossiped the more depressed Clementina became, and the more she shut herself away the greater the gossip grew. She now turned into a recluse, spending long periods in prayer, thoroughly neurotic and disturbed in her mind. In this depressive state she became even more a prey to Mrs Sheldon's malicious tongue. As Clementina grew worse Rome continued to take sides – usually hers. News that the Pretender's marriage was on the rocks spread through Europe doing untold damage to the Cause as a number of influential followers began to take Clementina's part.

James still loved his wife in spite of all the troubles that now engulfed his marriage and he tried to reason with her, but that only made her more hysterical and blind to reason. No effort of reconciliation had the slightest effect – Clementina just prayed and fulminated as summer turned to autumn in 1725. Finally, on 15 November, she packed her bags and drove to the Convent of Saint Cecilia, the religious house in which she had stayed when she first arrived in Rome. There she poured out her heart to the Mother Superior. Her husband was determined to bring her boys up as heretics, she told the nuns, and 'rather than permit such infamy, she would stab them with her own hand'.[6] The nuns were shocked and offered her sanctuary.

If the nuns were horrified, what a devastating experience all this must have been for a child not yet five: Charles watched the comings and goings and picked up scraps of the recriminations which were flying around the *palazzo* in the months that followed. The Pope, who himself had witnessed Prince Charles's heretical behaviour the day the boy refused to kneel before him, cut James's allowance and sent a bishop to try to discover the truth about the Prince's upbringing and the king's adultery. James was stung by such interference in his personal life and told the Pope to mind his own business – indeed, had he thought His Holiness could seriously believe this gossip, he said, then the papal emissary, bishop or no bishop, would have left by the window rather than the staircase.

The whole family and anyone else of influence was dragged into the squabble: while James wrote off to his wife's relatives, her father, the Queen of Spain and the Duke of Parma, and to the Duke of Ormonde and others, Clementina was composing her own version of the quarrel for anyone willing to listen. James even suggested to Prince James Sobieski at one point that Clementina should be sent home to Ohlau, but this never happened.[7] One of the queen's closest allies at this time was the fat, ambitious intriguer, Cardinal Alberoni, who repaid all the kindness James had shown him in the past, by visiting Clementina every day and helping her to pen 'wronged wife' letters to the King of France, the Queen of Spain, her sister, the Duchess of Bouillon, and anyone else who was likely to heed her complaints. As letters to her sister showed, separation from her husband covered up the weeping sores in her marriage if it did not actually heal them. Clementina told the Duchess of Bouillon:

Whatever happens, I assure you that I should rather choose to be silent under censure, than to offer the least thing which may prejudice either the person or affairs of the King, for whom I always had, notwithstanding my unhappy situation, and for whom I shall retain, as long as I live, a sincere and respectful affection.[8]

James, too, admitted that he felt no resentment against his wife, but demanded that she should return to him:

Return to reason, to duty, to yourself and to me, who await your submission with open arms, to restore you to peace and happiness as far as depends upon me.[9]

With his allowance from the Vatican reduced, James had to take his sons off to Bologna where it was less costly to live and he tried hard to persuade his wife to join them, but she refused. He even visited the convent to make her come back to him and the princes, but she received him with cool politeness. They spent some time by themselves in a room, then James left without a word to anyone and neither of them spoke later of what had been discussed.

All this was beyond the comprehension of six-year-old Charles as he watched his father being caught up in the social life of Bologna – a most uncongenial role for the dour, sad, exiled monarch, but very necessary for the sake of the Cause. Charles, now grown into a hyperactive child, spoilt but lovable, accompanied his father on many of these social outings. He had long outgrown the sickly start when it was feared that he might never walk, and managed to keep up with the tremendous pace of Bologna's social life. Peggy Miller has described this time in her biography of James:

Six-year-old Prince Charles must have had a constitution of iron, since he was invited to many functions along with the King his father. He danced with the newly married Contessa Popoli and with the little daughter of Senator Bargellini, 'admired by all the nobility for his gallantry and wit'. A magnificent ball was given in the Casa Marescotti in honour of his birthday on 31st December, and the light of thousands of candles, indoors and out, danced over the satins and diamonds of the guests in their gala costumes, while the King himself led a suite of English dances. There were more diversions for the carnival season in February, with a grand ball at the Casa Fibbia in honour of the King of England, at which twelve ladies, including Lady Inverness, danced – magnificently dressed and bejewelled in the Spanish style, a gesture which, no doubt, it was hoped the Spanish court would come to hear of. The Cardinal Legate of Bologna gave a sumptuous repast at his palace on the 22nd February and the King and the Prince of Wales, and even little Henry, attended a further ball at the Casa Fibbia on March 1. To this day Italian children keep late nights, but the social round of the small Prince of Wales in 1726 and 1727 in Bologna was, to say the least, extraordinary.[10]

James tried to maintain an air of Englishness around his sons. He 'always talked to them in English, saw that they ate English food [meaning roast beef, exotic in Rome], and wore English clothes'.[11]

One sad aspect of the Pretender's family was that it never saw itself as of a single nationality, let alone one family. The Pretender considered himself an Englishman, Clementina was Polish (and the removal of that stable element in her life was part of her trouble in Italy), Henry was an Italian through and through, and Charles Edward identified with the Irish thanks to his close and long association with Sir Thomas Sheridan, and later with the Scots among whom he felt so much at home during the early part of the '45 rising.

In Bologna, Charles showed himself at his best and Hay was not just being sycophantic when he said, 'The Prince is the finest child in the world, healthy and strong, and runs about from morning to night.'[12]

Spring 1727 brought James round to realizing that the impasse between his wife and himself must be broken, so he returned to Rome. Lord and Lady Inverness had had enough, too, and asked to be allowed to leave and, with heavy heart, James agreed. Even this was not enough for the unstable queen. All she said was that this was 'a great point, but not all'.[13]

James also tried to win the Pope over to his side by convincing him that Charles's faith had been safe, even in the Protestant hands of Lord Dunbar. The little Prince was duly taken before His Holiness and recited his catechism perfectly. James felt he had made his case, but Clementina refused to return to him and the boys. He soon returned to Bologna, where the princes joined him.

James tried hard to keep his affairs of state in motion without the help of Inverness, and at the same time to be a father and mother to his beloved Carluccio and Harry. He tried to compensate for the absence of their mother's love by being with them and leading as normal a life as was possible in the circumstances. One can hardly blame him for the fact that he overcompensated and spoilt them.

In the midst of this the unexpected intervened – George I died suddenly at Osnabruck on 11 June 1727, but the news took a whole month to reach James, losing him valuable time to make his bid for the vacant throne. Faced with the dilemma of his marriage or his throne he opted for the throne – and in the light of Clementina's obstinacy he can hardly be blamed. First he went to Lorraine, but the London government put pressure on the French to force him to leave, so he moved to Avignon, from where he might assess the temperature of the Cause in Britain. Alas, he found sympathy rather scant.

With tragic mistiming Clementina chose that moment to leave the convent as suddenly and with as little explanation as she had entered it, and travelled to Bologna, only to find James gone. Her sons were there: Harry, a toddler aged two, could not have known her, and Charles – still only six – probably had no more than a hazy, uneasy recollection of the woman who now hugged him and wept copious tears over him: after all, it had been eighteen months since she had lived with them. No sooner had she held them close to her than she abandoned them again to go off and pray, and this was the pattern the boys' lives followed during succeeding weeks – she would pour out her love, then leave them for long periods to travel around the countryside visiting churches, shrines and convents, praying, praying and praying yet again. Without their father's dull but stable hand, the poor children must have been terrified to be left to the mercies of this neurotic religion-obsessed woman.

From Avignon, James wrote to ask his wife to join him there, but she refused. In the midst of all his efforts to arouse interest for his Cause he managed to find time to send his sons advice on how they should behave. One short, pathetic response from the little Prince of Wales sums up the whole situation from the boy's point of view:

> Dear Papa,
> I thank you mightily for your kind letter. I shall strive to obey you in all things. I will be very dutifull to Mamma, and not jump too near her. I shall be much obliged to the Cardinal for his animals. I long to see you soon and in good health. I am,
> > Dear Papa,
> > > Your most dutifull and affectionate son,
> > > > Charles P.[14]

In this letter all the insecurity of Charles, the little lost boy, echoes through more than two centuries, a frightened child longing to have his father, his sole security, back with him, and in constant fear of sending his unstable mother into one of her neurotic rages. This one letter says more about Charles Edward Stuart's upbringing than all the words written about the Prince at the time or since.

James returned the following January, but there was no reconciliation with his wife. Two months later he poured out his despair to Lord Inverness:

> She leads a most singular life, she takes no manner of amusement, not even taking the air, and when she is not at Church or at Table, is locked up in her room, and sees no mortal but her maids or so; she eats meat this Lent, but fasts to the degree that I believe no married woman that pretends to have children ever did; I am very little with her. I let her do what she will.[15]

James was as solicitous of his wife as ever. Her fasting had now become alarming because she would no longer eat with the rest of the family but had her own little table set apart. From his own table, James, who had his own digestive problems, watched her pick at her food, noting carefully what she ate. He told Inverness with relief that she was eating a little meat that Lent, but a little meat was not enough to keep body and soul together: Clementina's fasting, starving and kneeling in prayer in cold, damp churches had damaged her health permanently.

James realized there was nothing he could do, however. There was no longer hostility between them, only a kind of fatalistic, tragic resignation. Clementina loved James and her boys in her own strange way, but it was as if a great door kept shutting them off from her. And she just could not bring herself to push it open and walk through.

James continued to try to make up to Charles and Harry for the absence of family life: he took them to visit their great aunt, the Dowager Duchess of Parma and they were admired everywhere, especially by any English travellers whom they met. The spy Walton was greatly annoyed by the success of the young Stuarts when he reported in April 1730 that Charles danced well and Harry sang sweetly at an assembly. 'This custom of doing homage to the two little boys gains every day among the young people travelling here, and is degenerating into a kind of tenderness and compassion for the two boys,' he wrote.[16]

In spite of his social success, young Charles continued to display an alarming need for reassurance that he really was loved. On 10 June 1729 he wrote:

Dear Papa,
I am glad you find the weather at Albano so favourable to your health, tho it hinders me so much longer from the Happinesse of seeing you. *Whether absent or present I hope you will always continue to love me.* My brother is very well and so is, Dear Papa,
                        Your most Dutifull Son,
                              Charles P.[17]

That summer James spent much time at Albano, away from the stifling heat and smell of Rome and, although he made an effort to persuade Clementina to be with him, she still refused. She had become completely overwhelmed by religion and preferred to stay near the Sant' Angeli church and the convent where the nuns had shown her so much sympathy. James tried hard to be a good father to his boys: even though state business took him away constantly, he took a close interest in the princes' everyday lives. That pride in his Charles and Harry shows in his letters. To Clementina he wrote:

> I am very impatient to see Harry in his Breeches, wch. will not be till Wednesday morning. Tho' I shall God Willing be with you tomorrow before 9 o'cloke at night. Dont come out to meet me, no more than Carluccio, to whom my blessing, as well as to his Brother. I continue well enough and I hope to see you tomorrow. I need say no more to yours of yesterday.
>
> James R.[18]

With Harry in breeches it was clear that the princes were growing up and were taking on their own personalities – shaped by their parents' relationship to them and to one another. Henry was gentle and studious; Charles was boisterous, a keen sportsman and no scholar, although he was not as ill-educated as is often claimed. He spoke English, French and Italian, but his Latin was poor. He read widely throughout his life and his general knowledge was good. Accusations of poor education seem to be based largely on the fact that his spelling and orthography were terrible. His mother's temper came out in him more clearly as he grew older, and his tutors found him impossible to handle at times. James recognized this problem and wrote to Hay on 12 August 1733:

> There is no question of crushing the Prince's spirit, and no danger of its being crushed, for he is mightily thoughtless and takes nothing much to heart; but I hope he will soon begin to think a little, and that then, with the natural parts God Almighty has given him, and the pains that are taken about him, I hope that he will be good for something at last . . .[19]

James and Charles grew very close to one another and took long walks together in Rome, talking all the time about how they might be restored to their throne. It was important that Charles should obtain some military experience since one thing was now certain, the Hanoverians would not give up their crown without a struggle. The chance came in 1734 when the Duke of Liria, son of James's half-brother, the Duke of Berwick, visited the Muti on his way to southern Italy to join the King of Spain's son, Don Carlos, who was fighting a campaign to win the throne of Naples. At almost the same moment Liria's father was killed in another campaign, so James sent Charles south to where the new Duke of Berwick was besieging the town of Gaeta: he thought the Prince would be a comfort to young Berwick and at the same time could gain some experience of war.

Clementina was terrified at the thought of her son going off to fight and reacted in her usual way – by rushing off to church to pray and ordering prayers to be said for his safety. James's response also was true to character – firmness mixed with weakness. Honour was everything and he begged Berwick to let him know how the Prince behaved. He need not have worried: Charles had a great ability to rub along with the common soldier and at Gaeta he won praise, although his determination to get into the heart of the fight gave Berwick some uneasy moments.

He returned to Rome in triumph and the months that followed should have been a time of great happiness for Charles Stuart, but they were not. His mother's health was failing alarmingly, she was wasting away through constant fasting, and her condition had become much more serious. Although it is difficult to diagnose at this distance in time and without much fuller detail of her medical condition, she was almost certainly suffering from some lung disease, very probably tuberculosis.

By the time the Prince's fourteenth birthday came round on New Year's Eve 1734, it was evident that she was dying and she received the last rites of the Church only twelve days later. Clementina was still quite lucid and asked to see her sons to plead with them never to abandon their Church for all the kingdoms in the world. Even at death's door she could think of her sons only within her own cramped religious confines. For another week she lingered, but at last, on 18 January 1735 death brought peace to Clementina: but her peace left Charles with his own relationship with his mother unresolved. Her religious zeal and the promise she extracted coloured his life later. He was to carry the scars of his love for her to his own grave.

Clementina's dear Carlusu wanted more than anything to be loved by his mother, but only at infrequent moments had she displayed the deep motherly affection that he craved. And every time he came tantalizingly close to being loved by her she abandoned him again to rush off on one of her long, lonely prayer vigils.

Clementina's greatest failure as a mother was that she did not teach her son how to love, and probably as a result he never was able to establish a lasting, stable relationship with any of the women with whom he became involved emotionally as a man.

That day, as Charles stood with his father and brother at a window, all three in sombre black, he wept inconsolably as his mother's coffin was carried from the Muti Palace to the Church of the Sant' Apostoli. It was too late for him to know a mother's love, and at that moment the Prince of Wales, so recently a fine young soldier, was a child again. He had been baptized on the battlefields of Gaeta and life. Above all, he had suffered a baptism of fire on the battlefield of love.

FIVE

CARLUCCIO – 'DUTIFULL SON'

Whether absent or present I hope you will always continue your love to me. My brother is very well and so is Dear Papa,

Yours most Dutifull Son
Charles P.

Letter from Prince Charles Edward Stuart to his father, 10 June 1729.[1]

Through the years following Clementina's death, as Charles was growing up, the King over the Water had two all-consuming concerns: money and the future of his sons. Women hardly entered into his reckoning, either for himself or his boys. Although James had been accused by his wife of being unfaithful, that was a figment of her troubled mind: he was in love with the woman he had married and lacked any deep sexual drive to push him into adultery during his marriage or into taking a second wife after Clementina's death. Unlike his randy old uncle Charles II, or even his father, the Pretender, James Stuart was a monogamous man with a high sense of moral values with regard to marriage, rather in line with those views which his great-grandfather, old James VI and I set down in *Basilikon Doron*.

As for his sons, only the younger boy, Henry, should have given him a sleepless night, for while the Duke of York was still in his teens his father was disturbed that he was going the way of Clementina. His tutor, Lord Dunbar, was sufficiently alarmed to send a report to the king describing Henry's odd lifestyle. The boy rose at six every morning to pray for a quarter of an hour with his confessor, Father Ildefonso, and the two prayed so loudly that the duke's staff could hear them in the next room. Henry preferred his devotions to dancing, and would abandon the dancing master after a couple of little minuets to go off and pray. He was constantly at church:

> When he rid a horseback he went out immediately after his lesson with Father Ildefonso. Then he dressed and went to Mass of which he heard two and sometimes three on holy days, and Saturday last four – to wit two with your Majesty one with the Prince and one by himself. When he hears Mass with the Prince he stays at prayers in the Chapel about a quarter of ane hour thereafter when the hour of dinner permits it. Since Lent he has heard sermon always twice, sometimes thrice, and perhaps once four times in a week, but of this last they cannot be absolutely positive.[2]

After dinner he couldn't wait to return to the chapel for another three-quarters of an hour on his knees and, later in the day, he was at prayer again.

> During the rest of the day he never reads a word on any subject nor could he probably do it, so that were not the course he is in ruinous to his health, as it certainly is, he would arrive at the age of 22 without having cultivated his understanding or acquired a reasonable degree of such knowledge as is the chief duty of his station at present both towards God and man.[3]

Henry's constitution, like his mother's, was delicate and that worried Dunbar too, but most alarming to the tutor was the young man's general state of mind:

> In reciting or relating his prayers he puts his mind in agitation, pronounces his words aloud and crowds them with great precipitation one upon the other and I often remark him when he goes abroad after dinner with a blackness about his eyes his head quite fatigued and his hands hot and the same thing when he comes from his prayers at night.[4]

Charles was different, very different, for he could take religion or leave it without giving it much thought. As for priests, he had little time for them.

Unlike his brother, Prince Henry always surrounded himself with priests, many of them young and handsome. Although there is no concrete evidence, it has been said that he had homosexual tendencies and certainly his friendships with priests like Father Lercari and Cardinal Gianfrancesco Albani worried his father. Needless to say this was all grist to the mill of Stosch and the other spies, just as Charles's coolness to women in 1745–6 was used by propagandists in Britain.

Andrew Lang certainly believed the stories about Harry's homosexual proclivities. He wrote that 'in a letter to Charles, James touches on some unpleasant set of circumstances known to the Prince and says, in effect, that Henry for whom marriage had been planned will never marry.'[5] Lang could not have been referring simply to the fact that Henry was to become a priest for that was a secret kept from the Prince of Wales until it actually happened, so the only interpretation possible is that, for one reason or another, Henry was not the marrying type. As James Lees-Milne points out, it is not out of the question that Henry 'was involved in some youthful liaison which would have seemed highly unpleasant to his father and which convinced him that since his younger boy was not of the marrying sort, he had better enter the Church and lead a life of cloistral celibacy'.[6]

All in all, it is hard to escape the conclusion that Henry was more interested in men than in women.

During his wife's lifetime, James, as the only real parent the princes had around them most of the time, poured out all the love he could to both of them to compensate for their mother's absence. He spoilt them thoroughly. Charles responded by becoming more difficult and flying into tantrums if thwarted. He grew to be as volatile as his mother, but never managed to cultivate his father's ability to control his temper, a failing which was to dog his relationships with men as well as women throughout his life.

Despite that he grew into a very normal boy in whose world dancing and girls played only a small part alongside sport and his growing preoccupation with his inheritance. Charles was already developing a deep sense of his responsibility as heir to the Stuart kingdoms, which occupied his mind above girls or anything else. He became a keen sportsman, and in the view of his father's secretary, James Edgar, 'improves daily in body and mind to the admiration and joy of everybody'.[7] He showed more interest in riding, playing golf, tennis and shuttlecock than in lessons and he trained himself to be an excellent shot through hours of practice potting bats as they flew over the *palazzo* roof at twilight.

James was immensely proud of his sons and whenever Jacobite sympathizers or others on the Grand Tour visited Rome he showed them off with delight. The visitors in turn were enchanted with both boys, but especially with the Prince of Wales, this fine young man who was to carry the hopes of the Stuarts into the next generation. Between the Muti's intrigue and gossip there were musical evenings and balls at which the princes were greatly admired, and these helped to create new interest in the Jacobite Cause.

Walton reported one such event at which Charles appeared in Highland dress sent to him from Scotland by the Duke of Perth. When the King of Poland's son arrived during the carnival of 1739 the Prince of Wales led the dancing dressed as a shepherd in white silk with white ribbons at his knees and on his shoes; on his head he wore a large white hat decorated with diamond loops and buttons.

All that sport and entertaining did not mean that the Prince had no time for the opposite sex: he had. But in their place. He loved balls and dancing and would have danced until he dropped, had the governors, who were in charge of him, not stopped him. Edgar noted the young Prince's passion for dancing. 'You would be surprised to see him dance,' he commented, 'nobody probably does it better, and he bore his part at the balls in the carnival as if he were already a man.'[8]

His father, now nearer fifty than forty, had quite deliberately set about training his son to take over the leadership of the Cause from him. The dancing, shooting practice and the expedition to the siege of Gaeta before his mother died, were all part of that process.

And as if to demonstrate his approaching manhood, Charles had his long, dark golden curls cut off when he reached the age of sixteen, and began to wear a wig, although he still combed his own hair over his forehead. His dark eyes continued to captivate everyone: like his great-uncle Charles II he was tall and well set, and walked with the unmistakable air of a prince. His father might be king by divine right, but Charles Stuart held the rank of Prince of Wales by that same divinity. It was said that whatever guise the Prince adopted, his appearance always had 'something of the stately and the grand'. The first down of manhood feathered his face, a fiery glowing red stubble, which would have become a Highland chief well.

Money was a perennial problem at the Muti, with the cutting of James's pension by the Pope during the quarrel with Clementina, serving to demonstrate just how dependent he was on outsiders. The French now had little use for him, so were spasmodic about providing financial help, and as for Spain, it had not paid him a penny for years and was unlikely to do so now.

If he hoped for his wife's riches at her death he was sadly disappointed: Clementina left the two boys some of her jewels and favoured Henry over Charles by giving him the income from her *rentes* in Paris, but all the rest went to the Roman Catholic Church. James did not benefit at all.

Settling his sons' future was to prove just as difficult for the King over the Water as balancing his finances, and it was at least partly with Charles's future in mind that he arranged for his elder son to go on a tour of northern Italy during May of 1737.

As far as the sixteen-year-old Charles was concerned, the object was simply to kill time while he waited for an answer from the Emperor whom he had asked to allow him to join the Austrian army which was then fighting the Turks in Hungary. With memories of Gaeta and tales he had heard told about his great-grandfather, John Sobieski's triumph in saving Vienna from the Turks, this was just what a hyperactive young man like Charles Stuart needed. Besides, the military campaigning experience would be of great value when the time came to make another attempt on his kingdoms. His father's reasons were quite different: he wanted to show his son off to people who could help the Cause as well as to possible future wives.

Travelling incognito as the Count of Albany, Charles made a really royal progress from petty court to petty court, wallowing in what has been unkindly called the 'splendour of that gilded *papier maché* Italy'.[9] To the Prince it was both real and royal. He reviewed troops like a monarch, he kissed ladies' hands with the panache of an experienced courtier, and he danced with the wives and daughters of petty dukes with the ease and elegance expected of a true prince of the royal blood. By every standard the journey was a success beyond anything his father could have hoped for: we would have knowledge of that even if we had no information about it from the Stuarts themselves (which we do have). The Hanoverians' strenuous spoiling tactics make it clear that the Prince was becoming a real threat to them.

They persuaded the Emperor to forbid his officers stationed in Milan to recognize Charles, and in Florence the British envoy tried to curtail the honours the Prince was accorded. Matters came to a head in Venice, where Charles was feted and treated as a reigning 'royal': when this news reached London the Venetian ambassador was given twenty-four hours to clear out and it took ten years for relations to recover.

Charles was now a handsome young man, with the grace of some of his Stewart ancestors and the dark good looks of his mother, and he behaved with such charm in female company that women were beginning to become captivated by him in spite of his cool detachment. The less interest he showed in the female sex the more they fell for him – that was to be Prince Charlie's lot all through life.

During the tour the Prince was accompanied by Henry Goring, later to be a valuable friend, Francis Strickland, to become one of the small band that accompanied him to Scotland, and Lord Dunbar to whom he was insufferably rude all the way. He refused to write home to his father often enough for Dunbar's liking, and indeed one wonders how he had time to put pen to paper at all. The Prince threw himself so wholeheartedly into the fun and ceremonial arranged by his hosts, especially the dancing, that Dunbar wrote home to complain:

As HRH cannot enjoy the diversion of dancing with any degree of moderation, but overheats himself monstrously on such occasions, I have refused a ball the public intended to give him here

tomorrow night, and have writ . . . that he would accept a
Conversazione . . . The later he comes home and the more he
wants to sleep, he will sit the longer at supper, so that it is not
possible to get him to bed of an opera night till near three in the
morning tho' he be home soon after one.[10]

Conversazioni instead of dances – Charles was short-tempered at the
best of times, but this was too much and he gave Dunbar hell for being
such a spoilsport. Undeterred by Dunbar's moaning, the Prince attended
state dinners and brilliant balls from beginning to end of the journey –
at Parma; Padua, Ferrara and Florence, Lucca, Pisa and Leghorn – but
disappointment awaited him back home: the Emperor refused to allow
the prince to join him on the Hungarian campaign.

Charles tried to hide his disappointment and boredom behind a hectic
social life in Rome, complemented by more sport and shooting
expeditions, but he yearned for that real action, which now seemed to
be simmering in the Jacobite cauldron, yet never ever quite came to the
boil. Such yearning to be at the enemy put considerable strain on the
relationship between the Prince and his father, who was sinking further
and further into morose acceptance of his lot and gloomy
disappointment.

Back in Rome Prince Charlie was at the centre of society, invited to
balls, the opera, and at every carnival or celebration he cut quite a
figure, dressed in the richest clothes – fine velvet breeches, silk shirts
with ornate ruffles and lace, gaudy waistcoats, silver embroidered coats
and shoes with silver and diamond buckles. Often he wore the Order of
the Garter and a diamond-studded Cross of St Andrew.

There were many Scots among those who came to pay him court.
John Murray of Broughton convinced Charles that the best hope for
the Jacobite Cause lay in poor, faithful Scotland rather than among
English nobles who paid the Cause only lip service. Murray was
greatly taken with the Prince and left a vivid description of the
young man as he first saw him:

Charles Edward . . . is tall, above the common stature, his limbs are
caste in the most exact mould, his complexion has in it somewhat of

an uncommon delicacy; all his features are perfectly regular and well turned, and his eyes the finest I ever saw. But that which shines most in him, and renders him without exception the most surprisingly handsome person of the age, is the dignity that accompanies his every gesture; there is such an unspeakable majesty diffused through his whole mien as it is impossible to have any idea of without seeing . . .[11]

Another visitor was the Earl of Wemyss's son, Lord Elcho, roughly the same age as the Prince, but when they stood back to back to compare heights, Charles (to his father's delight) was the taller of the two. At five feet ten inches he was above average height, but his slender figure made him appear even taller. Murray was to go into history as the Judas of Prince Charlie's story, the betrayer of the Cause, and Elcho was to abandon the Prince and write viciously about his meanness and bad behaviour to women, but at that time they were his warmest admirers.

The Stuarts were the talk of Rome and Charles made hearts beat just a little faster when he appeared at a splendid ball given by Cardinal Rohan, rigged out in Highland dress and wearing jewelled decorations that far outshone those of the women present.[12] At another ball the English poet, Thomas Gray, who was no lover of the King over the Water or his Cause, had to admit grudgingly, 'They are good fine boys, especially the Younger, who has the more spirit of the two, and both danced incessantly all night.[13] It is interesting that Henry, the quiet, reserved brother, was the one who caught Gray's eye. Perhaps Charles's flamboyance overawed the anti-Jacobite Englishman.

Thanks to all those visitors, by the time Charles was twenty, his attention was directed solely on winning back the Stuarts' crowns: Scotland was the focus of his aspirations. He had made up his mind that everything else, including love, would have to wait.

According to William Drummond of Balhaldy it was not a case of Charles disliking women – Balhaldy said the Prince took a definite vow of chastity, to which he held right to the end of the '45.[14] His whole life up to the time of the rising was devoted to restoring the family to their rightful thrones. Even the hunting expeditions and long, hard walks in the countryside around Rome were undertaken with the single objective of preparing himself for the task. He studied military strategy long into the night and at the end of most days, which usually meant in the small hours of the next morning, he spent a while playing his cello – his only recreation. These shooting expeditions and walks proved excellent training for what lay ahead on the marches and battlefields of the '45 and the five months spent as a fugitive among the Highlands and islands.

The King over the Water had more immediate concerns for his sons, especially Charles, in the late 1730s. Remembering his own late marriage, he was of the opinion that it was time to look for a wife for the Prince of Wales in order to secure the dynasty's succession. But James Stuart's wizened old mind could not conceive of anything as romantic as Wogan's journey through Europe in search of a bride, so it was more a matter of keeping an eye open for a suitable princess to turn up.

One surprising candidate who was brought to the Prince's notice was one of his Sobieski cousins, Marie-Louise de la Tour d'Auvergne, daughter of the Duc de Bouillon. A Sobieski would be the last bride James Stuart would be expected to desire for his son after his experience with Clementina and the fact that the family still haunted the Stuarts years after Clementina's death.

Clementina's sister, Charlotte, the one Wogan described as so pretty, with red hair and many admirers, had made a splendid marriage to the Duc de Bouillon, Grand Chamberlain of France, and a regular drinking and gambling crony of Louis XV. The Bouillons, who were descended from the great sixteenth-century French general, the Duc de Turenne, had for generations been close to the royal family, and Louise's grandfather was the man who went out on the balcony at Versailles in 1714 on the death of Louis XIV to announce, 'Le roi est mort: vive le roi.'[15] His son grew to be a trusted friend of Louis XV and the family lived in great style – and at great expense – and at the Hôtel de Bouillon, one of the most sumptuous residences in the French capital, at the Château de Navarre, near Evreux in Normandy, where the building and fantastic gardens designed by Le Nôtre were fit for a king – and often were enjoyed by Louis on hunting expeditions. They also had estates at Bouillon, near Sedan, in the north-east corner of France. With a matching lifestyle and huge gambling debts, it was little wonder that the duke was perennially short of money in spite of all the Sobieski wealth.

The Bouillon marriage was not a happy one, largely because of the duke's extravagance and persistent whoring and adultery. The women he slept with were rumoured to include his own stepmother who was actually younger than he was. In spite of the unhappiness that surrounded it, the marriage produced first a daughter, Marie-Louise, and then a son, Godefroy-Charles, who became Duc de Turenne and later succeeded his father as Duc de Bouillon.

Poor Charlotte was engulfed in unhappiness; her father, Prince James Sobieski, refused to have anything to do with her because she had married without his approval, so by the mid-1730s, when James Sobieski was growing old, Charlotte decided she must go to Poland in order to make her peace with her father and to endeavour to ensure a favourable mention for herself and her children in Sobieski's will.

Bouillon was glad to see the back of Charlotte and had no regrets when she never returned to him. He also alienated her children from her, leaving the poor woman to die alone in Poland.

While Charlotte was working so hard to win back her father's affection, her husband schemed and conspired to gain as much as he could, yet at the same time prevent his wife from returning to him.[16] As Sobieski's health failed the matter of sharing out the family estates at Zolkiew in Poland and at Ohlau in Silesia became urgent because Polish law laid down that only persons of Polish nationality could inherit land in Poland. If the matter should not be settled before the old prince's death, the Sobieski estates at Zolkiew would go to outsiders. But neither the Stuarts nor the Bouillons could agree on how the estates should be divided, so in order to salvage something from this impasse, Charlotte eventually sold off the Sobieski lands in Poland to one of her Polish Radziwill relatives who was eligible to take them over.

As part of Bouillon's complex machinations, always secretly playing one faction off against another and never letting his wife know what he planned, he sent his daughter, Marie-Louise, to Poland to butter up her grandfather and in the hope of marrying her off to the son of the King of Poland. When that failed overtures were made to a number of rich Polish nobles, but all came to nothing. Bouillon then suggested secretly that Louise should marry one of her Stuart cousins, which would have the great merit of keeping the Sobieski wealth within the family.

Old James Sobieski wept for joy at the enchanting thought of two of his grandchildren marrying – it would reunite the family, keep his wealth intact, and allow him to die a happy man. In Rome, however, James Stuart was far from enthusiastic: his younger son was much too young to think of marriage yet, and even the elder one could afford to wait. The suggestion came just at the moment the Prince returned from his triumphant progress through north Italy and the King over the Water probably felt that Charles deserved someone better, a princess of the royal blood perhaps. At the back of his mind there was always the question of restoration; in his response to Bouillon he set out his views on how his son's marriage might affect that:

> You will well appreciate that my restoration could some day depend on several alliances with my children, and that I could not answer either to God or to man, if by premature agreements I deprived myself of such resources for the restoration of my family.[17]

Insofar as Charles himself was concerned, he was not interested in Louise de la Tour or any other woman. He was happy to dance with women and talk to them at court functions, but he had no intention of allowing them to come too close. He was not ready for marriage yet, although on the evidence of his future conduct, he was interested enough in female liaisons, but never seriously interested in marriage other than for what he could get out of it. And all he really wanted was power, company and an heir.

Louise returned to Paris unmarried and, after Prince James died on 19 December 1737, the Bouillons and Stuarts could not agree on how to share his estate: they took their dispute to law and the result was unending costly litigation drawn out over the years that followed. Having saved something for her children by selling off the

Zolkiew lands, Charlotte died less than three years later, far from her husband and family; the King of Prussia solved the problem of the Silesian part of the estate by seizing Ohlau for himself.

In the end, thanks to delay and litigation, both Bouillons and Stuarts lost out, but remarkably little illwill resulted from the dispute, and the two families kept in touch.

Early in 1743 the duke wrote to the king in Rome to inform him that his daughter, Louise, was about to marry.[18] No doubt Bouillon took pleasure in passing on this news that his daughter was no longer available even if the Pretender were to come begging – little did he know what lay ahead!

James showed no pique at the news; he was delighted, especially as his niece was marrying into the great Rohan family, one of the most eminent in the whole of France, a family already related to the Stuarts through the Sobieskis. Louise's husband was Jules Hercule Meridiac de Rohan, later Duc de Montbazon and Prince de Guémené.

The Rohans may have been important, but Jules's immediate background was flawed to say the least. His father was insane and was kept locked up on one of their estates well away from Paris, so it was left to his mother, the formidable Madame de Guémené, to agree the terms of marriage, which not only apportioned the financial settlement, but also included a clause stating that the young couple were to live with her in her house in the Place Royale in Paris – *ils logeront chez Mme de Guémené*, wrote that court gossip, the Duc de Luynes who missed nothing that happened in royal circles, and very little outside them.[19]

Perhaps Madame de Guémené feared the influence Louise's father might have on her son, who after all was still only sixteen; perhaps she feared Louise might be a chip off the old block! She certainly displayed great foresight by insisting on that clause.

Madame de Guémené, an ambitious woman, wanted her son to be known as the Prince of Rohan, but that was too much for the French king, so he had to settle for the title of Duc de Montbazon. She also hoped that the formal betrothal might take place in the king's salon at Versailles, but had to accept the next best thing, the great Oeil-de-Boeuf salon just outside the king's rooms. The king, queen, dauphin, and princes and princesses of the royal blood were all present at the ceremony on Sunday 17 February 1743, which was worthy of the Bouillons' aspirations. De Luynes described in detail how it passed off with nothing more than the minor criticism that the young duke's outfit of silver brocade trimmed with gold lace was not appropriate beside his fiancée's dress of black and gold.[20]

The wedding ceremony followed two days later at the home of one of the bride's great-uncles, the Cardinal of Auvergne, whom James Stuart had helped to achieve this far from well-deserved distinction in the Church: he was known to neglect his religious duties and reputed to practise sodomy, and the fact that he lent the couple his bed for their wedding night led to considerable amusement and coarse jokes around the court. Maurepas's comment reflected gossip of the day:

> Seeing their old-fashioned proceedings and nose-to-nose love-making, all of a sudden the bed spoke, and told them that they lacked experience – that Monsieur le Cardinal went about it differently . . .[21]

Charles couldn't have cared less about his cousin's marriage: he was much more interested in the rumours emanating from Scotland that opinion there was turning in his favour and other reports from Paris that Louis XV would soon offer help.

James was accustomed to waiting, but Charles had no patience, simmering time and again at his father's fatalism and the way in which the king allowed himself to be treated by those countries which professed to support him. His father might wait while the changing winds of European politics blew over him, but Charles was in a hurry to get to St James's. The king tried to understand his son's impetuosity, but it disturbed him deeply. In a letter, written on 1 October 1742, he remarked that the Prince was 'quite wearied' of this country. He added:

> I don't wonder at it for his sole amusement here is to go out shooting, to which he has gone every other day during all this season before daybreak, whether fair or foul, and has killed a great deal of game, such as this place affords.[22]

James Edgar, now the King's Secretary of State, watched the two from close quarters and sighed wearily. Charles still refused to go to bed on many nights, but dozed in a chair, a tall, slim, athletic figure, with his riding coat thrown over him, all ready to set out with his gun at one or two in the morning. His servants were worn out, but not the Prince, who would return from these hunting expeditions and play his cello for hours.

'What a pleasure it would be,' Edgar told the Earl Marischal in a letter, 'to see better game than the shooting of Quails.'[23]

Better game was there to be hunted: in October 1740 the Emperor Charles VI died, sure in the knowledge that Maria Theresa would succeed him, but he reckoned without the European jackals, who were soon fighting over the carcass of Austria. With Britain and France supporting opposing sides this renewed the prospect that France might be persuaded to back a new rising to restore the King over the Water.

The Jacobites were riding high on a wave of hope at this time, buoyed by favourable reports from England and the death of old Cardinal Fleury who had blown cold on the Cause. Louis XV now took an interest in how the Jacobites might be of use to him, and decided that the time was ripe for a Jacobite rising in England. In great secrecy the devious French king made plans to invade England in the early part of 1744, conveniently tying up George II's army in Britain while the French were free to attack the Low Countries and German states. A Stuart was needed to rally Jacobites in Britain, but not until the French army under Maréchal Comte Maurice de Saxe was safely across the Channel.

In the words of Frank McLynn, one of the Prince's most recent biographers,

The trick was to acquire the Jacobite manifestos and declarations to the people of England without having Charles Edward in tow. By a sleight of hand Louis could contrive it so that the prince arrived in Paris only after the expedition's commander-designate, the Comte de Saxe had captured London. Charles Edward would then cross the Channel to ratify the French conquest.[24]

Tricks don't always come off and this one failed, largely due to a slip up by the French and the Prince's impetuosity. Louis sent Drummond of Balhaldy to Rome to obtain the manifestos he needed, but he would not give Balhaldy a letter inviting the king in Rome to send his son to France. James was highly suspicious since there was no invitation for him to be involved and no summons to France other than a remark by the Marquis d'Argenson saying that if Prince Charles wished to make his way to Paris on his own after 12 January (by which time the expedition would have left) then he was free to do so.

That was enough for Charles: he was determined to be on his way to France as soon as possible.

The king gladly drafted a series of commissions and manifestos to army, church and university leaders in England and Scotland as well as to the Lord Mayor of London and the lord lieutenants in Scotland. As he was now getting old – after all he was fifty-five – he knew he could not take an active part in a campaign himself, so he issued a Declaration of Regency on 23 December 1743, handing his kingdoms' safekeeping over to Charles until he himself would be able take them over. This declaration showed the deep trust as well as love that now existed between father and son:

James R.

Whereas We have a near Prospect of being restored to the Throne of our Ancestors, by the good Inclinations of Our Subjects towards Us, and whereas, on Account of the present Situation of this Country, it will be absolutely impossible for Us to be in Person at the first setting up of Our Royal Standard, and even sometime after, We therefore esteem it for Our Service, and the Good of Our Kingdoms and Dominions to nominate and appoint, Our dearest Son, CHARLES, Prince of Wales, to be sole Regent of our Kingdoms of England, Scotland and Ireland, and of all other Our Dominions, during Our Absence.

23 December 1743 in the 43rd year of Our Reign, J.R.[25]

Much less willingly, James agreed to allow Charles to set out for Paris. That Christmas the festivities, which normally barely ruffled the Muti's normal drab calm, concealed great activity as preparations were made for the journey. It is hard to believe that the Jacobites in the Muti were able to keep their plans secret since the building was always packed with spies, but perhaps they were all too full of good wine and food to stay awake to take in what was happening. As a result, no one, not even Prince Henry, got wind of what was afoot.

Charles announced that he was off to Cisterna on a shooting trip early in the New Year, and would take Harry with him. They were to set out on 9 January, and it was not in the least out of the ordinary for the Prince of Wales, who needed little sleep, to announce that he would be leaving before dawn. That morning a moving leave-taking took place in secret between the Prince and his father: as the two embraced the Prince said, 'I go, Sire, in search of three crowns, which I doubt not but to have the honour and happiness of laying at Your Majesty's feet. If I fail in the attempt, your next sight of me shall be in the coffin.'

Tears ran down the old man's cheeks. 'Heaven forbid that all the crowns of the world should rob me of my son,' he replied as he embraced the Prince. 'Be careful of yourself, my dear Prince, for my sake and, I hope for the sake of millions.'[26]

At this moment the bond between father and son was never stronger, all past differences were forgotten and the touching meeting in the dark palace that cold January morning was the apogee of the Prince's filial love, probably the high watermark of Charles Stuart's love for anyone.

But he was never to see his father again.

SIX

THE GIRL HE LEFT BEHIND

I have already seen the D. of Bullion, the P. of Turain and his sister, and Last night I supt with all that family . . . I am mightely well plesed with the D. of Bullion and his family.

Letter from Bonnie Prince Charlie to his father on first meeting his uncle and cousins, the Duc de Turenne and Louise, Duchesse de Montbazon, written on 11 January 1745.[1]

The news of de Saxe's impending invasion, which reached Rome at the end of 1743, breathed new life into Prince Charlie. The historian Andrew Lang wrote that the Prince, a man born to act, now saw the path to action ahead, and responded to it:

Given employment that he could understand, Charles rose gaily and strenuously to the needs and duties of the hour . . . now he had hopes and happiness.[2]

Few saw Charles leave Rome full of hope and happiness after that touching parting with his father, and Harry still knew nothing of the plan even after they were on their way. Charles had told him he planned to travel by a different route, accompanied by Francis Strickland, and they would meet up at Cisterna. When the Duke of York arrived, the Prince was not there and he was informed that his brother had suffered a fall from his horse and hurt his ribs slightly so he would not rejoin the party for some days. While the unsuspecting Henry waited, Charles rode on to meet Sheriden's nephew, Michael Sheridan, and John William O'Sullivan, an agreeable Irish colonel in the French army who had joined James's side, and all headed north as fast as they could.

Henry was understanding when he learned the truth, and agreed to stay on at Cisterna until the end of the month in order to give his brother time to reach Paris without discovery.

The brothers were too different in character ever to be close, but at this moment they were as affectionate towards one another as they were ever to be. Young Harry was carried away with admiration and, contrary to what one might expect from the reclusive, religious character, he wished fervently that he was going to France to be part of the action too.

'I can assure you Dear Brother (were the King but to permit me) wou'd make me fly through fire and water to be with you,'[3] he told the Prince. So determined was he to join Charles on the adventure that he planned to raise money on his share of the Sobieski jewels and join him.

Charles descended on Paris unannounced on 8 February 1744 after a marathon dash by sea from Genoa to Antibes and then overland through France. There had been frustrating delays at both the Italian and French ports, but he made up some of the lost time by covering the 730 miles from the Mediterranean to Paris in only five days. All those hunting expeditions around Rome had given him the fitness and stamina to leave his travelling companions trailing at his coat-tails.

'If I had been to go further,' he wrote home with considerable self-satisfaction, 'I should have been obliged to get them ty'd behind the chase with my Portmantle, for they were quite rendu.'[4]

Charles's companions were not half as 'rendu' as were Louis XV, his ministers and the Comte de Saxe when they learned that Charles was in Paris. The invasion had been delayed and the last thing they expected or wanted was the Jacobite Prince of Wales with them now that they were nearly ready to sail. They made the best of the situation: Louis insisted that the Prince should maintain his incognito, and so he was not to be received officially by the king.

That worried Prince Charlie, but he was so full of enthusiasm he was prepared to see the best side of Louis. 'I have mett with all that could be expected from Mr Adam (Louis XV) who expresses great tenderness and will be careful of my concerns,'[5] he told his father.

All was going as he wished, he said, and hinted at 'little intrigues' which would be to his advantage.

In his gloomy, empty *palazzo* in Rome, James still felt uneasy enough to write to Lord Sempill in Paris that 'the promises of France are not to be reconciled with her negligent and indifferent behaviour to the Prince'.[6]

Although the letters passing between father and son were still affectionate, differences in attitude which were to sour their relationship from now on were beginning to manifest themselves.

The secret of the invasion was soon out, and of course the French blamed the Prince for that. Still maintaining his incognito, Charles travelled to Gravelines on the Channel coast as the Chevalier Douglas, and revelled in the adventure of being a soldier again and mixing with people unrecognized for the first time in his life.

'Everybody is wondering where the Prince is, and sometimes he is told news of himself to his face, which is very diverting,'[7] he told his father, who doubtless saw little to amuse him in a prince of the royal blood playing hide and seek in such a way.

What Charles did not know was that the French were going off the idea: de Saxe, who was at Dunkirk gathering together a ragtag and bobtail force assembled largely from France's mercenary soldiers, would not even meet the Prince. French organization at sea was such a shambles that the fleet was only saved from being trounced by a far superior British Home Fleet under Admiral Sir John Norris because a storm blew up in the Channel and scattered it. At Dunkirk, these same Protestant winds devastated de Saxe's armada before it could even sail and he lost several ships, many of his supplies and a number of men. The expedition was called off and blame was conveniently laid on Charles's arrival which they said had blown the secret.

Worse was to follow – Louis declared war on Britain and sent his army off to Flanders without even telling Charles and de Saxe, who had avoided meeting the Prince, left the Channel coast. Only a token force was left at Dunkirk to fool the British into believing that the invasion plan was still on.

The expedition had fallen in with Louis's strategic plan nicely: by concentrating his troops around this section of the Channel coast, he was just a short march from Flanders, where he could quickly drive a wedge between Britain and her allies. In the words of de Saxe's biographer, Jon Manchip White the whole exercise had been 'nothing more than military vaudeville'.[8]

By the end of March 1744 Prince Charles found himself stranded at Gravelines, so furious that he wrote a letter to Lord Sempill threatening that if King Louis would not help further he would hire a fishing boat and sail to Scotland, where his faithful Highlanders would rally to his side.

'I would rather die at the head of these brave men,' he told Sempill, 'than languish in exile and dependence.'[9]

Wiser and older Jacobite heads counselled caution: the Earl Marischal, one of his father's trusted advisers but no friend of the Prince, tried to calm him, but Charles was not to be calmed, especially by dry old Marischal who always was every bit as determined as the Prince to do everything on his own terms.

When Charles moved back to Paris in May, still hoping to persuade Louis to allow him to join the campaign in Flanders, he found that the French king had gone off to the war without him and had no intention of inviting Charles to follow. Beside himself with disappointment and anger, Charles settled down in a house at Montmartre, and here a joyful reunion with his old tutor, Sheridan, took place at the beginning of June. Sheridan, now failing in health, was delighted to be with the Prince he adored and was especially happy that, in spite of all the disappointment he had been through, he found Charles in excellent physical condition. The Prince had filled out, to become both broader, more manly than when he left Rome, and taller: that surprised Sheridan since Charles surely had grown to his full height before he left Rome. Soon he discovered the secret. 'When I seemed surprised at it he let me into the secret,' Sir Thomas wrote. 'He showed me the heels of his shoes which he wears now of the usual size, whereas before he wore them remarkably lower than other people.'[10] As fashionable men at that time were wearing heels two inches high, this gave the Prince extra stature.

Sheridan's delight at being reunited with his beloved Prince did not last long: he quickly discovered that Charles was at 'the wine and play' with even greater gusto than rumours in Rome had suggested. Frustrated not to be able to appear in public as the Prince of Wales or to socialize as a prince of the royal blood, he had taken up with Alasdair MacDonnell, Young Glengarry, one of the most disreputable of the younger Jacobites – indeed one of the most despicable and untrustworthy men ever associated with the Cause – and the two were leading a wild life of drinking in the lowest taverns of Paris. There is no evidence that the Prince was womanizing, although in the circumstances one must suspect that he was having difficulty living according to the vow of celibacy he was supposed to have taken. Sheridan was deeply distressed at the influence this irreligious, amoral young man was having on the Prince, and discussed it with James's representative in Paris, Daniel O'Brien, but there was nothing either could do except protest and suffer. Sheridan grieved sorely over his protégé's behaviour.

Late that summer Murray of Broughton also turned up in Paris to find out what was happening, for in Scotland they had heard nothing but rumours and the chiefs were desperate to know what, if anything, was being planned. Murray has been blamed for urging Charles to come to Scotland, but this is not true: at secret meetings Murray told the Prince that support for the Cause at that moment was far less than Balhaldy and Sempill had led leaders on the Continent to believe. The Highland chiefs, especially, were of the opinion that the time was not ripe for a rising. Charles listened to all this, but in the end, told Murray he was more determined than ever to come to Scotland. Charles was beyond reasoning; his mid was made up: he would go to Scotland and neither the king in Rome nor the king in France would know of his plans until he sailed.

If the Cause was faring badly in Scotland it was not enjoying much success in France either: one supporter or another was constantly writing to James in Rome to complain about someone else – Balhaldy denouncing Sheridan as 'pernicious and useless', Sempill calling Sheridan an adventurer, Marischal criticizing all of them and Prince Charles as well. And the Prince was fed up with the lot of them and told his father so:

You may well imagine how out of Youmer I am: when for comfort I am plagued out of my life with tracasyrs [treacheries] from ower own People, who as it would seem would rether Sachrifise me and my Affairs, than fail in any private view. Lord John [Drummond] is one of those that has been plaging me with complaints but I quieted him in the best manner I could, saying that whatever is sed of our own people, tho' never so well grounded, was cutting our own throts, at the same time I am plesed that people should spake freely to me . . . The more I dwell on these matters, the more it makes me melancholy.[11]

King Louis was feeling pretty melancholy too. He was dangerously ill at this time and, on his recovery, was not one bit pleased to find the Pretender's son still with him. Charles had a good friend at the French court, the Bishop of Soissons, son of James's half-brother, the Duke of Berwick, who was then at Metz along with Louis, his army and his advisers, as well as his mistress, Madame de Châteauroux. It was Soissons's brother, the Duke of Liria, who had taken Charles to fight at Gaeta just before Clementina died, and Soissons was well disposed towards the Stuarts, so he was able to tell Charles that Louis not only had no intention of supporting him, but was growing tired of the Stuarts altogether. Louis's problem was that in his heart he knew he had let Charles down, so he couldn't easily send him back to Rome without losing face. Instead he cut off the Prince's money and hoped to 'starve' him out of the country.

He didn't understand the Prince's character: Charles simply stayed on and ran up more debts until, by the end of the year, the French would have paid all his bills gladly just to be rid of him. They wanted Charles to go to Avignon, although Rome would have been even more desirable, but finally Charles settled for a small pension and 'exile' at the Berwick estate of Fitz-James, a little to the north-east of Paris on the Calais road. The house was available because the Berwick relations were away at the time.

The Prince had no option but to accept, although he realized that exile at Fitz-James would be little better than imprisonment. But if that was to be the price of achieving his goal of restoration, then so be it – for that, he said, he was prepared to put himself in a tub like Diogenes if need be![12]

He was determined on one thing, however: before shutting himself away he wanted to meet his Bouillon and Berwick relations, who had been forbidden by the French king to entertain him.[13] Louis's excuse was that the Prince was living in France incognito so he could not be seen associating with any of his relatives. Matters were not helped by the fact that Bouillon had temporarily fallen out of favour with Louis and been exiled to his estates of Navarre, about halfway between Paris and Le Havre.[14]

At the beginning of 1745 Louis relented and at last Charles was permitted to meet his uncle, the Duc de Bouillon, and his cousin, the Duc de Turenne, for the first time. He took to them at once, and the following day had supper with them at their house, the Hôtel de Bouillon. This time his cousin, Louise, the girl his father had rejected as a bride for him, was also present, no doubt looking radiantly happy since she had just discovered that she was going to become a mother later in the year.

Next day he wrote a letter full of unconcealed excitement to tell his father all about it:

I have already seen the D. of Bullion, the P. of Turain and his sister, and Last night I supt with all that family and after supper i went to the Opera Ball in mask, along with the P. of Turein, Mr Montbason and P. Camill. I am mightely well plesed with the D. of Bullion and his family, with their sivilitys and expression towards me, and am very fond of the Prince de Turein, ho is really a very well behaved prety yong man every way.[15]

With Charles's aunt, Charlotte Sobieska, out of the way the Bouillons presented the picture of a happy, united family, something Charles Stuart had never known, yet had yearned for all his days. He now needed some blood relations around him and by good luck he had found them.

The Prince was delighted with his new family, and all thoughts of those ever-enduring, boring lawsuits over grandfather Sobieski's will were forgotten. He continued to see the Bouillons during the months that followed, and took greatly to Louise and her husband. Jules de Rohan was a year younger than his wife and more than five years the Prince's junior and, although heir to one of France's most powerful families, he was a rather shy, retiring young man – with the Princesse de Guéméné for a mother he had little choice to be anything else.

Prince Charlie's French family was now complete and they spent much time together, either in Paris or at Fitz-James. He grew to trust the Bouillons as he trusted no one in France, and they became his family away from Rome. The young Ducs de Turenne and Montbazon became his closest friends and he may have left us no indication of what he thought of Louise at that time, but clearly he lost his heart to her as she did to him.

The Bouillons visited him at Fitz-James and he returned to Paris to see them: he dined frequently at the Hôtel de Bouillon and enjoyed a very full social life with his cousin and Louise's husband.[16]

The king was annoyed to learn that Charles Stuart had been to a masked ball at the Opéra and made his displeasure known, but Charles took no notice. He continued to move between Fitz-James and Paris, attending masked balls under the guise of a German baron recently arrived in Paris. As he said himself, through the weeks that followed he was 'much hurried between balls and business'.[17]

It was recklessly audacious of him to continue to attend balls, especially those at Versailles, after being 'warned off' by King Louis, but Charles Stuart enjoyed taking risks. It was actually reasonably safe for him to turn up at these functions because there were always so many people present that danger of discovery was minimal, provided Charlie did not behave outrageously or draw attention to himself. He could not always resist that, however, and once went to a ball given by the king's daughters. On another occasion he had a narrow escape when Madame de Mézières, one of the most notorious gossips at the court, recognized him and forced him to admit his identity. Fortunately she does not seem to have passed the information on to anyone close to the king.

At a masked ball in the gallery just before the start of Lent 1745 he cheekily sat down close to Queen of France, Marie Lesczynska, and of course she was curious to know the identity of this elegant young man seated beside her. Charles was only saved by a quick-witted lady-in-waiting who told the queen he was her brother.

With his powerful Bouillon relations around to protect him, the Prince could always feel fairly safe, but never totally so, and that only served to add to his enjoyment.

The spring of 1745 was not devoted solely to entertainment; Charles was secretly at work preparing for his voyage to Scotland. How much the French actually knew of what was afoot is hard to discover, but one can scarcely believe that the tentacles of their great intelligence-gathering system were not able to probe deeply into whatever Charles Stuart was up to. It is very probable that they knew most of the plan, but decided to let it happen because an expedition by the Prince to Scotland on his own initiative, would provide another useful diversion to draw many of the Hanoverian forces away from mainland Europe. If it succeeded, so much to the good; if it failed then Louis could say with hand on heart that he had taken no part in it.

So Prince Charlie was left to get on with implementing his plan undisturbed. Under cover of continuing to ask Louis XV to permit him to join the French forces in Holland, he set about borrowing 180,000 livres to buy broadswords and muskets to arm the Highlanders who had been forced to hand in their arms after the '15 rising and were desperately short of weapons. The French also allowed him to hire an ageing sixty-four gun man-of-war, the *Elisabeth*, from a Dunkirk merchant, Walter Rutledge, and a sixteen-gun frigate, *Du Teillay* from Antoine Walsh.

The Duc de Bouillon and his family were as close as ever to Charles, who thought the world of them. In fact he tried to persuade his father to confer the Order of the Garter on the duke, who was now serving with the French army, and had invited the Prince to stay on his Château de Navarre. The Prince told his father:

I cannot but repet how good a Man is the Duc de Boulion, and how attentive and civil he is to me, which one can see esely is without affectation, *et de Bon Cour*.[18]

In May the French won a crushing victory over the British at Fontenoy: the demoralized Hanoverian armies were tied up on the continent and both Scotland and England lay open to attack. Charles realized that it was now or never and, at the end of that month, he and Sheridan met at Navarre to set in train final arrangements for the voyage to Scotland to raise the Highland clans.

While the others who were in on the plan gathered secretly around Nantes, Charles sat down at Navarre and wrote letters to his father, to King Louis and to his uncle explaining what was happening. The letter to his father was a justification for his action and the secrecy with which it had been planned; that to the French king was an explanation, a reprimand and at the same time an appeal for help; the affectionate letter to his uncle was one of thanks as well as an appeal for him to intercede with King Louis. The warmth of the letter to the duke showed clearly the deep affection Prince Charlie had formed for his new found family in the few months he had known them:

Navarre, 12 June 1745.

My Uncle and my Cousin.

As you are aware of what has happened to me in France you should not be surprised to see me leave in the same manner as I entered it, that's to say stealing away. I came here neither to see the country, not to be a charge on His Most Christian Majesty, but solely to make it easier to travel to those countries over which my birth gives me such clear rights . . . I am writing this to you from your castle of Navarre which you have so graciously lent me. I find it a delightful place and would willingly enjoy all its pleasures which you have provided, if the project of which I have just told you did not call me elsewhere. But no matter where I may find myself you can depend on the friendship and affection that I shall always have for you.

Your affectionate Nephew and Cousin
Charles P.[19]

The letters were dated 12 June, but were only sent a month later when the Prince was on the point of sailing. At that time he added a second note of farewell to his father.

Aboard the two borrowed ships the Prince carried a pathetically small number of weapons and men, only 1,500 muskets, 1,800 broadswords, 20 field guns, some powder, balls, dirks and some 700 men in all. To fortify them he took on board a good supply of brandy as well.

On the voyage the *Elisabeth* was damaged in a fight with a British warship which intercepted the Prince's ships and she had to turn back. As she carried most of his weapons and fighting men, Charles Edward landed at Eriskay in the Western Isles of Scotland on 23 July accompanied only by his closest associates, the little band which became known in history as the Seven Men of Moidart.

He was doubtless glad to see France disappear behind him as he set sail: his stay there had not been a happy one, and his only true friends in that country were his Berwick and Bouillon relations, especially his uncle, the Duc de Bouillon and his cousin, Turenne, who had been good and loyal friends. And no doubt he was sorry to leave Louise, who had treated him well and made his heart beat a little faster. If he had not had such important other matters on his mind he might have missed her more, far more, for she was the first girl who had stirred up feelings of love in him. But for now Prince Charlie's eyes were on the barren rain-drenched island which was his first foothold on his kingdom.

SEVEN

UNDER PETTICOAT PATRONAGE

I cannot think it an unreasonable Conclusion, that the Cause must needs
be bad, at least weak, when we find it so much under Petticoat Patronage.

The Female Rebels, an anti-Jacobite pamphlet published in 1747.[1]

Prince Charlie raised his standard on Monday 19 August 1745. It was a close thing, for when he arrived at Glenfinnan on the appointed morning, he found no more than a hundred and fifty Clanranald MacDonalds gathered around him: they were joined by MacDonald of Morar with an equal number of his men, but that was not enough to make an army with which to march on St James's. When the standard was due to be unfurled at one o'clock, the Prince's sparse little army looked no more than a sizeable party of Highland raiders.

The rallying place had been chosen carefully, for Glenfinnan lies at the top of Loch Shiel, a remote and empty place, yet accessible from three glens which open out from the dark, lowering mountains enclosing the gloomy loch. The Prince's mood turned as dark as the surrounding hills while he waited, but eventually the sound of distant bagpipes broke the silence over towards Cameron country. Every head turned to watch Lochiel march down the glen with seven hundred Cameron clansmen. Then MacDonnell of Keppoch arrived with another three hundred men. And of course, among the Camerons, was Jenny Cameron with the little band of her clansmen whom she had rallied personally for the Prince.

Jenny, or Jean Cameron of Glendessery to give her her proper name, was the first woman to come to the support of Prince Charlie: she was soon to be joined by many more for the handsome Prince proved irresistible to women.

Females were drawn to Prince Charlie not merely because of his handsome looks and the sad, but romantic tragedy of the ancient royal house. They found it easier to make the decision to support the Prince than their menfolk because they were not as involved in day-to-day politics and consequently tended to be more open-minded about such aspects of Jacobitism as divine right and religion. As a result they were much quicker to make up their minds to support the Prince and even those who belonged to families which traditionally favoured the 'other' side were prepared to come and admire this Prince who was risking all for his inheritance.

When he landed on Eriskay the Prince was young, immature and naïve, a man with little experience of love or war. He knew as little about the women of Scotland as they did about him. Although they may have been bred to have views on his Cause and either adored it or loathed it, they knew next to nothing about it or the young man who had arrived to defend it.

Most of the knowledge they did have was gleaned from gossip about life at the Pretender's court in Rome, based on hearsay, which was second- or even third-hand. All stories of the Jacobite Prince which were spread in Scotland before 1745 were far from impartial: if the source happened to be a returning follower of the Cause, they described Charles as a fine princely young man; if they emanated from one of the many Hanoverian spies who haunted the Pretender's *palazzo*, they painted a dark and ugly picture.

Thus females (and males too) in Scotland in 1745 were in a position to make up their own minds about which was the true Charles Stuart, the noble prince or the pompous young boor. Judging by the legend of the bonnie prince that Charles left behind, he clearly possessed that rare power to inspire devotion and generate love. However, on Eriskay and at Glenfinnan, Prince Charlie's mind was not on love, but on a determination to win back his father's crown – love would have to wait.

Women played a far greater role in the '45 than they have ever been given credit for. In every Jacobite house in the Highlands and Lowlands they kept the Cause alive while their men were away fighting for it. But theirs was much more than mere tea-table

Jacobitism, or quirky caprice like Isabella Lumisden's refusal to marry the engraver, Robert Strange, if he would not go and fight for Prince Charlie. It is impossible to say how many women played an active part in the '45, but Sir Bruce Seton listed eighteen women who were deeply involved and fifty-six regimental women among the prisoners taken by government forces.[2]

The wives of the leaders, Lady Ogilvy, the Duchess of Perth, Murray of Broughton's wife, Lady Cromartie and Lady Kilmarnock, all encouraged their husbands – in fact it was Lady Kilmarnock who persuaded her husband to join the Prince and of course that decision led to his death on the execution block. Some, like Lady Anne Mackintosh, came out in defiance of their husbands and raised clansmen for Prince Charlie's army, while Jean Cameron of Glendessary and Mrs Robertson of Lude, 'by instinct and by the example of her mother, Lady Nairne, a convinced Jacobite',[3] both raised men for the Prince. Other women like Lady Clanranald, Lady MacDonald of Boisdale and Flora MacDonald all gave surreptitious support to Charlie, while Lady Margaret MacDonald, wife of the Chief of Sleat in Skye, secretly gave hospitality to the Prince in her house while her husband was 'out' supporting Cumberland.

Although they did not involve themselves in any overtly treasonable activity, Lady Primrose and Lady Bruce of Kinross worked tirelessly to give practical help as well as to create a climate of opinion which would further the Cause during the '45 and after.

And all of these women were genuinely feared by Hanoverian officialdom.

The chief government official in Scotland at the time was Lord President Duncan Forbes of Culloden, who was well aware of their power when he wrote:

All Jacobites, how prudent soever, became mad; all doubtful people became Jacobites; and all bankrupts became heros and talked of nothing but hereditary rights and victories; and what was more grievous to men of gallantry, and if you will believe me, much more mischievous to the public, all the fine ladies, except one or two, became passionately fond of the young Adventurer and used all their arts and industry for him in the most intemperate manner.[4]

Jean, or Jenny Cameron as her Hanoverian detractors preferred to call her, became the focus of this fear of the Cause in the South. Many tales were told about Jenny, none to her credit, but in truth little is known about her presence at Glenfinnan other than that she was there on the great day. We know she was present because Aeneas MacDonald, the Paris banker who helped to raise the money for the rising and accompanied the Prince to Scotland, vouched for her presence:

> Here a considerable number of both gentlemen and ladies met to see the ceremony, among the rest was the famous Miss Jeanie Cameron (as she is commonly though very improperly called, for she is a widow nearer 50 than 40 years of age). She is a genteel, well-look'd, handsome woman, with a pair of pretty eyes, and hair as black as jet. She is of a very sprightly genius, and is very agreeable in conversation.[5]

What is less certain is whether, as James Caulfield described her in his *Remarkable Persons*, Jenny was 'the most fiery zealot' among the Prince's supporters, 'caressed and admired by the man whose esteem she so highly valued'.[6] She was said to have ridden on a bay gelding 'dress'd in a sea green Riding habit, with a scarlet Lapell trimm'd with gold, her hair tied behind in loose buckles, with a velvet cap and a scarlet feather'.

Certainly Prince Charlie took no notice of the effort this splendid woman had made on his behalf: that was left to Hanoverian scandalmongers when they learned of her presence at Glenfinnan and her loyalty to the prince. They said she spent the night with the Prince after the ceremony, and that from then on she followed him as his mistress all the way to Derby and back to Culloden.

Although such an assertion is complete nonsense, there is no doubting that Jean Cameron was a committed Jacobite. She was the daughter of Allan Cameron the third of Glendessary, and closely related to the Camerons of Lochiel, one of the great Highland families, thus had lived in the shadow of the Jacobite Cause all her days. She was born around the year 1714 in Morvern in the Highlands, an area to the south of Glen Dessary, from where the family took their name, and that would make her rather younger than Aeneas MacDonald's 40 to 50 years at the time of Prince Charlie's arrival in Scotland.

She may not have been in the first flush of youth in 1745, but neither was she 'far advanced in years' as the British spy Oliver MacAllester described her,[7] nor was she the wife of a Highland marauder known as Robert the Bruce, who was killed in a brawl, as Caufield claimed.[8] Several versions of Jenny's background have been given: one has her following her adventurer husband, an Irish colonel, to war on the Continent and returning after he was killed in battle in the Low Countries. In another she was married to an Irishman named O'Neal, who treated her badly as a result of which she divorced him and reverted to her family name. Yet another simply gives her husband's name as Cameron, and claims he died prior to 1745.

A grain of truth may lurk in some of the tales which were told about her, but MacAllester and Caulfield were not describing Jean or Jenny Cameron of Glendessary at all, but another Jenny Cameron of whom we shall hear more later – an understandable mistake in Scotland which no doubt contained many women of that name.

Whichever version, if any, of Jenny's story is correct she had returned to her native Inverness-shire, where her brother, John, was heir to the family estates and she was running the Glendessary lands during his absence on the Continent.[9] As soon as she learned of Bonnie Prince Charlie's arrival, Jean began to gather the Glendessary clansmen for the Prince and, with a woman's practical mind, also had rounded up a hundred fat bullocks to help feed the Prince's army.

Aeneas MacDonald scotches that first lie about sleeping with the Prince at Glenfinnan, for he saw her leave the field when the ceremony of raising the standard was over:

She was so far from accompanying the Prince's army that she went off with the rest of the spectators as soon as the army marched. Neither did she ever follow the camp, nor was ever with the Prince, but in public when he had his Court at Edinburgh.[10]

That is interesting: MacDonald states clearly that she did not follow the army, *but she was with the Prince in Edinburgh*, only in public it is true, but she did see him there. So the enthusiastic Jacobite, Jenny Cameron, may have hurried south to be among the women who thronged Holyrood to pay homage to him.

If this is true, Charles did not take any more notice of her than he did of all those other women who flocked to see him. Prince Charlie had too many other, more pressing, matters on his mind at that time to think of sex. He was only interested in clan chiefs and the soldiers they could bring to fight for him.

Charles lost no time after Glenfinnan: by a brilliant piece of strategy he outmanoeuvred Sir John Cope's Hanoverian army and struck south to take Perth and Stirling, where he spent the night of Saturday 14 September at Bannockburn House, the home of one of his most loyal supporters, Sir Hugh Paterson. Paterson's niece, Clementine Walkinshaw, was to play an important role in Prince Charlie's love life later, but there is no evidence to suggest that she met him at that time.

The following day he reached Edinburgh only to find the city bolted and barred against him. In those days the Scottish capital was a small, cramped city piled close to the Castle. The Nor' Loch, where Waverley Station now stands, had not been drained and the New Town was still unbuilt so the town was protected by the castle rock to the west, the loch to the north and city walls to the south and east. It was a 'braw hie heapit toun' exactly as the twentieth-century poet, Lewis Spence, has described it.[11] The city's entire population was crowded into high apartment blocks or 'lands', which lined the mile-long road that straggled downhill from the castle on its high rock to the ancient royal Palace of Holyrood in the shadow of Arthur's Seat. This backbone of the city comprised a single street with a succession of three names, the Lawnmarket, High Street and Canongate, collectively known as the Royal Mile because this was the thoroughfare used by Scotland's kings and queens over the centuries. Here, and in the closes and wynds that herringboned off it, much of Scotland's history was made.

On Sunday 15 September 1745 the city's douce Sabbath peace turned to turmoil.

When first news came of the Prince's landing, the authorities were confident they could destroy any Highland army, a view which was reflected in the pro-government newspaper, the *Edinburgh Evening Courant*, when it arrogantly dismissed Charles Edward's Highlanders. 'Not one half of them have tolerable arms, and are such a pitiful ignorant Crew, that such as have spread themselves to seek for Arms are fit for nothing: they can give no Account of their Designs, or even of themselves; but talk of snishing [taking snuff], K. James, Regent, Plunter [plunder], new brogues &c. and diminish daily.'[12]

By mid-September people were dancing to a different tune. At the head of his Highland army, and with one small victory behind him already, Charles Edward had given Cope the slip and was encamped just outside Edinburgh. Confusion was increased by the fact that the Scottish capital was in the middle of an election in which Whigs opposed Jacobites, but in this city of seven churches and several hundred drinking houses, politics was a matter to be debated rather than fought over. Nobody really wanted to go to war for either side. Walter Biggar Blaikie, an authority on the period, accurately described this political division in Edinburgh's society as a sentimental one.[13]

Appropriately, in a city which drank so deeply, the person in command was Lord Provost Archibald Stewart, by profession a wine merchant. Stewart came under deep suspicion because he was leader of the Jacobite party and, although Blaikie believed that the hapless Lord Provost 'did everything that was possible in a position of extraordinary difficulty',[14] he ended up in the Tower of London on a charge of treason and was held there for fourteen months.

One thing Stewart did do was keep his head while the rich rushed their valuables into the castle for safety or fled the city with them. In advance of the Prince's arrival, Edinburgh's walls were hurriedly strengthened, and mounted with cannon dragged up from ships moored in the port of Leith, but it proved difficult to gather up a force of volunteers to defend the city. When Lord Provost Stewart dithered, George Drummond, later to become one of the city's most redoubtable Lord Provosts, stepped forward and took command of the volunteer army, such as it was, and drilled it for action.

The drama reached its climax that Sunday morning, 15 September, normally a very sombre time in the Scottish capital, when the entire population was at (or should have been at) its devotions. Magdalen Pringle, or Madie as she was generally called, watched it unfold with the acute eye of an eighteen-year-old and wrote it all down in letters to her sister, Tibbie, back home at Nenthorn near Kelso, on the Scottish Borders:

> We were all much alarm'd with ye Fire bells ringing and drums beating to arms the time of ye Forenoon sermon. Ye Kirks, most of them dispers'd and Gardners and Hamilton's Dragoons march'd throw the town in order to go to Corstorphend to meet (and if they could) to Fight and overcome ye Highlanders.[15]

The volunteers drawn up on the street provided scant reassurance. They were a ragtag 'army' whose presence Sir Walter Scott later said did not rouse hearts so much as remind people of a passing knell. Without warning, gunfire broke over the city:

> To compleat ye Hubbub Terror and confusion ye Castle Fired six Great Cannons immediately upon ye back of ye marching &c. – this alarmed every body but upon enquiry it was found ye fired for ye Duke of Tuscany's being chosen Emperor and on no Deadly account. All Sunday ye town was in an uproar you can't easily conceive.[16]

Some women wept from fear; others leant out their windows and laughed or jeered. It was demoralizing for the volunteers, who were already terrified out of their wits, and Alexander Carlyle, who witnessed it, wrote: 'In one house on the south side of the street there was a row of windows, full of ladies, who appeared to enjoy our march to danger with much levity and mirth.'[17] The jeering women were soon silenced and the windows slammed shut when the troops trained their guns on them.

On Monday a subdued air hung over the city until a cry went up during the afternoon that the dragoons, who had marched out so confidently the previous day, were in retreat. From the castle walls and windows looking north from the city, Edinburgh folk watched the soldiers scurrying eastwards along the Lang Dykes, a pathway on the far side of the Nor' Loch, on the site of today's Princes Street. The episode, which became known scornfully as the Canter of Coltbridge, stirred the town into a new frenzy, which Madie witnessed:

> They fell to Barricading the Netherbow port, ye Drums beat furiously to Arms and ye Fire bell rang in a most dismal manner till five at night and everybody was in Terror for their friends the Volunteers.[18]

From then on the situation turned to farce as rumours raged like flames fanned by a high wind – the French were about to land; they *had* landed; 16,000 Jacobites were gathering outside the city. Then came a modicum of good news – General Cope, having been outwitted in the North, had raced his men back to Aberdeen and was now on his way south by sea. While this information was being digested in Edinburgh, a letter arrived from no less a person than Prince Charlie himself demanding Edinburgh's surrender, nothing less.

The Lord Provost called the citizens together in the New Church to decide what to do, and this meeting drew up a plan to play for time in the expectation that Cope would arrive to rescue them. Although it was now close to eight in the evening, four of the city's bailies were sent to negotiate with the Prince at his headquarters at Gray's Mill on the Water of Leith, only a few miles away. Charles's Secretary, John Murray of Broughton, was not taken in, and on his advice the Prince promptly sent the delegation back to Edinburgh with a brusque demand that the city must surrender by two o'clock in the morning or face the consequences.

While all this was going on, word arrived that Cope's fleet had been sighted at the mouth of the river Forth and he would soon be with them. Emboldened by such welcome news the meeting in the New Church ordered yet another bailie to go and recall the first delegation. It was too late; he met the disconsolate four already on their way back with Charles's two o'clock surrender demand in their pocket – and it was already past that hour.

Nobody had the faintest idea what to do next: the volunteer army had melted away and the Hanoverian commander, Lieutenant-General Joshua Guest, and his small garrison were safely tucked up in the castle, so the 'ports', or gates to the city were locked and everyone went off either to discuss the situation further or to sleep on it, in the hope that by some miracle Cope might appear by morning. The coach which had brought the deputation back from Prince Charlie's camp was sent back to its stables just outside the town walls, and Edinburgh settled down for what was left of the night. Unknown to them all, the Prince had set his Highlanders to watch the gates and wait. As dawn broke over Arthur's Seat the Netherbow Port was opened to let the coach leave for its stables outside the city walls, and Lochiel and his Cameron men rushed the guard and seized the gate. Without a shot being fired or a drop of blood spilt, the Scottish capital was the Prince's – all of it except the Castle where Guest continued to hold out and fire his guns towards Holyrood from time to time. This proved little more than an annoyance to the Highlanders, who referred to the castle thereafter as that 'damned angry bitch'.[19]

On the morning of Tuesday 17 September the Prince himself arrived to take possession of the capital in his father's name. He didn't dare ride within gunshot of the Castle, but followed a circuitous route to the south of the city. Passing along what is now Grange Loan and pausing only to drink a glass of wine at Grange House with his loyal supporter, Sir William Dick, he skirted Duddingston Loch to St Anthony's Well, where he dismounted in order to take his first look at Holyrood, which symbolized home to the Royal Stuarts: this was a palace with especially close family associations for Charles, since it had been rebuilt at the time when his grandfather, then Duke of York, was in Scotland as commissioner for his brother, Charles II. James had contributed much to the making of the new palace.

With all the comings and goings of the night before, the young Prince had managed to snatch no more than a couple of hours' sleep, but he showed no trace of weariness as he acknowledged the cheers of the host of people who crowded round him now. As news of his arrival spread, the crowd grew, cheering him all the way, waving white ribbons of the Stuarts, and jostling to kiss his hand. He wore Highland dress, but with red breeches and was flanked by the Duke of Perth on his right and young Lord Elcho on his left. Charles Edward Stuart looked handsome – even his enemies had to admit that.

John Home, no friend of the Jacobites, viewed Charles on the ride into Edinburgh with an eye as sharp as a portrait painter:

The figure and presence of Charles Stuart was not ill suited to his lofty pretensions. He was in the prime of youth, tall and handsome, of a fair complexion; he had a light coloured periwig with his own hair combed over the front; he wore the Highland dress, that is a tartan short coat without a plaid, and on his breast the star of the order of St Andrew. [He] mounted his horse, either to render himself more conspicuous, or because he rode well and looked graceful on horseback. The Jacobites were charmed with his appearance.[20]

By the time Charles reached Holyrood the courtyard was crammed with onlookers, many of them women, who shouted, 'Long live the Prince' and 'Long live the royal House of Stuart'.[21] He acknowledged their cheers gracefully, but already was impatient to get down to the task of planning his next move.

While the Prince settled into Holyrood the town was beside itself with excitement. At the mercat cross around one o'clock Charles's father was proclaimed King James VIII and III of Scotland, England, Ireland and – rather tactlessly in view of Charles's hope that King Louis XV might send him help – France as well. Poor James, 'Mr Misfortune' all his life, had nearly been crowned at Scone during his 1715 invasion, but that coronation never took place and he was forced to return to the Continent with nothing more than loyal addresses from the Provosts of a few of the towns he had passed through. There was no hesitation, no dithering now. Threatened by Highlanders brandishing guns 'of innormous length', swords, old Lochaber axes and 'pitchforks and some bits of sythes upon poles',[22] the herald was forced to read the proclamation, then manifestos and declarations were read, a trumpet sounded and bagpipes resounded joyfully over the applause and cheering of the throng. As the proclamations were read, the wife of John Murray of Broughton, the Princes's Secretary in Scotland, rode among the people, handing out white cockades with one hand, while holding a sword in the air with the other. Edinburgh was a capital city again, and her citizens loved it.

'The joy seemed universal,' wrote James Maxwell of Kirkconnell. 'God save the King was echoed back from all quarters of the town. The ladies particularly distinguished themselves on this occasion.'[23]

It is interesting that so many observers refer to the role of women in these incredible events, proof of how successfully Prince Charles won them over. Madie Pringle confirms that women were wild about Charlie and were prominent among those who 'huzza'd' every declaration. At every crowded window, she said, they waved and showed great loyalty, but added carefully, 'Don't imagine I was one of those Ladies. I assure you I was not.'[24]

Behind Madie's exhilaration, her letters tingle with the danger of being under Prince Charlie's spell at this moment, partly because she was aware that her good pro-Hanover family would be shocked and angry beyond words to discover she had been consorting with rebels and traitors. Madie cared about what her family thought, but paid little attention to other possible consequences, for she was too young to remember the vengeance the government brought down on those who supported the Jacobites during the 1715 Rising. She defied her family and the authorities to let herself be drawn to look admiringly at the Prince, yet she stopped short of allowing herself to be presented to him, although it is apparent from her letters that she would dearly have loved to have done so.

'All ye Ladies are to kiss ye Prince's [*hand*]' she told her sister, Tibbie. 'I've an inclination to see him but I can't be intro-'. Unfortunately Madie's letter breaks off halfway through the word *introduced* and the rest has been lost.[25]

Madie Pringle was not alone in her infatuation: in mid-September 1745 it was said that two-thirds of the men in the city were Hanoverians, but (with some exaggeration no doubt) nearly every woman was for the Prince.

It was not simply a matter of silly young girls becoming caught up in Prince Charlie's web: mature women, many of them belonging to respectable anti-Jacobite families, crowded to their windows to see him, or rushed into the street to touch his coat as he rode by. If they were important enough they schemed to be invited to the palace so that they might kiss his hand, much to the disgust of those few Hanoverian ladies who managed to keep their heads and resist Prince Charlie's charms. One who remained impervious wrote to tell her daughter how much she was alarmed by the Prince's influence over women. 'The Young Gentleman that we have got amongst us busses [*kisses*] the ladies so that he gains all their Hearts', she recounted in a secret letter from Edinburgh. Then she added a prophetic thought: 'We must certainly have the Duke of Cumberland to kiss the Ladies and fight these Dogs or there will be no living here for honest people.'[26]

Heaven knows, few hearts missed a beat and no one sought to be kissed by the plump, pompous, unattractive Hanoverian prince, William Duke of Cumberland, when he arrived among them early the following year to lead King George's army against the Prince.

Charles Stuart cannot be accused of 'bussing' the women of Edinburgh when they came to see him. As Elcho said, far from encouraging women admirers, Charles positively discouraged them. From the moment the Prince set foot in Holyrood and fashionable ladies began to rush to kiss his hand, Elcho recalled that 'his behaviour to them was very cool'.[27]

Charles Stuart looked like a prince and behaved like a prince, mixing extreme courtesy with cold hauteur of one whose family believed they ruled by divine right and were beings set apart from the nobility, let alone from the common people. Unfortunately in Edinburgh this attitude was sometimes mistaken for disdain. Other supporters as well as Elcho noted it, and feared for the effect it might have on the Cause.

How wrong they were. The less attention Charles Stuart paid to these women, the more they fell at his feet until almost every female in the city was his slave. And the oftener he rode aloofly past or received them coolly, the greater their adoration grew. When the 'bonny prince' moved among them, Scotswomen's excitement seems to have risen in direct proportion to the offhandedness with which he treated them. They gossiped about this in Edinburgh at the time, so that poor Charles lost out twice over – while his manner drove female admirers into ecstasies of devotion, it allowed his enemies to accuse him of being unfeeling towards women and even uninterested in them.

Madie continued to follow the Prince's every movement and to chronicle all she saw for the benefit of her sister at Nenthorn. Next morning there were new excitements to report when her friend Madie Nairne was shot:

Madie Nairn [*Mary, daughter of Jacobite supporter Baron Nairne*] who was looking over Lady Keith's window along with Katie Hepburn. On ye other side of ye street there was a Highland Man and a Boy standing with a Gun in his hand which Gun went off and shot in at ye Window and ye Bullet went in at Mady Nairn's head. luckily the strength of ye ball had been spent by its Grazing on ye wall so that it stuck and did not go through her skull or she must have Died instantly. Mr Ratray has taken out ye Ball and sow'd up her wound he thinks her safe if she keeps free from a Fever. The Prince has sent several messages to inquire after her which has help'd not a little to support her spirits under ye Pain of her sore wound.[28]

Mary Nairne survived and died unmarried in 1774.[29]

The Prince was barely installed in the palace when he received word that Sir John Cope had landed with his army. 'Has he, by God,' said Charles, and at once set about preparing for battle. Near Prestonpans on the following Saturday, 21 September, he and his Highlanders won a great victory over Cope, and the following day he marched back into the city – now *his* undisputed capital (the Castle apart, since it still held out) – with colours flying, bagpipes playing and drums beating. If Charles Stuart was a much-admired, handsome prince when he first entered the city on Tuesday 17 September, he was cheered to the echo as a victorious hero on his return to it the following Sunday. Again the streets were jammed with ecstatic supporters. Windows in the Canongate were filled to overflowing, and white cockades were everywhere. As it was the Sabbath day, the Prince sent word to ministers in the city that they were free to hold services as usual if they so wished. Many did not, and one of the few who did, offered up a somewhat ambiguous prayer for King and Prince. 'Bless the King,' he said. 'Thou knows what King I mean; may the crown sit long easy on his head, &c. And for this man that is come amongst us to seek an earthly crown, we beseech Thee in mercy, to take him to Thyself and give him a Crown of Glory.'[30]

Displaying great sensitivity, Charles ensured that the wounded and prisoners were treated well after the Battle of Prestonpans, and ordered that there should be neither festivities nor bonfires in the city to mark his victory. The wounded or dead Hanoverians at Prestonpans, or Gladsmuir as the Jacobites called the battle, were his father's subjects every bit as much as were the soldiers of his victorious army.

With his army encamped at Duddingston, a few miles east of the city in those days, Charles again took up residence at Holyrood: for six glorious weeks Edinburgh had her own royal court where, if no king actually reigned, at least there was a regent who possessed all the power and majesty of a monarch. Charles Edward issued manifestos and declarations in his father's name, he received his subjects at levées, and reluctantly he attended balls in the great gallery from whose walls monarchs of Scotland through the ages looked down. The court of Bonnie Prince Charlie may have been as much a sham as those hundred and more portraits of the Prince's ancestors, which had all been painted by one man, Dutchman Jacob de Wit, between the years 1684 and 1686, but it gave back to the citizens the pride and sense of nationhood many felt they had lost at the Union of the Parliaments 38 years before. This brief sunburst of Stuart glory was a royal court as real as when Scotland had a king of her own living in this same palace.

The Prince's court sent the good folk of Edinburgh – especially the women – into rhapsodies. Miss Threipland of Fingask could not wait to put pen to paper when she returned from seeing Charles:

> Oh, had you beheld my beloved Hero, you must confess he is a gift from Heaven; but then, besides his outward appearance, which is absolutely the *best figure* I ever saw, such Vivacity, such piercing Wit, woven with a clear Judgement and an active Genius, and allowed by all to have a Capacity apt to receive such impressions as are not usually stampt on every brain; in short, Madam, he is the *Top of Perfection and Heaven's Darling.*[31]

The Bonnie Prince was anxious to push ahead with his task of sending German George back to Hanover, and met with his advisers every morning to plan his march into England and to raise more men and money for the campaign. Afterwards he usually dined with his principal officers in public. Lord Elcho wrote:

> Their [*sic*] was always a Crowd of all sorts of people to See him dine. After dinner he rode out Attended by his life guards and review'd his Army, where their was always a great number of Spectators in Coaches and on horseback. After the review, he Came to the Abbey, where he received the ladies of fashion that came to his drawing room. Then he Sup'd in publick, and Generaly their was musick at Supper, and a Ball afterwards.[32]

In spite of Charles's reluctance to spend time with the ladies, the court at Holyrood glittered from the very first night after his arrival, when his officers persuaded him to give a ball. The Prince was not at all keen and refused to dance, causing annoyance among his leaders who were disturbed that this might harm his popularity, especially among the women whose support was so important to the Cause. O'Sullivan, who had been at the Prince's side all the way from Rome, was greatly worried about this standoffishness. O'Sullivan commented:

> The Prince went to see the Lady's dance, made them compliments on their dance and good grace, and retired; some gents. followed

him and told him, yt the knew he loved dancing, and yt the Ball was designed for him to amuse him; 'its very true', says the Prince, 'I like dancing, and am very glad to see the Lady's and you divert yr selfs, but I have now another Air to dance and until that be finished I'l dance no other.'[33]

But Charles Edward was far happier surrounded by his soldiers at Duddingston than in the midst of fawning men and women in the palace, so he spent much of his time at the camp, planning with his leaders, or reviewing his men. In spite of his coolness towards them, women continued to pester him even at the army camp: they crowded out to Duddingston just to gaze at him – which must have been a great embarrassment to a young man accustomed to a predominantly masculine environment. Needless to say Madie Pringle was among those admirers who went to watch him review his troops: on Wednesday 10 October she visited Duddingston and reported back to her sister ecstatically:

He was sitting in his Tent when I came first to ye field. The Ladies made a circle round ye Tent and after we had Gaz'd our fill at him he came out of the Tent with a grace and Majesty that is unexpressible. He saluted ye Circle with an air of grandeur and affability capable of Charming ye most obstinate Whig . . . we were all extremely near to him when he mounted and in all my Life I never saw so noble nor so Graceful an appearance as His Highness made, he was in great spirits and very cheerful.[34]

Madie loitered at the entrance to the Prince's tent with all the fine ladies, among whom that day was Lady Nithsdale, daughter-in-law of the Jacobite heroine who had helped her condemned husband to escape from the Tower of London on the eve of his execution at the end of the '15 Rising, as well as Lady Ogilvy, whose husband was a member of the Prince's council, and the staunchly Jacobite Lady Traquair.

Madie took in every detail of Prince Charlie's appearance as was only possible for a girl who, if not actually in love with him, certainly was lost in admiration:

He was dressed in a Blue Grogrum Coat trimmed with Gold lace and a lac'd Red Wastcoat and Breeches. On his left shoulder and side were the Star & Garter and over his right shoulder a very rich Broad Sword Belt. his sword had ye finest wrought Basket hilt ever I beheld all Silver. His hat had a white Feather in it and a white cockade and was trimmed with an open gold lace . . . his Highness rides finely and indeed in all his appearance seems to be Cut out for enchanting his beholders and carrying People to consent to their own Slavery in spite of themselves.[35]

Madie decided she preferred him in this Lowland garb to the Highland dress in which she had seen him earlier.

The gathering of women at Duddingston, notabilities rubbing shoulders with girls of very ordinary families, proves that if women had fought wars in the time of Bonnie Prince Charlie, the Prince would have had considerably less difficulty rallying an army to his standard at Glenfinnan at the start of the '45. But women didn't go to war – at least not as part of the fighting force – and it was left to the men to decide whether to stay at home or to join in the Jacobite rising.

Prince Charlie's brief stay at Holyrood has been called unkindly his 'little hour of royalty',[36] but it was more than that – much more. This was the high point of the century of the Jacobite Cause, the peak of Charles Edward Stuart's life, the moment when the legend of Bonnie Prince Charlie was born.

Prince Charlie was young, success lay all around him, and he believed himself and his Highlanders invincible. At that moment Scotland belonged to the handsome Prince and he belonged to Scotland. There was hardly a woman who was not just a little bit in love with him then, and many had lost their hearts completely.

EIGHT

CONQUEST AT BANNOCKBURN

Le Prince Edouard était en Ecosse, y épouse suivant le usage du pays, une d'elle aux meilleur maison de ce pays . . . ce premier marriage n'étant pas fait suivant les rites de l'église Romains, ce prince crût pouvoir ensuite le regard comme nil, et il epousa in italie la Princess de Stolberg-Gedern

Memoir sent by Charlotte Stuart to the French king in 1774.[1]

As night fell on Edinburgh on the last day of October Bonnie Prince Charlie rode out of Holyrood: next morning the last of his Highlanders followed, leaving the capital empty and Holyrood once again the silent, echoing place it had been for generations. Even those who believed the Prince was on his way to restoring his father to his rightful crown in London felt a heaviness in their hearts.

For women at every level of society, who had enjoyed the Prince's 'reign' at Holyrood, it was a moment of particular sadness, but especially so for old Lady Bruce of Kinross, who had made her house at the Citadel of Leith the principal centre of Jacobitism in the capital. Lady Bruce, born Magdalene Scott, who was the widow of Sir William Bruce of Kinross, had been familiar with the Jacobite movement ever since King James VII and II fled over the water in 1688. She was a girl of eighteen at that time and, although now past her seventy-fifth birthday, her enthusiasm for the Cause burned with as much bright youthfulness as ever.

Until the end of her life on 24 June 1752 her home was open house for Jacobites to exchange information, to receive comfort or financial help, or just to get their stories off their chest. Lady Bruce was rich and generous, quietly handing out money to deserving Jacobites who visited her. No one knew more of this quiet generosity than Robert Forbes who, in drawing up her accounts, once wrote, 'I have not reckoned up a guinea, half a guinea, or a crown, which I had from time to time from my Lady Bruce as a necessitous sufferer happened to come in the way.'[2] Much of her open-heartedness went unrecorded.

Magdalene Bruce's greatest piece of generosity towards the Jacobite movement was to make it possible for Robert Forbes to gather together 'a collection [as exactly made as the iniquity of the times would permit] of speeches, letters, journals, etc., relative to the affairs, but more particularly the dangers and distresses of Prince Charles Edward Stuart'. These were eventually published in three volumes under the title *The Lyon in Mourning*.[3]

Forbes, a young Episcopalian clergyman and ardent Jacobite, was captured early in the rising on his way to join the Prince and was thrown into Stirling or Edinburgh Castle, or perhaps he was incarcerated in each at various times. When he was freed Lady Bruce invited him to stay at the Citadel and there he worked for a number of years, collecting the reminiscences of supporters both during and after the rising. Forbes was appointed Bishop of Ross and Caithness in 1762 and died at Leith on 18 November 1775.[4] Without Lady Bruce and Robert Forbes, the history of the '45 and its social impact on the Highlands would be much poorer.

In the south the welfare of the Cause was in equally safe hands, where Lady Primrose made her house in Essex Street, off the Strand, in London, a centre of Jacobite activity. Here leaders of the Cause in England and from the other side of the Channel met and plotted, and kept in close touch with the king in Rome and the Prince in Scotland, France and Flanders during and after the '45 rising.

Lady Primrose was born Anne Drelincourt, one of sixteen daughters of the Dean of Armagh, and was the widow of the third Viscount Primrose. She is said to have become interested in the Jacobite movement because she was descended from an illegitimate child of Louis XIV of France and could claim kinship with Prince Charlie. There is a traditional story told in the Rosebery family, to which the Primroses belong, that her royal ancestor was found, Moses-like, floating down the Seine in a box of orange blossom.

At the time of the rising Anne Primrose had been a widow for four years and was deeply committed to the Cause in England, where her opinions carried much weight. Chiefs and other prominent Jacobites who were held in London after the rising were able to visit her house fairly freely and she gave much financial help to clansmen who were in need, just as Lady Bruce did in Leith.

When the Prince rode south women were discouraged from accompanying the army, and the orderly book of Lord Ogilvy's regiment actually forbade them, but many went in defiance of the order.[5] Such orders did not apply to someone as important as Lady Ogilvy, and she accompanied her husband. The Duchess of Perth and Secretary Murray's wife also accompanied the army, the secretary's wife dressed in tartan and fur hat to match that of the troop of hussars her husband had raised. She also carried 'pistols at her syde sadle'.[6]

Lady Perth was always mounted on her horse, ready to ride off 'as early as the hardiest cavalier among them'. It was said that when Carlisle surrendered she was all for hanging the townspeople because they did not open their gates immediately they were ordered to. At Derby she raged and stormed and 'stamped like a fury' and called the Prince a poltroon 'almost to his face'.[7] Even allowing for the fact that these words were written by an enemy of the Cause, it is clear that the Duchess of Perth was made of tough stuff!

That ultra-respectable Victorian historian, Andrew Lang, is reputed to have given credence to the tales of the Prince's women followers by quoting a letter from an unidentified woman in Preston in which it was said that Mrs Murray of Broughton, Lady Ogilvy, 'the mistress of one MacSheridan, a popish priest', and Jenny Cameron were seen driving in a coach and six. 'The young Pretender seem'd very sick and faint, and is very assiduously ministered unto by Jenny Cameron,' she added.[8]

The manner in which females flocked to Prince Charlie's support frightened the Whigs and it angered and frustrated them as well, because they had no way of retaliating in like manner. Prince Charlie was leading an exemplary life as far as sex and women were concerned, so the only way was to invent mistresses and affairs, or to whip up scandal by embroidering wild tales around real women, especially poor Jenny Cameron, who was easy prey for these spoiling vultures.

The more outrageous the story the more widely they spread it; the greater the lie the louder they trumpeted it. Jenny Cameron, whose only crime was to be first in the field, was vilified and lampooned unmercifully.

The Hanoverians very quickly latched on the value of Mrs Cameron as an anti-Jacobite propaganda weapon, and she became a cornerstone of their campaign to discredit the Prince. Portraits and cartoons were circulated, scurrilous stories were put about, and poems, books and plays appeared in which she featured usually as an Amazon or a whore whom the Prince kept in tow.

Hogarth pilloried her and so did many inferior artists, nearly always depicting her in a tartan coat, with drawn sword in her hand, and either carrying a miniature of the Prince or wearing a white rose. Henry Fielding scourged Jenny Cameron with his pen in *Tom Jones*, when he had Squire Western's daughter, Sophie, mistaken for Jenny by the innkeeper at Upton. Sophie's maid was outraged:

Mrs Honour, having scolded violently below-stairs, and continued the same all the way up, came in to her mistress in a most outrageous passion, crying out, 'What doth your ladyship think? Would you imagine that this impudent villain, the master of this house, hath had the impudence to tell me, nay, to stand it out to my face, that your ladyship is that nasty, stinking wh-re (Jenny Cameron they call her), that runs about the country with the Pretender?'[9]

Nothing was too vile to write about this highly respectable woman: the song they made up about her ran to many verses, a few of which give a good idea of the picture the Whig versifier wished to portray:

> Ye'll a' hae heard tell o' Bonnie Jeanie Cameron,
> How she fell sick, an' she was like tae dee.
> An a' that they could recommend her
> Was ae blythe blink o' the Young Pretender!
> Rare, O rare, Bonnie Jeanie Cameron!
> Rare, O rare – Jeanie Cameron!

111

The doctor was sent for, to see if he
   could cure her,
Quickly he came, he made no delay,
But a' that he could recommend her
Was ae blythe blink o' the Young Pretender!
   Rare, O rare, Bonnie Jeanie Cameron!
   Rare, O rare – Jeanie Cameron!

To Charlie she wrote a very long letter,
Stating wha were his friends an' wha
   were his foes,
An' a' her words were sweet an' tender
Tae win the heart o' the Young Pretender!
   Rare, O rare, Bonnie Jeanie Cameron!
   Rare, O rare – Jeanie Cameron!

O, scarcely had she seal'd the letter
   wi' a ring,
When up flew the door, an' in cam' her king.
She pray'd to the saints, bade angels
   defend her,
An' sank intae the arms o' the Young
   Pretender!
   Rare, O rare, Bonnie Jeanie Cameron!
   Rare, O rare – Jeanie Cameron![10]

The verse was doggerel, the sentiments unworthy of any decent man, but Whig pamphleteers stopped at nothing to discredit Prince Charlie. As Charles Edward's great partisan, Compton Mackenzie wrote, 'The more infamous the lie, the more tenacious it is of life.'[11]

If he heard any of this scurrilous nonsense, Charles ignored it. He reached Derby by the beginning of December and was only a few days' march from London where panic reigned everywhere. England had been a disappointment, with morose people in morose towns offering no welcome. There was little support forthcoming even from the English Jacobites and the leaders and men of the

Prince's army were becoming dispirited. Only Charles seemed to be in good spirits.

Then came the bombshell: his leaders met together at Lord Exeter's house in Derby to discuss the situation and decided that, with the Hanoverian armies gathering against them, it was too dangerous to march further south and risk being trapped and destroyed. The Prince was alone with John Hay in his room, unaware that any meeting was taking place. He had just put on his bonnet and was about to leave when Lord George Murray strode in and announced in his usual brusque manner that it was high time to think what they were going to do. Charles was dumbfounded and asked what he meant: he understood it had been resolved to march on to London. No, Murray told him, the chiefs all considered that they should retire to Ashbourne and join up with the army they believed was following from Scotland.

Charles turned on his general. 'To retire, Lord George, to retire. Why the clans kept me quite another language and assur'd me they were all resolved to pierce or die.'[12]

A council was called and one by one the members told him that they agreed with Lord George – all except the Duke of Perth, which may account for the anger of Lady Perth when she called the Prince 'a poltroon',[13] presumably for not following her husband's advice. Secretary Murray of Broughton was absent and had not attended a meeting since he quarrelled with Lord George at Carlisle, but he happened to walk into the room by chance. Seeing the assembled council, he turned to leave, but Charles called him back and told him angrily that his chiefs were trying to force him to return to Scotland instead of marching directly to London. What was the secretary's opinion? Broughton believed they should turn back.

The Prince lashed all of them as traitors and, although he told them he would accept their decision, he spent all day trying to win the chiefs over one by one – without success. That night he called his council together again and informed them with ill grace that they would return to Scotland, but henceforth there would be no more councils of war: he would neither ask for nor take advice, but would be accountable only to his father.

The following morning, Friday 6 December – called Black Friday in London where the entire population was in a state of panic, but Black Friday in Derby too – drums beat the men to arms, bagpipes played and the Highland army marched out of Derby. Most of the men believed they were on their way to London and it was only later that they realized they were heading north.

By nine o'clock the town was almost empty of her unwanted guests. When all but the rearguard had left, the Prince appeared quite suddenly at the door of Lord Exeter's house, mounted a black horse, and rode rapidly past the marching columns until he reached the front of his army. One observer thought he looked as if he wished he had been twenty feet underground.

Derby marked a major turning point in Prince Charlie's life. All the way north he rode silently and sulkily on his own, apart from his men and separated from his generals by an ever-widening gulf of distrust, which in some cases grew to hatred. From that moment in Derby when (Perth's protest apart) none of his commanders spoke up for him, Charles Edward Stuart changed and the new Prince who emerged from the disappointment of retreat was to be reflected in every action he took throughout the remainder of his life.

The women, who had trudged all the way from Edinburgh to Derby and must have been as weary as their menfolk, were sent to the van of the retreating army while the Highlanders gave a bloody nose to part of Cumberland's army which had caught up with them at Clifton near Penrith.

On 20 December 1746 (the anniversary of Charles' birth by the Old Style Calendar), the Prince celebrated his twenty-sixth birthday,[14] but there was not much to celebrate that day as he and his army sullenly recrossed the Esk river back on to Scottish soil. For some hare-brained reason he left the Manchester regiment and a hundred or so men in French service behind in England to defend Carlisle Castle, which was indefensible against Cumberland's big guns. Carlisle soon surrendered and many of these men were marched off to gaol and ultimately to death. Along with them were were some fifty-six women and girls and at least fifteen children, many of them from Scotland, who had been left behind probably because it would have been too difficult to get them back across the flooded Esk into their home country. These miserable followers of their men were sent to gaols in Chester, Lancaster and York to await their fate.[15]

The Prince who abandoned these soldiers and their women to Cumberland's mercies when he re-entered Scotland was a very different man from the high spirited young commander who had crossed the Border on 8 November and ridden into Carlisle in triumph ten days later.

Return to Scotland also marked a watershed in Prince Charlie's sexual life. It was after this that the man who hitherto had little or no appetite for women, even when they threw themselves at him as they had done in Edinburgh, first sought out female company.

If Balhaldy was right in his assertion that the Prince took a vow of chastity until his family was restored to their throne, then this was the moment when he began to slough it off.

The Prince probably never did make that vow, certainly in so many words, and he did not make any formal renunciation of it now; more likely, it just happened that up to that moment he was too preoccupied with his campaign to think of female company, but now he became aware of a need for a woman's comfort.

Frank McLynn believes that we cannot assume that Charles was a male virgin before the '45 and certainly he may well have bedded his cousin, Louise, in France. 'But it is clear,' McLynn adds, 'that in his positive phase, on the upward climb to the meridian at Derby, women were unimportant to him.'[16]

Prince Charlie could not return to Edinburgh because it had been reoccupied by King George's army the moment the Jacobites left, and Hanoverian strength was concentrated on the eastern side of the country anyway. So the Prince decided to follow the same route north to the Scottish border and then to strike west to Dumfries and through Nithsdale to Glasgow, where he planned to raise money from the well-heeled but sullenly anti-Jacobite merchants. It rankled with him that when he tried to raise a levy of £15,000 in the city before the march south, he had managed to squeeze little more than £3,000 out of them, yet as soon as his back was turned the citizens promptly raised a regiment of militia against him. Glasgow was not for Charlie and did not hesitate to say so.

The chosen route took him through the Whig heartland of Lowland Scotland, close to Covenanting country where old people could still remember the scourge of the Highland Host during his grandfather's religious persecutions. Those Killing Times of James VII and II were still remembered with anger.

However the Stuarts had some friends here too, notably the Maxwells of Nithsdale, who made him very welcome. Pausing only for a day's hunting at Hamilton, he arrived in Glasgow on 26 December to a frigid reception. The streets, though thronged with people standing several deep, were so silent that the cheers of the Highland soldiers died on their lips when nobody joined in.

Prince Charlie spent eight days at Shawfield House, a merchant's house in the city, during which time he worked hard to win the heart of the city, but with little success. Glasgow's Provost proudly recorded that the Prince made five or six appearances without getting so much as a cheer from the humblest citizen. 'Our very ladys had not the curiosity to go near him, and declined going to a ball held by his chiefs; very few were at the windows when he made his appearance and such as were declared him not handsome.'[17]

Every day the Prince went to great lengths to show himself off to the folk of Glasgow, dressing extravagantly in fine clothes brought from France when he appeared among them, and displaying the warmest side of his nature, although he could not have felt comfortable in this unfriendly city.

He even took notice of the ladies, something very different from his response to them in Edinburgh, a small band of whom waited on him as he ate in public twice a day with a few of his personal officers at a table spread in Shawfield drawing room.

Among those who might have been dancing attendance on him at Shawfield House was Clementine Walkinshaw, the daughter of John Walkinshaw of Barrowfield and Camlachie, and his third wife, Katharine, daughter of Sir Hugh Paterson of Bannockburn. Both the Walkinshaw and Paterson families were loyal Jacobites, who had long been supporters of the Cause.[18]

Clementine was Barrowfield's tenth and youngest child in a family which comprised only girls. She was born in 1720, although the *Dictionary of National Biography* gives her birthdate as 1726,[19] and of her early background only one thing is sure – she was named after Clementina Sobieska, as were so many other girls at that time. There is no proof of a claim that Queen Clementina was her godmother, or that she held the infant Clementine at the font.

Nonetheless the Cause had been part of her family's life since long before she was born. John Walkinshaw of Barrowfield had been out in the '15 rising, was imprisoned, but afterwards fled to France, where he joined King James at Bar-le-Duc. He was involved in the preliminary negotiations with Prince James Sobieski for Clementina Sobieska's marriage to the Pretender and was sent to Vienna by James to complain to the Emperor about the detention of the bride at Innsbruck on her journey to Italy. Walkinshaw was constantly embroiled in the Cause, which probably gave rise to a story that Clementine was born in Rome and grew up there, although Henrietta Tayler gives it as her view that she was much more likely to have been born at Barrowfield or Camlachie.[20] An absurd Victorian story describes her as Charles Edward's 'little playmate'.[21] Clementine was Roman Catholic and spent part of her youth in France or the Low Countries, where she received much of her education.

Given such a staunch Jacobite background it was hardly stretching the truth greatly for W.D. Norie to claim, 'It is almost certain that Clementine Walkinshaw was one of the fair Glasgow lassies who waited on the Prince at Shawfield House, and it is more than probable that arrangements were made for a future meeting at Bannockburn.'[22]

By 2 January 1746 Charles had had enough of Glasgow and as a final demonstration of his strength he held a great review of his troops on Glasgow Green before marching out of the city the following day. While his soldiers were stationed around Stirling he made Bannockburn House, now occupied by Clementine's uncle, another Sir Hugh Paterson, his own headquarters.

Whether or not he and Miss Walkinshaw had already met in

Glasgow may be disputed, and she herself suggested that she did not meet him until he arrived at Bannockburn. The memoirs which her daughter, Charlotte, laid before Louis XV and XVI state categorically that she was presented to him there:

> Le prince Charles Edouard prit son quartier general au château de Bannockburn chez le Chevalier Paterson. Le Seigneur lui presenta toute sa famille. Mlle de Walkinshaw sa nièce fut du nombre de demoiselles présentées.[23]

All that is certain then is that they were together at Bannockburn, but the question of whether he bedded her there too is debatable, and probably always will be: There are no firm facts, only hints, from his enemies or her family. Dr William King of Oxford, one of the leaders of the Jacobites in England, turned violently against Clementine. 'When he [the Prince] was in Scotland he had a mistress whose name was Walkinshaw,' said King bluntly.[24] And Lord Elcho also claims that they met at Bannockburn House and she 'there and then became his mistress'.[25] Neither says that the two simply met at Bannockburn, but that she actually *became his mistress*.

Is there a hint as to what happened at Bannockburn House to be found in the fact that Clementine did not marry during the years after the Prince left? Her portraits show her to have been an elegant woman in her mid-twenties, poised and confident, and likely to catch some young man's eye. She was reputed to have been wooed by John, 5th Duke of Argyll, but that seems an improbable match – he was Presbyterian and she was Catholic; his family as staunchly loyal to Hanover as hers were to the Stuarts over the Water.

Religion and political affiliations would make it difficult in eighteenth-century Presbyterian Lowland Scotland to find a suitable suitor for an aristocratic Roman Catholic Jacobite girl, and Walkinshaw of Barrowfield had ten daughters to match up with husbands. It is interesting that only four out of the ten Walkinshaw girls found husbands, and two of these were cousins. A liaison with Prince Charlie at Bannockburn House in 1746 could have made it especially hard for Clementine to find a suitable or willing suitor.

Another interesting aspect of the Prince's stay among the Walkinshaws and Patersons is that a Jacobite family would normally boast about having the Prince under their roof, but Clementine's relations kept mum on the subject – might that have been because they felt they had been compromised by the liberties Charles Stuart had taken with the youngest daughter of the house? They would not be at all pleased about the 'honour' for which Clementine had been singled out, but would close ranks and not breathe it to anyone in the world.

When Clementine decided later to go to the Continent, ostensibly to enter a religious house, they reacted with cruel anger. Taking their lead from their mother, the entire family cut her off from the moment she left Scotland. Such a reaction indicates more than mere religious grounds as was suggested by an unnamed friend in a letter to Clementine: 'All the world believe that, by the advice of the false and foolish priests, you left your friends and lovers and everything to go in to a convent, So you pass for a priest-ridden weak girl.'[26]

'Lovers' is a strange word to use unless there were other affairs as well as the one with Charles, and Clementine's morals disturbed or even disgusted her strait-laced family.

Clementine Walkinshaw may have been priest-ridden, although she never gave the impression of being so, but she was not weak; in fact it was more probably Clementine's strength of character that her mother feared. Clementine, the most Jacobite of the girls, was going to the Continent, where there were many Stuart followers, including Prince Charlie, and old Mrs Walkinshaw feared, or perhaps had some solid knowledge of the fact that her daughter was likely to be drawn into their web.

Charles and Clementine were lovers by the time he left Bannockburn House after a week to begin the siege of Stirling Castle and defeat General Henry Hawley at Falkirk on 17 January, but soon he was back at Bannockburn, where he went down with a miserable 'fluish cold accompanied by a high fever'.[27]

This was the first day's illness the Prince had suffered since his arrival in Scotland the previous July, but it was not to be the last now that he was depressed and worried about the way the campaign was falling apart. His army failed to take advantage of its victory at Falkirk and this brought on one of those illnesses to which he tended to succumb whenever he was under stress.

And on hand with cinnamon possets and sympathy was Clementine Walkinshaw, who had lived in Europe and consequently could speak French and listen to him with understanding.

She and her friends at Bannockburn helped him to forget his troubles so successfully that he even missed a meeting he had arranged with Lord George Murray. He sent a message, saying, 'I was just ready to get on horseback and make you a visit, but have been overpersuaded to let it alone by people who are continuously teasing me with my cold.'[28]

The tone of the note suggests that he was easily 'overpersuaded'.

If Charles and Clementine were not lovers in the fullest sense of the word before, this would be the moment, as he recovered, when the relationship slipped from comforting companionship into something much deeper and Clementine gave herself to him. He needed Clementine more than ever as he recovered, for the situation with his army and his generals was worsening by the day. There were numerous desertions and the leaders behaved just as arrogantly as they had done at Derby, urging the Prince to retreat into the Highlands rather then face Cumberland before he had time to organize his army as Charles wanted to.

Eventually they sent a message to the Prince putting this to him. Charles, clearly on a knife-edge anyway, exploded. He banged his head violently against the wall and cried, 'Good God! Have I lived to see this?'[29]

He left Bannockburn House on 1 February and marched north to disaster at Culloden on 16 April: it was the end of the last real attempt to win back the crowns of Scotland, England and Ireland.

Before he departed from Bannockburn, one of the few places he had felt among friends since his arrival in Scotland nine months before, Clementine promised him that 'if his great political ambitions came to nothing and he ever needed her, she would be his to command'.[30]

Many allegations have been made over the years to suggest that Clementine Walkinshaw bore Prince Charlie's child as a result of their liaison at Bannockburn, and one of these stands out as containing a germ of possibility.

In the remote churchyard of Finsthwaite at the southern end of Lake Windermere in the Lake District of England a simple white cross marks the grave of a young woman whose death is recorded in Finsthwaite parish register:

> Buried, Clementina Johannes Sobiesky Douglass, of Waterside, Spinster, May the 16th, 1771.[31]

The story, as told in Lakeland, is that this was the child of Charles Stuart and Clementine Walkinshaw, and that she arrived in Finsthwaite about the year 1746 accompanied by two servants. Her surname, Douglass, was one which Charles Stuart's favourite aliases, and her first name was that of his mistress and his mother. The girl's other names, Johannes Sobiesky, were also linked to Prince Charlie's mother's Polish ancestry. And in the district the girl was always referred to as the Princess.

Writing a century ago, a Miss A.M. Wakefield, said:

> The proverbial oldest inhabitants remember their fore-elders speaking of her as *the Princess* and that she as a young woman came, somewhere about 1745, with two servants, and resided in extreme privacy as a sort of lodger at this lonely Waterside farm which, however in former days boasted more importance than it possesses at present.[32]

Another account has her arriving in 1746 accompanied by a Mr James Douglass,[33] and she had with her a medal commemorating the marriage of James Stuart and Clementina Sobieska in 1719.

The Finsthwaite Princess lived first of all at the 600-year-old farmstead known as Jolliver Tree or July Flower Tree, which was then occupied by James Backhouse and when he died she went to live with the brother of Backhouse's wife at Waterside, Newby Bridge, close to Finsthwaite. She remained there until her death in 1771.

Unfortunately no reference to Clementina Douglass has been found in family papers apart from her signature as a witness to the will of Edward Taylor, owner of Waterside Farm, which was drawn up on 28 April 1770. On this she signed herself *Clementina Douglas*. Just a year later the Perpetual Curate of Finsthwaite, the Revd George Simpson, buried her in the lee of the little church in the village, where she lay almost forgotten for two centuries – almost, but not quite.

There is a tale told that during the latter part of the nineteenth century when a grave adjacent to that of Clementina Douglass was being opened a lock of golden hair was found in her grave, and this was taken as proof that the Princess might well be Clementine's daughter, for Walkinshaw had fair hair. As no firm source has ever been given and the fair hair link to Clementine is a very tenuous one, the gravedigger's alleged discovery takes us no nearer to the truth of the Finsthwaite Princess.

The Finsthwaite grave remained unmarked until 1913, when Canon Charles Gale Townley, honorary canon of Carlisle Cathedral and a descendant of a noted Lancashire Jacobite family, raised a subscription to erect the stone which now stands over it.[34]

In the absence of hard facts, there has been a lot of speculation, much of it wildly wrong, about the true identity of the Princess. It has been said she was one of three ladies who were with the Prince when he arrived at Kendal on 22 November 1745 on his march south to Derby, that she was a Russian princess, a granddaughter of John Sobieski (Prince Charlie's grandfather), a sister of Charles Edward, the daughter of a Jacobite follower, or even that she was a lunatic boarded out in this secluded spot by some aristocratic family.[35]

If the child belonged to Clementine and Charles, or to some other supporter of the Cause, Finsthwaite was a perfectly logical place to send her for safety because, although it was in the very centre of a nest of highly placed Jacobite supporters, it was remote from tongues that might betray her identity. Sizergh Castle, nearby, was the home of the Strickland family, who had been closely linked to the Stuarts over the Water for generations and one of whom accompanied the Prince to Scotland in 1745; Levens Hall was the family home of

James Graham, who had looked after the affairs of James VII and II's illegitimate daughter, Lady Katherine Darnley, who had mortgages on property in the Newby Bridge and Cartmel areas; and the family of Francis Townley, one of Charles's most trusted officers, had their roots nearby.

Most important of all, the Backhouse and Taylor families, with whom Clementina Douglass lived in Finsthwaite, also had strong Jacobite connections.[36] They were related by marriage to the eminent English Jacobite, Dr William King of Oxford. When she first arrived in Finsthwaite the Princess stayed with the Backhouses and later went to live with Edward Taylor, at Waterside. So Dr King must have known all about these people and probably about the Finsthwaite Princess, if such a person existed, as well.

If Clementina Douglass was the fruit of Clementine Walkinshaw's affair with Charles at Bannockburn House she could not have been born before September or October of 1746. She would certainly have been an embarrassment to the Walkinshaw family in those unsettled times, and Jacobite supporters would have rallied to keep her out of sight of prying Hanoverian eyes. The fact that Clementine had borne an illegitimate child could also explain her family's unkind treatment of her and the fact that she never found a husband.

If Clementine had another lover, perhaps an important Jacobite, before she met Prince Charlie, the child might have been his, and there would be every reason to board her out with friends in this remote Lakeland village. An interesting conjecture is that the child was the daughter of Charles Douglas, fourth and last Lord Mordington, who was one of 127 prisoners found guilty at Carlisle in 1746 of being involved in the '45 rising. He died in 1755 and his daughter might have been settled at Finsthwaite after this for economy,[37] although that would not tie in with the dates traditionally given for the girl's arrival at Finsthwaite, nor would it explain why she was called a princess.

If the theory were true that Clementine Walkinshaw was the mistress of Charles Douglas or some other Jacobite, it would explain why Dr King and the English Jacobites always spoke so virulently against Clementine. We are usually told that Clementine Walkinshaw was distrusted because her sister, Catherine, worked in the household of the wife of Frederick, Prince of Wales, and many supporters of the Cause in Britain believed that Clementine was passing on Stuart secrets to the London government through her sister. Clementine was disliked beyond all reasonable limits to the point of hatred, so that one must ask, did the Jacobites know some dark secret that lurked in her life before she came to live with Charlie in Ghent?

No epithet was too severe – King described her as 'a wench . . . without any elegance of manner' and even 'an harlot, whom he . . . neither loved nor esteemed'.[38]

Lady Primrose, who was so generous to all Jacobites in need during and after the '45, could not say a kind word about Clementine, and Isabella Strange, a fanatically loyal supporter of the Prince, refused even to see Clementine or her daughter, saying, 'Oh, the vile jades. If ye bring them here I'll put the door in their face.' Yet she did meet his adulterous wife, Louise of Stolberg, in 1788.[39]

Such harsh words surely had some foundation, and the unanswered question is – was the Finsthwaite Princess a dark secret known only to the English Jacobites? If that is so, it would be a good reason for leaving the grave unmarked until Canon Townley came along a century and a half later. And they would certainly not have approved of the wording he put on the simple white cross in Finsthwaite churchyard in 1913:

In memoriam

Clementina
Johannes Sobiesky Douglass
of Waterside
Buried 16th day of May 1771

BEHOLD THY KING COMETH

No earthly king came for Clementina Douglass, the Finsthwaite Princess.

NINE

'COLONEL' ANNE AND HER REGIMENT

The people of England and the soldiers, were pre-possessed with a notion that Lady Mackintosh was a woman of monstrous size, had always rode at the head of her regiment, and that she charged with it in the battle of Culloden, fully accoutred and mounted upon a white horse; but this was far from the truth, for she was a very thin girl, never saw the men but once, and was at her own house the time of the action.

Description of 'Colonel' Anne by Alexander M. Mackintosh, author of *The Mackintoshes and Clan Chattan*.[1]

The Duke of Cumberland could not have been more delighted. On 2 February 1746 he wrote at once to the Duke of Newcastle to give him the good news: 'We have taken 20 of their sick here, and the famous Miss Jenny Cameron, whom I propose to send to Edinburgh for the Lord Justice Clerk to examine, as I fancy she may be a useful evidence against them if a little threatened.'[2] The capture of the now notorious Jenny Cameron was a great coup for King George's leaders who were rounding up stragglers and camp followers from Prince Charlie's army at Stirling after it withdrew to the Highlands.

The Prince had frittered away much of January at Bannockburn apart from brief forays to oversee the siege of Stirling Castle and to scatter General Henry Hawley's army at Falkirk on 17 January. Unfortunately the Falkirk victory did little for morale among the Highlanders or Charles's leaders and, instead of following up their success, the Prince was persuaded to agree to retreat into the Highlands to regroup his army.

125

It was after the Highlanders left that Jenny was captured – but unfortunately she turned out to be the wrong Jenny Cameron. In Edinburgh the woman's questioners were left red-faced when they discovered that she was a milliner in Edinburgh who had come to Stirling to see one of her kinsmen who had been wounded. There she was arrested along with a number of other women, and the news was passed to Cumberland without waiting to question her.

What questions the Lord Justice Clerk asked and what answers she gave went unrecorded, but Mrs Cameron was held in Edinburgh Castle until the following November. On her release she discovered that the notoriety her name had brought her was excellent for business and she wisely admitted nothing of her reputed intimacies with the Prince and the Duke of Perth, nor did she deny them. According to a contemporary account, all Edinburgh soon was 'crowding to buy her Ribbands, Gloves Fans, etc.' Milliner Jenny was described as neither young nor handsome, but a woman of wit and good sense.[3]

As late as 1786 Jenny was still boasting of her role as a notorious courtesan: she was a strange figure in Edinburgh, dressed in tartan trews to hide a wooden leg she wore to replace a leg she lost probably as a result of being run over by a cart, and now boasted openly that she had not only been bedded by the Prince while he was in Scotland, but had followed him to France where he dismissed her and she had to beg her way home. Disowned by her family, Jenny fell on hard times and ended her days begging for tobacco and ale in the High Street. She was found dead one morning on a stairfoot in the Canongate.[4]

Prince Charlie knew as little about her as he did about the real Jenny Cameron.

About the only piece of good news the Prince received during his time at Bannockburn was the arrival of six hundred Mackintosh clansmen to join his depleted army shortly before Falkirk, men raised by an ardent female supporter, Lady Anne Mackintosh. Legend confers the rank of 'Colonel' on Anne Mackintosh, and presents her as an Amazon, boldly riding out and raising the clansmen while her husband was out fighting for the Hanoverians, but the truth – as so often in Highland tales – is very different.

The picture of 'Colonel' Anne which has gone into history, comes from Sir Walter Scott's pen, showing a strong-willed woman riding among her troops, dressed in Mackintosh tartan trimmed with lace, a blue bonnet on her head, and carrying a pair of pistols at her saddle. From Allan Ramsay's portrait, painted only a few years later, a graceful young woman with a pretty oval face looks confidently out. She has high cheek-bones, large dark eyes and a firm mouth which betrays determination behind just a trace of a smile.

Lady Anne was a loyal supporter of the Cause, and could hardly have been otherwise since she was born a Farquharson of Invercauld in Aberdeenshire, and the Farquharsons had always supported the King over the Water. In 1741, at the age of eighteen, she married Aeneas Mackintosh of Mackintosh, known as The Mackintosh, who had Jacobite sympathies, but was in the compromising position of having held a commission as commander of one of the three new companies of the Black Watch since December 1744.[5] As a result he did not come out for the Prince when the standard was raised at Glenfinnan, but swithered before eventually deciding to remain with the Black Watch.

A dispute between The Mackintosh and Ewan Macpherson of Cluny over the chieftainship of Clan Chattan, and Prince Charlie's decision to put Cluny in command of Clan Chattan men in his army, has been given as the reason why Mackintosh did not join Prince Charlie.[6] But as a commissioned officer of the Black Watch, Mackintosh would have sworn an oath of loyalty to King George, an oath on which no Highland gentleman could go back.

For whatever reason, Mackintosh did not follow Prince Charlie on his march south to Derby, and as a result was dubbed weak and unfaithful. It is perfectly possible, however, that this was another hedging of Highland bets – if The Mackintosh could not break his word and raise his clan for Charlie, then his wife could.

Lady Anne needed no persuading; as early as 16 October she had sent a letter to the Jacobite Duke of Atholl making her position clear. Andrew Lang describes Anne Mackintosh as the worst speller of her century and her letter to Atholl confirms his opinion:

My Lord Duke. The beraer of this is a Very Pretay Fellow, Brother to Mcenzie of Killooway. He had a Compannay Resed for the Prince's servace, but was handred by Lord Siforth to keray them of, which meks me geve this trobal to beg of your Grace to geve hem en ordar for rasing his men, & thene he can wouse a littel forse. My God praeserf Your Grace, and all that will searve ther Prince and contray, which is the ernast woush of

Your Grace Most Affnett, & obd. Sarvant,
A. McIntosh[7]

Through October and November Anne Mackintosh rode among the Chattan clansmen and by December had raised more than six hundred men who marched south to join the Prince at Stirling, in time to fight in his front line at Falkirk on 17 January.

Charles bowed to the leaders again and marched north into the teeth of the bitterest part of the Highland winter, which made his journey difficult and slow. A month and all but a day later, on Sunday 16 February, he arrived at Moy Hall, near Inverness, home of Lady Anne Mackintosh, the 'belle Rebelle' as she was known to fellow supporters of the Cause.[8] At Moy a real Jacobite welcome awaited the Prince: James Gib, Master of his Household, told how Lady Anne insisted on feeding Charles's entire household of more than seventy men. 'There were always ten covers upon the Prince's own table, and eight covers upon another table in the same room for the aide-de-camps,' he recalled. 'Lady Macintosh's supper was exceedingly genteel and plentiful.'[9]

After supper the Prince retired to bed, weary after the long day's ride through snow, but there was little rest for him or his men. Lord Loudoun, who held Inverness for the Hanoverians, and Sir Alexander MacLeod, had heard of the Jacobites' arrival at Moy and, tempted by the £30,000 reward and glory Prince Charlie's capture would bring, decided to take Moy by surprise. They sealed off the town to ensure secrecy, increased the garrison at the castle, then slipped quietly out with Loudoun's own regiment and as many other men as they could muster.

The Dowager Lady Mackintosh, mother of The Mackintosh, who lived in Inverness and learned of the plan, sent young Lauchlan Mackintosh, a boy just into his teens, to try to overtake Loudoun's men and warn the Prince. The boy followed stealthily behind the Hanoverians until they reached a point where the road divided and, while Loudoun was making up his mind which route to follow, Lauchlan managed to slip past unseen and raced to Moy Hall to raise the alarm.

Prince Charlie was awakened and when James Gib came out of the house into the bitterly cold night, 'he saw the Prince walking with his bonnet above his nightcap, and his shoes down in the heels; and Lady Macintosh in her smock petticoat running through the close [courtyard], speaking loudly and expressing her anxiety about the Prince's safety.'[10]

O'Sullivan watched her. 'No woman in the world cou'd be in the condition yt poor Lady Mccintosh was in, running about like a mad woman in her shift' he said. 'Every man she saw she took him for the enemy.'[11]

'Colonel' Anne may have panicked, but she quickly gathered her wits together and arranged for thirty of her clansmen to lead the Prince a mile along the shore of Loch Moy and conceal him in a wood while she herself hid the Prince's valuables in another wood close to the house and in her attic.

Earlier in the evening she had taken the precaution of sending the Moy blacksmith, Donald Fraser, 'a Cliver bould fellow'[12] and four men to keep guard on the Inverness road. Fraser posted his men on either side of the road among peak stacks and when the advance guard of Loudoun's army approached under MacLeod the five Moy men shouted the war cries of various clans and fired their muskets. In the darkness the enemy mistook the piles of peats for Jacobite soldiers and, thinking the whole of the Prince's army was about to charge them, they turned and fled back to Inverness.

The Rout of Moy was a victory in which there was only one casualty, MacLeod's piper, Macrimmon, reputed to be the best piper in the whole of Scotland, who fell at his leader's side. It was said that before leaving Skye, Macrimmon with the second sight, composed the famous lament, *Cha till mi tuille* – I'll return no more.

When the rout was over Lady Anne 'who was not well recover'd of her fright . . . wept bitterly when she saw the Prince'.[13] Charles showed no ill effects of the escapade at the time, but later contracted 'such a cold as stuck to him very long'.[14] It was soon to have repercussions.

The Rout of Moy reverberated through the Hanoverian ranks and many deserted immediately afterwards. Loudoun tried to put the best face on it that he could, but he could do nothing to stop MacLeod being 'very much laughed at when he came back [to Inverness].'[15]

As a result of the 'battle' at Moy the Highlanders were able to march on Inverness and Lord Loudoun took fright and fled with his army across the Beauly Firth by the Kessock ferry to the Black Isle of Ross-shire. With the town in Jacobite hands the castle at Inverness soon surrendered and the Highland capital was the Prince's.

Scottish weather proved treacherous for Charles, once again he caught a terrible chill, which O'Sullivan called a fever, but it was something much nearer to pneumonia. He managed to travel to Lord President Forbes's house at Culloden and then to Inverness on Tuesday 18 February, where he slowly recovered at the home of Lady Anne's mother-in-law in Church Street. Lady Mackintosh, whose vigilance had saved him that night at Moy Hall, now nursed the Prince back to health and from then until 14 April he stayed there or at Thunderton House in Elgin.

He enjoyed life in the Highland capital and, according to Elcho, 'very often went shooting, and sometimes gave bals at night, where he danced himself, and Endeavour's to keep up the peoples Spirits that approach'd him'.[16] So much for his being withdrawn in women's company all the time he was in Scotland during the '45.

The Prince's attention was well rewarded: the Mackintosh household accounts for this period include two sizeable purchases of 'white Riban' for Lady Mackintosh and her womenfolk to make white cockade emblems for the Jacobite supporters to wear.[17]

The Highlanders were in great spirits and seized Fort Augustus, laid siege to Fort William, then made a daring raid into Atholl, which came within a whisker of re-taking Blair Castle for the Prince. They now set out to take care of Lord Loudoun in the far northern counties, and a cat-and-mouse chase began, which ended with

Loudoun finally cornered by the Duke of Perth and defeated at Embo, near Dornoch. Loudoun escaped, but the Mackintosh chief was among those captured. Prince Charlie, who was staying with the chief's mother at Inverness at the time, released him into the hands of his wife, 'Colonel' Anne, saying that he could not be more secure nor more honourably treated.

When husband and wife met Lady Anne said:

'Your servant, Captain.'

'Your servant, Colonel,' The Mackintosh replied.

Loudoun fled to Skye – the first to escape over the sea to Skye – while his officers and men who managed to get away sought refuge in Sutherland, where the Earl of Sutherland was loyal to Hanover. The earl fled but his wife remained behind at Dunrobin Castle and welcomed the Jacobite army warmly – clearly the Mackintoshes were not the only family in which a husband and wife had opposing views and were not afraid to show them. But it was always the husband who was for Hanover and the wife who wore the white cockade of the Stuarts.

So March ended on a high note for Prince Charlie, his health was improved and his armies had been highly successful – but then April brought a series of misfortunes, culminating in disaster on the battlefield of Culloden. First the Prince took ill again, this time at Elgin, with what has been suggested was scarlet fever.[18] O'Sullivan called it 'a spotted favor'[19] and the Prince was starved and bled. Although very seriously ill for several days he 'got up the ninth or tenth day, against the Doctors advise', but he was still very sick.

Worse still, food and money were short and morale was low among the clansmen in spite of every effort Charles made personally to raise it. The Prince was on bad terms with Lord George Murray as usual, and the army no longer had the air of a force on the way to victory. Matters were not helped by the loss of the ship the *Prince Charles* which arrived at this moment with money and men from France.

The Duke of Cumberland was closing in and by 14 April he had crossed the Spey and was past Nairn. The same day the Prince again set up his headquarters at Culloden House: on the following day he made up his mind to fight – against the advice of his commanders –

and chose Drumossie Moor for his battlefield – also contrary to the view of his leaders. As this was Cumberland's birthday and he believed the duke's men would be celebrating and off guard, the Prince decided to make a surprise night attack on the Hanoverian army, but the affair was botched, so it was a weary, dispirited, hungry, demoralized Highland army that met the enemy on Charlie's chosen field on 16 April.

From the first Cumberland's cannon devastated the Highland ranks, but the clansmen's commanders would not let their men charge until the enemy came closer. When at last the Highlanders could be held in check no longer, the order to charge was given and the clansmen rushed straight into devastating musket fire and bayonets. Culloden was lost and Prince Charles was forced to flee, leaving the remnants of his devastated army to find their own salvation. Some made for the hills, some for home and others for Inverness, but none expected the vengeance that was to be brought down on them and their families.

For two days following the battle the wounded were left lying alongside the dead on the field, in outhouses, or any shelter to which they were able to crawl. Then began the systematic murder by shooting, bayoneting or by setting fire to the huts in which they lay. There was no question of treating the wounded mercifully: the victors asked no questions and as a result a great many innocent men and women were murdered simply because they happened to be there.

According to James Ray, who produced a scurrilous history of the rebellion, many important ladies were in Inverness preparing to celebrate the Prince's victory when news of the defeat reached the town. Lady Gordon, Lady Ogilvy, Lady Kinloch and old Lady Mackintosh were among them and 'Colonel' Anne might have been there too, although she was more likely at home at Moy Hall. The ladies were 'preparing to dress for a ball in the evening, after the rebels had gained the victory; but the King's Red-Coats were so rude as to interrupt them, and lead them to a dance they did not expect,' Ray wrote.[20]

Whether this is an untruth (like most of the rest of Ray's

'history') or not, Lady Ogilvy was certainly taken prisoner and ended up in Edinburgh Castle from where she escaped the following November dressed as a servant girl. After a number of adventures, one of which involved her in being mistaken for the Prince when she was in male disguise, she managed to reach Europe safely.[21]

Poor old Lady Mackintosh was held prisoner in Inverness while Cumberland slept in her house in the bed the Prince had occupied only days before. 'Colonel' Anne was apprehended at Moy and had her money taken from her, then was forced to ride back to Inverness, where she counted fourteen murdered men, women and children on the way. If Hawley had had his way she would have met the same fate: he said he would gladly 'honour' her with a mahogany gallows and silk cords. But Lady Anne was well treated in Inverness, perhaps because her husband had been a Hanoverian, and she was able to give surreptitious help to a number of prisoners in the town.

The men captured in or around Inverness fared worse than 'Colonel' Anne, for when the gaols were overflowing, the churches and ships moored nearby were all filled and no one was allowed to take food or drink to any prisoner for two days. John Farquharson of Aldlerg took down the story of one of them. 'What a scene open to my eyes and nose all at once,' he recorded. 'The wounded feltring in their gore and blood; some dead bodies covered quite over with pish and dirt, the living standing to the middle in it, their groans woud have pirsd a heart of stone.'[22] When the Provost and ex-Provost of the town protested to Hawley they were literally kicked out of the door and down the stairs on to the street.

To offer sympathy to Prince Charlie or his soldiers in Inverness was to risk one's life, but that did not stop women like Anne McKay, a young Skye woman, from performing brave acts of humanity. Anne lived above a cellar in which two wounded prisoners, Robert Nairn and Ranald MacDonald of Belfinlay, one of the Clanranald MacDonalds, were held, and she smuggled supplies to the men all through the summer of 1746 and the winter of 1746–7. In March 1747 a group of ladies in the town hatched a plot to help Nairn to escape, but unfortunately Belfinlay was still too badly injured to join him. Anne was brought before the officer in charge, but refused to give information even when she was offered ten guineas reward. She was ordered to be kept standing upright for three days and three nights, bribed with food from time to time to persuade her to confess, but still she did not break. If Anne's punishment seems harsh, think what the Hanoverians did to their own side – the soldier on guard duty the night Nairn escaped, received five hundred lashes.[23]

Cumberland's cruelty spread through the whole of the country. 'In several parts of the Highlands in Scotland the soldiery spared neither man, woman, nor child, particularly those under the command of Major Lockheart, Caroline Scott, etc.' it was written. 'The hoary head, the tender mother and the weeping infant, behoved to share in the general wreck, and to fall victim to rage and cruelty by the musquet, the bloody bayonet, the devouring flame, or famishing hunger and cold. In a word, the troops sported with cruelty.'[24]

In time the cruelty abated and the troops turned their attention to the prize of prizes that Cumberland sought, Charles Edward Stuart himself. Although the suffering continued for the Highlanders, and the clanswomen bore their share of it, their loyalty to their Prince remained as firm as ever. In defeat Charles Edward Stuart continued to be their Bonnie Prince, and there were many who were still prepared to risk their lives to help him to escape.

TEN

THE ROMANCE THAT
NEVER WAS

> *Though the waves leap, soft shall ye sleep,*
>   *Ocean's a royal bed,*
> *Rocked in the deep Flora will keep*
>   *Watch by your weary head.*

> *Speed bonnie boat, like a bird on the wing,*
>   *'Onward', the sailors cry:*
> *Carry the lad that's born to be king*
>   *Over the sea to Skye.*

The Skye Boat Song has immortalized the escape of Bonnie Prince
Charlie dressed as Flora MacDonald's maid, and turned it into
popular mythology.[1]

Wherever he went Prince Charlie always gathered a band of
admiring women around him; in victory they were there to
cheer, in defeat they grieved for him. But soon after the battle of
Culloden their solicitude took on a very practical dimension and in
this they were as closely attuned to his needs as were the clan
leaders.

The Prince was in a pitiful, confused state as he rode from the
battlefield at Culloden, having had no sleep for days, little to eat and
was dressed in clothes which were dirty and tattered. When he
reached Borrodale in Arisaig, the wife of MacDonald of Borrodale
produced a new Highland rigout for him to wear, and thanks to that
at least he began to look like a Prince again.

Unaware of the brutality and chaos he had left behind, Charles hoped to rally his broken army at Fort Augustus, but there he found no men to rally. As he pushed on south and west towards the coast, a bitter, uncompromising letter of resignation from Lord George Murray, written the day after the battle, confirmed that there would be no regrouping, no continuing the fight. The campaign was over and he was a fugitive with a price of £30,000 on his head. His only hope was to escape to the western islands and try to make his way back to France, where King Louis might be persuaded to help him to mount another campaign. His supporters persuaded a Skye boatman, Donald MacLeod of Galtergill, to take him back to the Outer Hebrides, where the adventure had begun eleven months before, so by the morning of 28 April, he was in the safest place in which his friends could hide him while they sought out a boat to take him back to France or round the north of Scotland to Norway, from where he could make his way back to Paris.

Fortunately Cumberland lost the scent after Culloden, and it was the middle of May before the enemy knew with any certainty that Charles Edward was on the outer isles. That gave him some respite, but from then on the chase gathered momentum, with the Army, Navy and militia companies of clansmen, which had been raised by a few clan chiefs, relentlessly scouring the islands and seas around them for him. These regular servicemen and militiamen all came under the command of Major-General John Campbell of Mamore (later to become fifth Duke of Argyll), but they included the cruel and notoriously anti-Jacobite, Captain Caroline Scott of the Army and Captain John Ferguson of the Royal Navy ship, HMS *Furnace*. Either would have been delighted to collect that £30,000 reward.

For six weeks HMS *Furnace* and other Navy ships patrolled the seas around the Hebrides and Army search parties prowled on land: they knew the Prince was somewhere on the Outer Hebrides and in time they would find out where, for King George's forces were remarkably well informed – torture, burning, threatening and killing had proved marvellous persuaders. Yet, for all their intelligence skill, the fugitive always remained out of their reach.

Prince Charlie's guardians were so successful in helping him to evade his enemies that he managed to enjoy three much-needed weeks' of respite, hidden away at a remote place called Corodale in South Uist during June. In this glen, cut off from the main part of the island and almost invisible from the sea, he spent idyllic days shooting, hunting, drinking and conversing with the clan chiefs. Clanranald organized the Corodale interlude, but almost every clan member of importance visited him, so his whereabouts was well known to the clansmen if not to the Hanoverians. Charles was well fed and well looked after, for Clanranald's wife, 'Lady Clan', sent him shirts, a silver cup and other presents, while Lady Boisdale had food and clothing delivered to him secretly.

Even Lady Margaret MacDonald, the wife of Sir Alexander MacDonald, Chief of Sleat in Skye, who had remained loyal to King George, sent Prince Charlie newspapers, clothes and a present of fifty guineas. While she was secretly helping the fugitive, her husband was with the Duke of Cumberland at Fort Augustus and his clansmen were searching the islands with the militia companies which the Sleat Chief had raised.

Thanks to the generosity of all these Highland women the Prince now looked like a well-dressed Highland chief, clad in a fine quality, if rather stained, kilt with tartan coat, plaid and brogues. In spite of the rest at Corodale his health had deteriorated badly by now, because of the endless physical and mental strain he had undergone during the months since Derby.

Inexorably the net closed in as a great final sweep of the islands of North Uist, Benbecula and South Uist, was begun. The plan was for one group of soldiers to start at the north of North Uist while a second combed the islands northwards from the southern tip of South Uist. By the time they met, not an inch of these islands, where they knew the Prince was hiding, would have been missed, and there was no way Prince Charlie could have escaped the net.

The chiefs realized that it was imperative that Charlie should leave at once: the Corodale interlude was over, so a plan was devised to get the Prince off the island, a scheme almost certainly masterminded by Hugh MacDonald of Armadale, who was captain of the militia company conveniently stationed at the northern end of South Uist, at the ford, the only easy crossing to Benbecula, the island on which the Clanranald chief's house was situated. Hugh was a secret supporter of the King over the Water and had been the first person to kiss the Prince's hand when he landed on the Scottish mainland in 1745. It was said that Hugh met the Prince by chance then[2] – perhaps so, but it was very probably the same 'chance' as brought other clan chiefs to Moidart at that moment.

For a Jacobite who wore the uniform of a Hanoverian militia officer, the South Uist–Benbecula ford was a most convenient place to be in late June 1746.

Hugh MacDonald, known as 'One-eyed Hugh', reportedly because he had lost an eye in a boyhood accident or while fighting for the King of France (no one was quite sure which, if either, story was true), had another great advantage – he had a step-daughter who was able to travel between Uist and Skye without arousing suspicion.

Flora MacDonald was unaware of it, but she had been chosen to spirit Bonnie Prince Charlie over the sea to Skye and safety. Even if she had known of the plot she could never have dreamed that it was to create a legend and make her one of Scotland's greatest heroines – and even more surprising, that it would link her name romantically to Prince Charlie in the minds of most of the world for ever after. Whatever history says, however often it is proved that she and the Prince were never in love, the popular myth remains that the meeting of Flora MacDonald and Prince Charlie was one of the most romantic moments in the lives of both of them. It was not: they met at an isolated, run-down hut and their conversation was utterly mundane. There was deep affection but no love between them, yet the risk Flora MacDonald ran to help the Prince amounted to an act of great devotion.

Of the Prince, all that can be said of their association is that he showed Flora more respect than he did to almost any other woman he ever met – and he expressed his thanks to her, which was more than he did to anyone in his adult life.

As for Flora, to her dying day she never told what she thought of Prince Charlie, nor did she reveal her feelings towards him. We can only divine what these were from the way her story unfolded.

Although she was living in Skye in 1746, South Uist was home to Flora: her mother, Marion, had been married to Ranald MacDonald of Milton in South Uist – quite close to Charlie's Corodale hideout, but on the other side of the island – and Flora was born there in 1722. When Flora was only a year old, her father died, leaving Marion with two young sons and Flora to bring up by herself. One of her sons died accidentally, and in time Marion married again. Her new husband, a Skye kinsman 'One-eyed Hugh', helped her to raise her surviving son, Angus, and daughter, Flora, until 1745, when Angus married and Hugh handed over Milton to him and moved back to Skye with his wife. Flora settled with them at Armadale in the south of the island.

In 1746, when the Hebridean peace was broken by soldiers and sailors hunting for Charles Edward Stuart, Flora happened to be back on South Uist visiting her brother, and on the night of 20 June she was helping him out by tending his cattle at the summer pastures. This meant staying overnight at his remote shieling, or summer hut, at Alisary on Sheaval hill.

It seems odd that Angus should allow his sister to stay alone overnight at a lonely hut in the mountains when the island was full of soldiers, but the fact remains that Flora was there all by herself that night – in the right place at the right time. Perhaps Angus was in on the plan too.

The more probable of the two versions told of what took place at Alisary[3] relates that Flora was awakened by her fellow islander and kinsman, Neil MacEachain, who brought the Prince and Captain Felix O'Neil to her. She said she was surprised, yet admitted much later that she had previously met O'Neil at the Clanranald chief's house at Nunton when he asked what she would give for a sight of the Prince. She said she answered 'that as she had not that Happyness before, she did not look for it now, but that a sight of him would make her happy, tho' he was on a hill and she was on another'.[4]

Flora was a quiet, sensible girl, not given to gossip. She was very circumspect ever after when she talked of her encounter with Prince Charlie: at first she wanted to protect those who were most closely involved, but even later when secrecy did not matter, she still did not boast about her meeting with Prince Charlie.

The Prince himself explained the escape plan to Flora, and the other two tried hard to persuade her to help: O'Neil even offered to marry her if she feared for her good character, but she was able to resist that. It was Charles himself who won her over by assuring her of the 'sense he would always retain of so conspicuous a service'.[5]

While Prince Charlie, O'Neil and MacEachain hid in the mountains, Flora set out for Nunton to make arrangements for the journey, proving that Clanranald and Lady Clan were deeply involved in the plot too – like all Highland secrets, this one was already known to many. As she crossed from South Uist to Benbecula she was arrested by the militiamen on guard at the ford, but of course it turned out that her stepfather was captain of the company at that very place – another remarkable coincidence.

She stayed overnight with her stepfather and while they were having breakfast together the following morning the militiamen brought in another prisoner – none other than Neil MacEachain who, she thought, was safely in hiding with the Prince. Later she learned that Prince Charlie, with his usual impatience, had sent Neil to find out what was delaying Flora, and Neil was stranded at the ford because the tide was high. As a result he was taken by the militiamen.

Neil appeared to be as surprised as Flora to see her and to discover that his captor was 'One-eyed Hugh' whom he knew well. Flora whispered to Neil that she would soon be on her way to Nunton and told him to take the Prince to Rossinish at the south-eastern corner of Benbecula, where she would rendezvous with them.

The first plan had been to hide the Prince on a small island off the north coast of Skye, but that was abandoned as too dangerous, so it was decided to take him to the Chief of Sleat's house at Monkstadt on Skye, disguised as Flora MacDonald's Irish maid Betty Burke, and from there to smuggle him back to the mainland.

At Clanranald's house, Flora and Lady Clan sewed furiously to make Charles's disguise, a quilted petticoat and a gown of calico printed with sprigs of flowers, a white apron and a dun-coloured cloak with a hood which would hide his face. Stockings, buckled French garters of blue velvet and shoes completed the disguise.

By Friday 27 June, when all was ready, Flora set out with Lady Clanranald and Lady Clan's young daughter, Margaret, to sail round the island to meet the Prince at Rossinish. With MacEachain, O'Neil and Flora's brother, Angus, all sat down to enjoy the first real meal Charles had eaten for several days. He was in great spirits and turned the alfresco picnic into a banquet at which he made Flora sit formally on his right and Lady Clan on his left. All the miseries of the past days were forgotten as they laughed and talked while they ate heart, liver and kidneys, all roasted on a spit.

As the Prince drifted easily into that relaxed feeling of utter security which he had known at Corodale, a messenger arrived with news that General Campbell had landed close to Nunton with 1,500 men to search the island. In panic everybody rushed to their boats, grabbing whatever they could carry from the picnic, and crossed Loch Uiskevagh to relative safety. About five in the morning the picnic was resumed, but no one had much appetite for the, by now, cold food or conversation.

Lady Clan rushed home to explain her absence to Campbell and Captain Ferguson: she said she had been visiting a clanswoman's sick daughter, an explanation which may have been accepted by the general, but it did not take the suspicious Ferguson in.

On the other side of the island in the meantime frantic finishing touches were being put to the plan to get the Prince away from the Outer Hebrides. Flora was handed a letter from her stepfather to her mother, saying:

My dear Marion:
I have sent your daughter from this country lest she should be in any way frightened with the troops lying here. She has got one Bettie Burke, an Irish girl, who, she tells me, is a good spinster. If her spinning please you, you may keep her till she spin all your lint; or if you have any wool to spin, you may employ her. I have sent Neil MacEachan along with your daughter and Bettie Burk to take care of them. I am, Your dutyful husband.
Hugh MacDonald[6]

That night, Saturday 28 June, Flora dressed Prince Charlie in his costume as Betty Burke, not without difficulty for he insisted on wearing his own breeches and waistcoat underneath, and wanted to take his pistols hidden under his skirt. Flora drew the line at that and insisted that they be left behind. If they should be searched the pistols would give them away, she told him.

The Prince meekly handed over the pistols and made a joke of it. 'Indeed, Miss,' he answered, 'if we shall happen to meet with any that will go so narrowly to work in searching as what you mean, they will certainly discover me at any rate.'[7] Considering how dangerous it was to give Charles Edward Stuart orders on anything, that was a brave thing for Flora to do, but he accepted her decision meekly. This was one of the few moments in his entire life when Prince Charlie ceased to be a prince by divine right who took orders from no one. And Flora MacDonald clearly was a woman with authority.

As a gesture she allowed him to keep his 'crab stick', a cudgel which was his comforter and protector wherever he went.

Charles must have been at a low ebb for he caved in again when Flora told him the passport only permitted Neil MacEachain to accompany them, so he would have to leave his friend Felix O'Neil behind. After making only a token protest he accepted her decision and at eight o'clock that Saturday night the three – Prince Charlie, Flora and MacEachain – set out in a boat rowed by a scratch crew which included three militiamen from the companies supposed to be out hunting the Prince on the island.

Prince Charlie was on his way over the sea to Skye and safety from immediate capture.

After rowing until they were well clear of the island the men raised the sail and the small boat sety sail for Skye through the short Hebridean summer night. As a strong north-west wind blew up, the voyage became most uncomfortable and the passengers huddled in the bottom of the boat for shelter. Flora eventually dozed off into sleep with the Prince guarding her carefully 'lest in the darkness any of the men should chance to step upon her'.[8] Charles was in good spirits and shared some milk with the crew, but saved a half-bottle of wine for Flora. He sang Jacobite songs as they approached Skye in a thick mist, which suddenly cleared to reveal a couple of militiamen on the shore. The boatmen rowed like fury and hid the boat in a cleft in the sheer black cliffs of the north-west corner of the island to rest and ensure that they were not being followed. They then rowed the last few miles across the mouth of Loch Snizort to a small beach just above Uig, close to Monkstadt, the home of MacDonald of Sleat.

It was now Sunday afternoon and the whole island was either at church or quietly passing the Sabbath day at home. 'One-eyed Hugh' had planned the escape wisely and chose a Sunday deliberately for the Prince's arrival in Skye because he knew the coast would be at its least well guarded and there would be few people on the roads.

MacEachain and Flora left the Prince in the care of the boatmen while they hurried to Monkstadt to tell Lady Margaret MacDonald the fugitive had arrived. There can be little doubt that she was expecting him, for Mrs Margaret MacDonald of Kirkibost had arrived from North Uist only the day before and her husband would very likely have been in on the plot too. When Kirkibost's wife landed she was searched with embarrassing thoroughness, as if the militia were checking that she was not a man in disguise. A possible explanation for that is that the militia on Skye also knew of the Prince's imminent arrival in disguise, and wanted to be able to say with hand on heart that they had been looking carefully for the Prince – if the authorities did not believe them, let them ask Mrs MacDonald of Kirkibost. When the Prince landed at the same place the following day no one stopped him.

Whatever the truth, Kirkibost's wife was at that moment dining with Lady Margaret, but unfortunately a young lieutenant of the militia was also there. Flora was introduced to the officer and while she talked calmly to him Lady Margaret excused herself, saying she had some urgent business to discuss with her factor or land agent, Alexander MacDonald of Kingsburgh. The chief's wife was in a state of panic, but fortunately was able to summon a clansman, Donald Roy MacDonald, to Monkstadt as well. Donald knew every inch of the island and every place to hide.

It was decided to take the Prince to Kingsburgh's house for the night and, without arousing the militia lieutenant's suspicions, Flora excused herself and joined Kingsburgh and Neil MacEachain to walk to the factor's house. The relative safety of Skye restored Charles Edward to his arrogant princely self and, when Neil joined him, he ordered the poor man to go back and fetch his case of knives which he had left behind on the boat. When Neil protested that it would be dangerous to do so, the Prince gave every sign of flying into one of his passions, so Neil obeyed.[9] On the way to Kingsburgh's house they met a number of people on their way to church, but Charles continued to take long mannish strides in spite of his female disguise, so that Kingsburgh was compelled to leave the road and lead him across fields to avoid the eyes of the curious islanders.

After a night at Kingsburgh's house the Prince was taken to Portree, where he was to meet a new set of guardians who would eventually help him to make his way to the mainland. Flora left the Prince at Portree in the early hours of Tuesday 1 July, and never saw or heard from him again. As they said their farewells Charles told Flora, 'I believe, Madam, I owe you a crown of borrowed money.' She told him it was only half a crown, which he repaid, then kissed her hand and said, 'For all that has happened I hope, Madam, we shall meet in St James's yet.'[10]

Charles had met Flora eleven days before and for three of these he had been in her constant care. He loved and trusted the MacDonalds and Flora was a MacDonald. She was no doubt in his mind when he sent a brief note to thank them for their care – something unusual for Prince Charlie who took so much for granted. It was delivered to Donald Roy:

Sir, – I have parted (I thank God) as intended. Make my compliments to all those to whom I have given trouble. – I am, Sir, your humble servant.
James Thomson[11]

Donald Roy hurried to Armadale in the far south of Skye to show the letter to Flora and afterwards it was burned in case it fell into enemy hands. That was the only thanks Flora received from the Prince, but she expected no more: she did not rescue Bonnie Prince

Charlie for thanks or glory, but as a matter of Highland honour, the same principle as motivated so many of her clansmen.

As for her relationship with Prince Charlie, love did not enter into it, but respect did – deep respect for this man who was heir to the royal house of Scotland. That and a natural Highland response to assist anyone in trouble was enough. When she met Frederick, the Hanoverian Prince of Wales, in London later, he asked her why she had dared to help his father's enemies. Flora answered 'that she would have done the same thing for him had she found him in distress'.[12]

There was no love in a sexual sense on the Prince's side either. Yet he showed Flora enormous respect in many ways and was generous and protective towards her, at times almost as if he was the one who was the protector. He also seems to have been a little in awe of her to judge from the way in which he obeyed her order to leave his pistols behind and accepted her decision to abandon Felix O'Neil, although that must have been a terrible blow to him.

It is in the small things that his feelings towards Flora MacDonald are best revealed. Even 'our lady', the name by which he called her, shows how highly he regarded her, and on the voyage to Skye he shielded her from the sailors as they moved about the boat in a storm, and he kept his last precious half-bottle of wine for her. Then at Portree, where the rain came down in torrents and soaked all of them to the skin, Donald Roy commiserated with him, but Charles only replied, 'I am more sorry that our Lady should be abused with the rain.'[13] Later he handed a piece of sugar to Donald Roy before he left, saying prophetically, 'Pray, MacDonald, take this piece of sugar to our Lady, for I am afraid she will get no sugar where she is going.'[14]

Prince Charlie's last thought that night at Portree was for Flora. Before he parted from Donald Roy he said. 'Tell nobody, no, not our Lady, which way I am gone, for it is right that my course should not be known.'[15] It was not that Charles did not trust Flora: he was simply determined that she should be able to answer, when questioned, that she had no idea where he had gone.

And so Flora MacDonald disappeared from Prince Charlie's life, but not from his story.

Flora was arrested on Saturday 12 July, less than two weeks after her final farewell at Portree, and a year's imprisonment lay ahead of her, but even as she was taken aboard HMS *Furnace* off Armadale for her first questioning by Captain Ferguson, she was already a legend in her own right, not just a fragment of Prince Charlie's heroic story. She was already a heroine.

Not that the Hanoverians showed her much respect. For all their eavesdropping and skill at retailing gossip as fact, the Whig satirists missed the Prince's liaison with Clementine Walkinshaw at Bannockburn House completely, the only sexual relationship in which he was involved during the entire course of the '45. They made much of Jenny Cameron, whom he scarcely knew, and now Flora MacDonald was added to their armoury of propaganda.

A mezzotint was circulated, showing the Prince flanked by Jenny and Flora, with the caption from John Gay's *Beggar's Opera*:

How happy could I be with Either
Were t'other dear Charmer away.

Even today the world finds it hard to believe that Flora MacDonald was not one of Prince Charlie's great conquests.

ELEVEN

DEAREST COUSINS

*I am as sick as a dog, dear heart. I have not been able to sleep this
morning, but that doesn't matter. Tonight at midnight I shall be cured of
all my ills . . . Yes, dear love, I am never happy but when I am in your
arms.*

Letter from Louise, Duchesse de Montbazon to her cousin, Charles
Edward, when their affair was at its height.[1]

For two months after Flora was arrested the hunt continued for
the Prince as he was passed from clan to clan and hideout to
hideout until eventually the French ships *l'Heureux* and *Prince de
Conti* made contact with him and he sailed for France on 20
September. As he left, those Scotswomen who had given their
support so freely were mostly in gaol, uncertain what their fate
would be.

After being questioned by Captain Ferguson and General
Campbell, Flora MacDonald, who had no love for ships, was taken to
Leith in HMS *Eltham*, while the authorities deliberated what should
be done with her. On the very day that the Prince sailed for France
she was transferred to HMS *Bridgewater* to spend another comfortless
month on board ship agonizing over what might happen to her.

Compared with others Flora was lucky: she was close to the
Jacobites' best friend, Lady Bruce and, although not allowed ashore,
was permitted visits from all the fawning young Jacobite ladies of
Edinburgh who flocked aboard to ask about the Prince's escape.
When one of them, Lady Mary Cochrane, was stranded on board the
Bridgewater one day when a storm blew up, she whispered in Flora's
ear that she would remain on the ship all night with pleasure if she

might have the honour of sharing a bed with 'that person who had been so happy as to be guardian to the Prince'.[2] Flora agreed to the suggestion.

Old Lady Mackintosh, 'Colonel' Anne and Lady Gordon of Park, who were arrested in Inverness, had already been freed, but Lady Ogilvy was now locked up in Edinburgh Castle where MacDonald of Kingsburgh was also held prisoner. In November Lady Ogilvy escaped dressed as a servant maid and after an unsuccessful attempt to sail to Holland she travelled to London and escaped to France.

Flora MacDonald was taken by sea to London towards the end of November, but the authorities still had not made up their minds about what should be done with her. Captain Knowler of HMS *Bridgewater*, on which she was still being held, was worried in case he might have to put her aboard one of the notorious disease-infested prison ships where Jacobites were being held in the most appalling conditions.

Flora escaped the prison ships thanks to the trust she built up with Knowler, who sent a letter to his superior officer asking for her to be taken to London rather than to the *Royal Sovereign*, which he said with superb understatement, 'would not be very agreable to her'.[3]

She was sent to the house of one of the government messengers-at-arms, along with a fortunate few people of quality, who were considered less likely to try to escape. These messengers-at-arms, who acted as couriers between Whitehall and government officials in Scotland and elsewhere, had trusty prisoners billeted in their houses and were allowed to charge their 'guests' for their keep. Some made a very good thing out of it, but when all was said and done, a messenger's house was better then Newgate, Southwark or the Tower of London.

With Flora in various messengers' houses were a number of other women, including Lady Clanranald, Lady Mackinnon, Lady Frances Steuart of Goodtrees, Lady Stewart of Burray, and Mrs Katherine McDougall. None of them were ever brought to trial, although they were threatened with it, but all were held until the summer of 1747.

Lady Cromartie, Lady Traquair and Mrs Patrick Wallace were allowed to stay in the Tower of London with their husbands.[4]

The regimental women, wives, lovers and camp followers, met with less gentle treatment, and their plight was greater because many of them had young children with them. Those who were taken at Carlisle were sent to various prisons and some were transported to the colonies. At Chester there were 20 regimental women and 11 children prisoners ranging in age from infants to fifteen years old: Lancaster held 19 women and 4 children and York had 8 women.[5]

In his *Collected Papers on the Jacobite Risings*, Rupert C. Jarvis has woven a rich fabric of a story of three of these prisoners from threads partly discovered half a century earlier by Sir Brian Seton and partly by himself in the Cumberland county records. Ann Layread from Inverness, Margaret Straughton from Aberdeen and Jane Mathewson, whose home has never been discovered, were all shut away in Whitehaven house of correction and, while the master of the house was away, they 'made their escape by undermining the Foundation of the House of Correction'. They vanished and nothing more was recorded of what happened to them. Jarvis speculates on how they managed to walk or stow away in a ship and get clean away. And did they ever reach their homes so far away in Scotland, he asks?[6]

Detail is always tantalizingly meagre in the official reports on these unfortunate women who gave so much for Prince Charlie and their menfolk. Jarvis cites a Cumberland Quarter Sessions Register report of the period, which records simply:

To victualling the woman & three Children for
    thre weeks that belong'd to the Dragoons   9s. 0d.

to a gill of wine for the Child that dyed   6d.

A coffin to the child that dyed   4s. 0d.[7]

It is known that at least twenty-eight women were transported, possibly not sentenced for their own direct actions, but because they chose to follow their loved ones into the virtual slavery that transportation to the colonies meant in those days. The transport, *Veteran*, carried twenty women and several children when it sailed for Antigua in 1747, but they were lucky enough to be captured by a French Privateer and released.[8]

Alongside those women who suffered cold, hunger, brutality and fear at the hands of 'Butcher' Cumberland's men and through the process of King George's merciless legal system in ghastly prisons, one should not forget Jenny Cameron who suffered and went on suffering from the cruel pens of the Whig propaganda merchants. In August 1746, while Charlie was still hiding in the Highland heather, a scurrilous *Brief Account of the Life and Family of Miss Jenny Cameron* was published, and this cruel pillorying of the woman who did nothing more than raise a few clansmen continued long after the rising had become history. *Tom Jones* was not published until 1749, three years after Jenny Cameron had ceased to be a weapon against the Jacobites, yet Fielding felt it worthwhile to weave her into his tale of the period of the '45.

When another Jacobite threat, the Elibank Plot, failed in the early 1750s and Dr Archibald Cameron, brother of Lochiel, was executed in 1753 – the last man to die for taking part in the '45 rising – a *Life of Jenny Cameron* was appended to a pamphlet about him.

These word portraits of Jenny were as vicious caricatures of the poor woman as were those that the cartoonists drew, usually highlighting her military and Amazonian qualities. The *Life of Jenny Cameron* published at the time of Cameron's execution has her present at the battles of Prestonpans, Falkirk and Culloden, where she was seen at the head of her soldiers 'leading them on through fire and smoak to the very muzzles of the enemies' guns, never flinching from any danger, but, like another Amazon, with the most undaunted bravery inspiring her men with courage by her own example.'[9] Appropriately, it also contained a protrait of Jenny in tartan doublet and trews, fully armed and – an extra touch here – a gun in her hand.

In the doggerel of the day there she was, exhorting the Prince, first to go out and fight at Prestonpans:

> . . . and lo! an heroine was seen,
> Calm was her aspect, masculine her mien;

All ears attended, for upon her tongue
Good nervous sense and soft persuasion hung.
Thus she reply'd. Why makes my Prince delay?
This instant haste and march your troops away;
At our approach each hostile town shall yield,
Nor dare the Lowland youth dispute the field;[10]

She was at Culloden, too, on the right wing of Charles's army,
'brandishing her blade' with gusto and the most effective but
improbable results:

At length great Rich[11] the furious Fair
oppos'd
To save his men, and with the heroine clos'd;
His fury on her buckler she sustained,
And still her ground against the chief
maintained.
But when he saw the fair one's beauteous face,
Her charmful eyes, her mien, and ev'ry grace,
Back he some steps retreated, sore amaz'd.
And on the Fair with admiration gaz'd;
Urg'd by success she follows him apace,
And thought her sword had conquered, not her
face;
Still she pursues, and with one furious blow,
Lops the left arm of her yet wond'ring foe'
Far stream'd the gushing blood from out the
wound,
And the lopt limb lay quivering on the ground.
Another blow she aim'd, but numbers rose,
To save their leader they themselves expose,
And the same blow design'd the Chief to've
slain,
Laid two brave youths, expiring; on the plain;
Now to her troops the maid again withdraws,
Too brave and too successful for her cause.[12]

And when the day and the Cause were both lost, Jenny was still there, pleading to die with her men. But Jenny was spared – by the humane Hanoverian soldiers no doubt:

> The Cameronian maid long strove to fly,
> And, when surrounded, begg'd in vain to die.
> Thus in one day rebellion, vanquished, fell,
> And her rapacious sons were sunk to Hell;
> But vagrant Charles escap'd by shameful flight,
> And bid his hopes of Empire all good-night.[13]

The 'real' Jenny Cameron settled quietly in the Scottish Lowlands, in Lanarkshire, close to Kilbride (now the new town of East Kilbride), where she paid £1,500 for the mansion house of Blacklaw and its neighbouring lands of Rodinghead, all of which she renamed Mount Cameron.

It is clear that nobody believed the Whig propaganda about her affair with the Prince, for she was accepted by all the leading families of the area and was even visited by the famous anatomist and royal physician, William Hunter. Jenny was an intelligent woman who 'showed in her conversation on a great variety of subjects, that she had a discernment greatly superior to the common'.[14] She kept her own two-wheeled chaise and attended the parish church regularly, and when she arrived in Kilbride, she brought with her several Gaelic-speaking orphan girls whose fathers had fallen in the '45. She taught them herself and brought in a tutor to teach them English.[15]

Jenny Cameron was still a handsome woman at this time as David Ure, who must have known her or talked to many local people who did, testifies: in his history of the area he said she retained 'to the last the striking remains of a graceful beauty'.[16]

While their women were suffering in their different ways, the men who had followed the Prince and been captured were subjected to even greater cruelty. Some were released eventually, but many were transported or sentenced to a gruesome death – to be hanged, not until they were dead, but to be cut down alive and have heart and bowels gouged out and burned. The body was then to be quartered and the head displayed as a warning to others.

Lords Balmerino, Cromartie and Kilmarnock were put on trial before their peers at Westminster Hall and all three were condemned to death, but because they were nobles, they were sentenced to be beheaded. Cromartie's life was spared, but Balmerino and Kilmarnock were executed at the Tower of London. Old Lord Derwentwater, who had been caught during the '15 rising and escaped, was captured again in 1745, but this time his luck ran out: he was executed on the warrant issued in 1715.[17] The last peer to be executed at this time was Lord Lovat.

At the headsman's block, Balmerino spoke for many who had come out for the Cause, when he said, 'I might easily have excused myself from taking arms on account of my age. But I never could have had peace of conscience if I had stayed at home when that brave Prince was exposing himself to all manner of dangers and fatigues both night and day.' Of the Prince himself he said, 'I must beg leave to tell you of the incomparable sweetness of his nature, his affability, his compassion, his justice, his temperance, his patience and his courage, which are virtues seldom found in one person.'[18]

Sweet nature, affability, compassion, justice, temperance, patience and courage – by the time Balmerino made his dying speech all that was in evidence of these fine character traits was courage – and that was of a reckless nature unlikely to do him or his Cause any good. But who can blame Bonnie Prince Charlie for losing all his finest qualities during the months that followed his return to France, his dream of a Stuart restoration destroyed.

He landed at Roscoff on the north Brittany coast on the afternoon of 11 October New Style, 29 September by the Scottish Old Style calendar. By one of those ironies of history this was the very port at which his great-great-great-grandmother, Mary Queen of Scots, disembarked when she was brought to France as a child in 1548.

Charles was already a hero from end to end of Europe, acclaimed by crowned heads, adulated by the nobility of France, and adored by the common men and women. His return to Paris was as glorious as his entry into Edinburgh the day he rode back from routing Cope's army at Prestonpans, yet all that glory did nothing to bring him the help he sought.

The first person Charles wanted to meet was King Louis to ask him to mount a new expedition to Scotland while interest still ran high among the people there, but the French king cannily distanced himself from the returning hero. He would gladly have ignored the Prince completely for he had given very little help in 1745 and his conscience must have been troubling him, but he could not afford to do this because of the enthusiastic reception the returning hero was being given by the people of Paris. So at first Charles had to be content with a meeting with his own brother, who was as overjoyed as the French nation to welcome him back. The young Duke of York was so delighted to see his brother that he rushed forward to hug him, and a Highlander, thinking this was someone trying to assassinate the Prince, nearly killed him.

Henry showed great consideration for his brother and even ordered the Prince's beloved dog, Marquis, to be brought all the way from from Navarre, where it had been left in the care of the Bouillons during the rising, to be reunited with his master.

Henry was so full of admiration that relations between the two were warm to begin with, but the Prince's closest followers soon began to undermine this brotherly love by suggesting that the Duke of York had not done enough to push the plan for a French expedition to be sent to Scotland in support of the rising.

Charles could hardly wait to contact his uncle, who was at Fontainebleau with the king, and would be a vital intermediary in arranging a meeting with Louis. The Prince was as fond of the Bouillons as ever and, while he was skulking in Scotland, there had been rumours that he had managed to reach France and was lying low at the house of his cousin, Louise, Duchesse de Montbazon in the Place Royale.[19]

On 19 October, just eight days after he landed, the brothers were invited to Fontainebleau where they were warmly received by Louis XV, the queen and the dauphin, not as princes of the royal house of Stuart, but as Count of Albany and Baron Renfrew. Charles was irked not just at having to maintain the stupid incognito, but because Louis refused to see him alone, giving him no chance to put his case for a new rising.

The ministers of state, who had done little for the Stuarts hitherto, now took their lead from the king, and entertained the Prince to lavish dinners and suppers over which he told his story again and again. Then on the evening of 23 October he was invited to supper with Madame de Pompadour, the king's mistress, a lavish affair at which the Duc de Bouillon was present. During the evening the door opened suddenly and the king walked in, an unprecedented honour, and talked informally to those around the table for two hours. Louis was expansive, well disposed to 'le Prince Edouard' and generous: he even indicated that he would make one of his houses available for Charles to live in while he was in Paris.

The Pompadour dinner was the high point of the Prince's glorious return; within weeks relations with Louis and his ministers had soured as it became clear that they intended to do nothing worthwhile for the Cause, and the Prince did not hide his feelings of anger and contempt for king and ministers.

Soon the bonds between the brothers and between Charles and his father loosened too. James tried to give his son 'good advice' on every subject – on handling the French, on the supporters he ought to keep around him and, when the Prince began to think of marriage and the succession, of suitable brides.

In the marriage stakes, Charles aimed high – he thought one of Louis XV's daughters or the Infanta of Spain would be a great coup for the Cause, but of course these were impossible dreams. Then there were rumours of a proposal to an Austrian archduchess, but that also proved a non-starter, and for a dizzy moment the Prince hit on the brilliant idea of solving the problems of succession and restoration at one blow, by marrying the Czarina of Russia in return for a dowry of twenty thousand troops to invade Britain.

Nothing was too far-fetched, but unimaginative old King James in Rome soon brought his son back to earth:

As long as we are abroad, it would be a jest to think that you could have either a Daughter of France or Spain, and I should think that during our misfortunes we may be very well satisfyed if you can marry a princess of the same Family as my Mother, & I doubt if you could have even one of them, except you nick the time in which the Court of France may be willing to do all in their power to soften the turning you out of France.[20]

A princess of Modena seems a surprising suggestion from James in the light of his own rejection there by his cousin Beatrice, a generation earlier, but time had healed that wound.[21]

All this put pressure on the homosexual Henry, who was afraid of women, and terrified his father might force him to take a wife, or his brother would force him to join in the riotous drinking and whoring orgies in which he and his friends were now indulging. George Kelly, that despicable old clergyman who had been one of the Seven Men of Moidart on the 1745 expedition to Scotland, was one of the worst offenders, even suggesting to Henry openly at dinner one day that he too should take up whoring.[22] Henry was appalled and, already estranged from his brother who hectored and humbled him constantly, could take no more of this humiliation, so when Charles went off to Madrid to try to enlist the king of spain's support, he seized the chance to make arrangements to escape from his brother and from marriage.

His departure was even more cunningly planned than Prince Charlie's had been from Rome in 1743, and his scheme worked brilliantly. Henry invited Charles to dine with him on the last day of April 1747, and arranged for the meal to be prepared, the table set and the house brilliantly lit to await his brother's arrival, but when Charles arrived there was no host to receive him – Henry was already hours on the road to Rome, and it was only after several days that he sent his brother a letter telling him where he had gone.

Henry still gave no reason for his departure, and it was not until the following June that he realised how completely he had been duped. Henry Stuart had not just gone to Rome, he had arranged to become a priest and was now to be a cardinal of the Catholic Church:

I know not whether you will be surprized, My Dearest Carluccio, when I tell you that your Brother will be made a Cardinal the first days of next month. Naturally speaking you should have been consulted about a resolution of that kind before it had been executed but as the Duke and I were unalterably determined on the matter, and that we foresaw you might probably not approve of it We thought it would be showing you more regard, and that it would be even more agreable to you, that the thing should have been done before your answer could come here and so have it in your power to say it was done without your knowledge or approbation.[23]

The red hat and betrayal by his father and brother left the Prince stunned. Paralysed by the shock of it, he shut himself away for hours, and it was 10 July before he felt able to sit down and write the letter telling his father that the news had been a 'dager throw my heart'.[24]

It was a mortal blow to the Cause as well, as everybody was aware, including – perhaps especially – James and Henry Stuart.

Charles, whose health tended to break (just as his father's did) under strain, went into a deep depression that summer, and began to drink more heavily than ever. All this was very worrying to his friends and it was probably with that in mind that arrangements were made through the Rohan family for him to use one of their houses at St Ouën. Charles's cousin, Louise de la Tour, was of course married into the Rohan family.

St Ouën was perfect, far enough from the court for him to be able to drop his incognito most of the time, yet close enough to Paris to accept the many invitations that were showered on him. He was still at the centre of Paris society, bombarded with invitations, and Englishwomen came over from London just to gaze on him.[25] It offered an extra *frisson* of excitement because the King of France had hunting forests for his own exclusive use close by, and Charles was able to poach on these. St Ouën did much to raise Prince Charlie's spirits: so too did the rout of the Duke of Cumberland by the French at Laffelt in the Low Countries that summer.

By autumn it was obvious to all who saw him that Prince Charlie was in the warmest good humour, his spirits higher than they had been since he landed at Roscoff a year before, but few knew the reason why. Charles Stuart was deeply in love for the first time in his life. He had fallen madly for his cousin, Louise, the girl who had been proposed as a bride for him and rejected ten years earlier, and whom he had met for the first time when he first came to France before the '45.

Cousin Louise was married, of course, to the Duc de Montbazon, one of Charles's closest friends, and she was the mother of a two-year-old son. The affair began around the time of Louise's twenty-second birthday and her portrait, painted at this time, shows her dressed as a shepherdess and holding a little dog. It depicts a plain but strong face with a small, rather hard, set mouth and large almond eyes, which look out disapprovingly on the world. Louise does not have the appearance of the innocent she might be judged to be from her letters, and she had already experienced life: after all, she had travelled to Poland and undergone the maturing, but unedifying experience of being offered unsuccessfully around the marriage market there. Looking at the picture one wonders if her future mother-in-law might not have read what was to come in Louise's face when she insisted on that clause in the marriage contract, insisting that she and her husband were to live at the Guéméné house in the Place Royale.

And yet, having said all that, it is not possible simply to dismiss her as a scheming wife, betraying her husband while he was away at the war. From her letters and the course of the affair, Louise emerges as an innocent in many ways, a victim of the kind of deep and full love which leaves no room for choice. She had the misfortune to have inherited that Sobieski determination to go her own way, which Charles also possessed in a high degree. Her main fault was exactly the same as Charles's and it was to cause her great hurt as the affair reached its climax.

At the time the Prince was twenty-seven, still a tall athletic figure, who, to the astonishment of his brother had actually fattened out and looked fitter after his adventures in the Highlands following the rising. He was compared to the popular and handsome Charles XII of

Sweden and, as his portraits of the time showed, he was every inch a warrior prince. No one noticed the pimples on his chin or that his face was beginning to fill out to the roundness of the heavy drinker, which it was to take on later. Heroes are not judged by their appearance and those who looked at Prince Charlie at this time saw what they wished to see. To men he was a man whose achievements were awesome: to women he was irresistibly romantic.

We do not know exactly where or when the affair began although we know how it ended, and we have not a breath of it from any of the people who observed at that gossipy French court because one did not talk about these things. The only word of it that we have from the Prince himself is what Professor Bongie, who has chronicled the affair, describes as 'a rather strange autobiographical fragment . . . probably Bonnie Prince Charlie's only formal attempt at fiction'.[26]

On Louise's side the only evidence is a bundle of undated, hastily written notes, which lay almost unnoticed among the Stuart Papers in the Royal Archives at Windsor for generations until Professor Bongie transcribed them and put them into their probable date order during the 1980s – although the nineteenth-century historian, Andrew Lang *nearly* discovered them, writing in his biography, 'There are traces also of an affair with Madame de Montbazon, whom Charles compromised, it appears, by firing off two pistols, on what occasion is not known.'[27]

Andrew Lang confused matters by quoting from the Marquis d'Argenson's *Journal*: 'The Prince is amusing himself with love affairs. Madame de Guéméné almost seized him by force: they quarrelled after a ridiculous scene.'[28] There was a quarrel with Louise's mother-in-law: but it was far from being a love affair, and it came much later in the story of Louise's romance.

Louise's letters were never meant to be seen by anyone other than the person to whom they were sent. She asked Prince Charlie to burn them as she had destroyed his to her, but he did not do so, and they ended up being bundled together with his other papers and found their way into the British royal archives.

These are not love letters in the usual sense of someone sitting down to write billets-doux reciprocating the tenderest affection, or musings on moments of deep pleasure or passion. Neither are they the vicarious 'morning after' reliving of the sexual ecstasies of the night before. The letters are hurried, confused, pleading and above all spontaneous, written by someone whose mind is often in such turmoil that punctuation is forgotten and no thought is given to grammar or spelling. Often Louise was prostrating herself at his feet, pleading for him to come to her. The letters were undated and unsigned and not all were sent to Charles: some were addressed to intermediaries involved in the complicated arrangements for the night-time assignations and through whom she begged for Prince Charlie's love.

Unfortunately this is a one-sided dialogue. We have to listen to Prince Charlie through Louise's thoughts and pleas, but it is not hard to hear what he has been saying. The ladies of Edinburgh had taught the Prince nothing about love: he was as inexperienced with women as ever and, if the story of his vow of chastity is correct, he was a virgin at the time as well, but that is unlikely in the light of the Clementina Walkinshaw liaison. All in all Prince Charlie comes out of Louise's letters as immature, demanding, irresponsible and impossibly petulant – in other words the Prince who was the bane of his father's life and a thorn in the side of the French king as well at this time.

When did the affair begin? And where? We can only guess at that, but all the evidence points to that summer of 1747 when the Prince moved to St Ouën, depressed and solitary, after severing the bond that had united him to his family. It would have been natural for him to turn then to his second family in France, the Bouillons, but his uncle was at court much of the time and his cousin, Turenne, was at the battlefront with his regiment.

There was no shortage of entertainment, however: with many of the eligible young men away at the war, the returned hero Charles, was in great demand. Invitations rolled in from all sides, including his cousin, Louise, and her mother-in-law, Madame de Guéméné. He even went to stay at the Bouillons' estate at Navarre, and it is possible that the romance blossomed there, or at his own house at St Ouën – or perhaps at both. The Prince himself says no more than it was at 'a country house whose name I forget'.[29]

It was not a case of love at first sight, for Charles had got to know Louise well when he first came to France before the start of the '45, but probably he and Louise drifted into love then, during long summer days – and idyllic evenings – when they were together in the beautiful gardens of Navarre. With Prince Charlie's reputation as a novice at love, it is hardly likely that the affair was premeditated: Charles needed someone sympathetic to whom he could pour out his heart that summer and Louise was there to listen and, in the beautiful surroundings of Navarre, sympathize. Comfort simply merged into love.

They were able to meet throughout that autumn because Charles was living at St Ouën, next door to Louise's ageing great-uncle, the Duc de Gesvres, which gave the pair ample opportunity to be together. One day they were seen strolling through the gardens of the Duc de Gesvres's house accompanied by several gentlemen, Charles was obviously enjoying himself and kept taking pot-shots at the duke's partridges every now and then.[30]

St Ouën was perfect for secret assignations and, better still, whole nights together. Louise was highly sexed and highly experienced and in her bed the Prince, suddenly felt stirrings of sexual need within him, and soon love was raging inside him, totally beyond control. It would not be putting it too strongly to say that Prince Charlie soon loved Louise de la Tour to distraction.

It was very probably at St Ouën towards the end of October that their child, a son born the following July, was conceived, and soon Louise began to suffer from morning sickness, which continued right into the New Year. Prince Charlie was so besotted by then that he didn't care in the least about the scandal that would be unleashed when news of the love-child leaked out. For Charles nothing mattered except that he loved Louise de Montbazon: he was prepared to give up everything for her, even the Sobieski inheritance, over which the two families had been haggling since grandfather Sobieski's death a decade before.

At the end of October, in the euphoria of possessing Louise totally, he was prepared to give her anything. He rarely wrote to his father these days except on the most important business, but on 30 October he sent a letter to Rome, enclosing a memorandum compiled by the Bouillons. Louise and her brother had been 'extremely Ronged', he told James, and he wished to put matters right. 'I was not au fet of these Matters,' he told his father, 'I telt them I woud send their Paper to you, recomending it ernestly to yr. Consideration, and being entirely resolved to yeld my shere iff yr. Majesty thinks it resonable.'[31]

James thought it far from reasonable, especially as he was now as hard up as he always was, and his son was running up debts while still refusing to accept the pension the French had offered him. He replied accordingly, cleverly side-stepping the Sobieski inheritance issue and turning it on to their own financial position. He rubbed in the point that charity should begin at home:

I should much approve your kind & generous dispositions towards your Cousins, if you had not nearer Relations than they, who should be much dearer to you, & who are in want, while they are in plenty & riches.[32]

That was not what Charles had in mind at all, especially since a 'nearer relation' could only refer to Henry, with whom relatins were now at breaking point.

The Bouillon greed was staggering for they were immensely wealthy, but wealth never stops people wanting more. Louise even wrote directly to James, but he would not yield. If she wished to pursue the matter then a court of law could decide, he said, or an even better way would be through a papal tribunal.

That brought Charles to his senses: 'I must beg yr Majesty's pardon,' he had to write, adding 'I never intended to relinquish any of my rights but as far as it was found just and that if you agreed to it.' Charles must have hated the taste of that particular piece of humble pie, but he had to swallow it. He ought to have been grateful later that he had not signed away his rights to the family inheritance, but no doubt he was not.

When Louise could not be with him at St Ouën, Charles made regular visits to the Place Royale to spend nights in bed with her, always risking discovery by his lover's ever-watchful mother-in-law and the houseful of servants, all asleep under the same roof. Inevitably the comings and goings of a closed carriage near the Prince's house at St Ouën at odd hours of the night, carrying an unidentified man muffled up in a white riding coat, attracted attention and one of the porters at a nearby house decided to investigate. On approaching the carriage he found himself looking into the muzzle of a pistol and ordered to keep away.

He reported the incident to the police, who feared that this might be a Hanoverian attempt to assassinate the heir to the Stuarts, so they informed the Minister in charge of security, the Comte de Maurepas. This was a very serious matter for, if the hero-Prince were to be murdered, it would be a terrible embarrassment to the French authorities, therefore Maurepas ordered the Paris chief of police, Lieutenant-General Nicolas-René Berryer to set up a full surveillance operation at once.[33]

The Prince's staff were advised of the strange comings and going outside their master's house, and their uneasy response served only to deepen police suspicion. They said they had not advised Charles of the mystery, which ought to have struck the police as odd, but it didn't.[34]

For several weeks a comic opera police surveillance operation was pursued both at St Ouën under the commander of the St Denis district, a man named Rulhière, and at the entrance to the city, where an officer named Poussot was in charge.

After a week without the closed carriage being spotted again, Rulhière decided to cover every road leading to St Ouën. This brought success: on 7 November the carriage, which had been first reported, was seen again, arriving a little before midnight just outside the Duc de Gesvres's house. There it waited until a coach and four, lit up with torches, suddenly emerged from the grounds of Prince Charles's house, then the carriage drove off soon after with two men in it.

A description of the carriage was hurried to the police at the Paris boundary, and there the vehicle was intercepted and tailed all the way to the rue des Minimes, a street behind the Place Royale, close to the rear of the Hôtel de Guéméné. Having checked carefully that the coast was clear, the driver called out that it was safe and a passenger got down and disappeared into the carriage entrance of a house.

The carriage then drove to the rue Sainte Marguerite in the Faubourg St Germain, where the second passenger got out and went into the premises of an English wigmaker at the sign of the *Cornet d'Or*. A quarter of an hour later the same man came out and dismissed the coachman.

It was all most mysterious, but the Paris police were determined to get to the bottom of it. Rulhière reported that he intended to continue his observations and would not fail to report his findings back to his superiors. He watched assiduously and over the following days both he and Poussot submitted details of every movement of mysterious vehicles outside the Prince's house at unusual hours. Slowly they built up a picture of what was happening.[35]

In addition to the visits to the rue des Minimes their meticulous detective work revealed that the man the coachman visited was one Stafford, a member of the Prince's household, who lodged at the rue Sainte Marguerite, but that didn't really take them any further towards solving the riddle of who was travelling between St Ouën and Paris.[36]

Two nights later the plot thickened when a drunken carter named Chevalier decided to hitch a ride on a coach which had just overtaken him on the St Ouën road, but no sooner had he jumped on to the back of the carriage than one of the passengers appeared, brandishing a rapier and threatened to run him through if he didn't get off. The carter jumped down, cursing his attacker, but he cleared off when the man with the rapier ran at him. After warning the mounted police on the road, the carter, overfull of Dutch courage, returned and flagged down the carriage and offered to fight, but again he was routed when the man with the rapier reappeared, now wielding a sword.

The carter took to his heels crying, 'Murder, I'm being murdered,' and the police patrol, which now arrived, identified the man with the sword as one of Prince Charles's valets. They took the valet's part in the quarrel, and offered to clap the troublesome drunkard into jail, but the valet, who turned out to be none other than Daniel O'Brien, said to let things be as he was on secret business for the Prince and was anxious to get to his master.

The carter must have been very drunk indeed, for he returned to the fray and claimed that O'Brien had a pistol as well as the swords, and was about to draw it when the police arrived on the scene. Yes, O'Brien admitted, he did have a pistol, but he was allowed to go on his way. From then on the police treated the mysterious carriage that drove from St Ouën to Paris by night with great respect.[37]

The strange nightly rendezvous with the hired closed carriage outside the Prince's house continued and, taking great care to hide among the undergrowth – a most uncomfortable assignment for Rulhière's men on these damp November nights – the police at last felt sure they had identified the two nocturnal travellers as O'Brien of rapier, sword and pistol, and none other than 'le Prince Edouard' himself. But this was absurd, Rulhière pointed out.

Rulhière and Poussot pieced the story together, leaving Charles out of it, and tried to fill in the blanks as best they could. The house in the rue des Minimes to which the carriage drove, belonged to a family called Dampierre, and the passenger entered the back of the house. Since the Prince's valet was involved it was safe to assume that whatever was going on was taking place with the knowledge of the Prince himself. And as a son of the Dampierre house was a lieutenant in the guards it was surmised that he, and not Charles Stuart, was the second man.[38]

Rulhière was now more or less satisfied that nothing more need be done – 'This business which has disturbed St Ouën and me as well has to some degree been cleared up', he told his chief. *En quelque sorte éclaircie* were the words he used.[39]

What no one realized was that the passenger in the carriage simply passed through the building or its grounds to the back of the Place Royale. There an accomplice waited to let him into the Hôtel de Guéméné and lead him upstairs to the apartment and arms of the waiting Louise. Rulhière had been correct in his first surmise, the second passenger was the Prince.

The return journey was the reverse of this process.

Maurepas had to be told, of course, and he ordered Berryer to write to the Prince's secretary: if nothing else this would let Charles know that the French were looking after his safety, and Berryer made this point when he wrote to Secretary Kelly.

'I promise you that the singular circumstances merited attention and that we neglected no precautions, however slight, relating to the person of the Prince who is dear to all Frenchmen.'[40] He had intended to add that the Prince would no doubt be amused at this careful surveillance of his staff, but thought better of it and omitted it from the letter he finally sent.[41] Perhaps that was wise.

Through the months of October and November and even into December Charles and Louise enjoyed nights together without regard to the risk they ran. Charles was delighted at the prospect of becoming a father and knelt beside his lover and talked to the child in her womb: the prospect of fatherhood made him more passionate than ever, but he simply could not understand Louise's worry about how she would ever explain the child away to her husband.

As winter set in with frost and icy roads life became more difficult for the lovers, so Charles rented a house in the rue du Chemin du Rempart in Paris, which was much more convenient to the Place Royale. A worse inconvenience arrived on the scene with the return of Louise's husband from the war, making it much more difficult for Charles to visit her bedroom. Fortunately the Duc de Montbazon, like other young officers back from the front, threw himself into the hectic court life of balls, the opera and supper parties, which went on interminably – his wife seemed to take second place, and a poor second place at that. Perhaps the marriage, which of course had been arranged as most marriages were in their social class, had not turned out as well as it might have done, but the Montbazons were still together and the slightest whiff of scandal would have appalled such great families as the Bouillons and Rohans.

Louise knew they could no longer come and go virtually as they pleased: the Prince had to lurk outside until the coast was clear, and he often did not even manage to get into Louise's bedroom until one in the morning, or even on occasions, three o'clock. In spite of the cooperation they must have had from servants inside the Hôtel de

Guéméné as well as from Prince Charlie's own men, it became more and more difficult.

Charles Stuart could not bear to be thwarted in any way; even when his life was in danger in Skye when he was disguised as Flora MacDonald's maid, he had refused to take proper care when soldiers hunting for him were around and refused to carry some of the baggage as any maid would have been expected to do. Now he acted in the same foolhardy way, and instead of becoming more circumspect, he turned truculent and reckless if he was refused entry. He became madly jealous of Louise's husband and made her promise on her word of honour that she would always belong to him, Charles and would never let her husband near her.

This put the poor girl in a terrible situation for she was pregnant, and if she was ever to have a chance of passing off the Prince's baby as her husband's she would have to sleep with him. This, Charles simply would not allow her to do. Louise bore the brunt of all this, and many of her letters in the Royal Archives at Windsor date from this period. She spent her time grieving over his arrogant behaviour, assuring him of her undying love, yet suffering his insane jealousy and begging him to come to her again. To her, he remained 'le comble de mes plaisirs' – the crowning point of her happiness.[42]

There were narrow escapes when he created scenes if he could not have access to his lover's bedroom whenever he demanded it, and once he even fired his pistols in the street. Louise, pregnant with her love-child, hiding the situation from her husband, and distracted with love, was in a constant state of fear of being found out, but she could not bring herself to end the affair.

Inevitably, the police were not the only people who became alerted to the nightly ongoings around the Place Royale. Tongues were beginning to wag in court circles, but in the most circumspect way, for the affair must have been known to many, yet so far as we know Louise's husband never got wind of it. It could be of course that his mother, who ruled the family with a rod of iron, ordered him to continue as if all were normal in order to give people no excuse to talk.

Inside the Hôtel de Guéméné Louise's formidable mother-in-law, well aware of what was going on, at last felt something had to be done to stop Louise's scandalous behaviour. Rather than create a scene, she decided simply to drop a few remarks to show that she knew what was happening, and that, she hoped, would be enough to halt the affair. Louise was scared nearly to death and immediately reported the incident to her lover:

> I am more dead than alive my dear love. Madame de Guéméné has just announced openly at the dinner table that noises were being heard inside the house every night. From today she will put someone on guard and the whole house must be on the alert. Many other remarks were made in a manner which fills me with apprehension. I feel deeply that this will test our love sorely and I am simply miserable because of it.[43]

Even in this letter, written in a state of anguish, Louise took care to beg her lover not to think ill of her and that she would not presume to tell him what to do, but she hoped for the best. She feared that Charles might react in an ill-considered manner, and she knew in her heart that her mother-in-law would not let the matter rest there. Louise closed the letter by telling Prince Charlie, 'If you could see the state I am in, you would pity me.'

Pity was not an emotion with which Charles Stuart was familiar. In her troubled mind Louise must have feared there would be worse to come.

TWELVE

A DAGGER IN MY HEART

Consider that soon I shall give birth (to our child) and I may die as a result. But that does not matter if I cannot see you. At least do not thrust a dagger into my heart by refusing to send me your news! . . . Adieu, my dear love, write to me as you promised.

Letter from Louise to Charles Edward at the end of their affair, when she was awaiting the birth of their child.[1]

In spite of her mother-in-law's threats, Louise continued to smuggle passionate little messages to her lover, but she was left with almost no one she could trust, and it became difficult to admit the Prince to her bedroom with Madame de Guéméné's spies watching everywhere in the house. Charles became more paranoid than ever, unbalanced and beside himself with rage and jealousy. To be kept waiting in the street was a crime committed against him personally by Louise, and he taunted her with being unfaithful and threatened to abandon her. Louise wept and pleaded with him to continue to come to her for she loved only him. She tried to persuade him to visit the Guéméné house socially during her mother-in law's after-dinner receptions to allay suspicion, but this he flatly refused to do.

There was no compromise in the mental make-up of Charles Edward Stuart: whoever was not openly and wholeheartedly for him was against him, and anyone who thwarted him in the slightest degree was his enemy. He had to see Louise on his own terms and if he could not, then she was to be regarded as one of the enemy too.

We do not have his side of the correspondence, apart from a few petulant drafts written when he was unable to gain immediate admittance to her bedroom,[2] since Louise destroyed his letters as they had agreed. But we do have hers, which speak eloquently for both sides and add an interesting sidelight on Prince Charlie's character – in spite of all her requests to him to burn them, he didn't. Charles Stuart in love might consider himself a prince, but he certainly was no gentleman.

So it continued through January with stolen meetings and recriminations, which brought a response of more tears and pleadings from Louise. For Louise every assignation was begged and yearned for in advance, and treasured afterwards, but to Charles Stuart, it was a princely right. Each love tryst was a royal command to be obeyed at once and without question.

In reply to one of her notes he told her, 'Although I love you to distraction you should know I am my own master and when I am pushed to the limit nothing will stop me . . . Come, woman! You must understand that you are agreeable to us only while you yield to our pleasures. This may be my last visit. Adieu.'[3]

And Louise capitulated every time, even when she was calling him 'le plus ingrat et le plus adorée de tous les hommes'.[4]

And yet, when they were together Charles could be tender and full of romance. His heart was as loving as any expectant father could possibly be and, as he cradled his head in her lap, he continued to tell the unborn child he would always love it.

At the middle of January the court was due to move to Marly, taking all the cream of society with it, and Louise's husband planned to spend some days there. It would be a golden opportunity for the lovers: unknown to them it also provided Madame de Guémené with her chance to spring the trap she had been busy setting for the lovers.

With Jules out of the way, Louise settled down in her bedroom to wait for her lover as usual on the night of Tuesday 23 January 1748: as she waited she was joined by an old friend and confidante, Anne-Françoise de Carteret, a member of a well-trusted Jacobite family, who was privy to all the secrets of the affair. As they chatted Louise became uneasy, then as time wore on a niggling worry grew at the back of her mind, a worry which in time turned to thoughts of black despair. There was something wrong. Her father had called on her mother-in-law earlier in the evening and the two were still shut away in a room downstairs, talking. Louise was convinced that it all had to do with her and Charles.

She was sure they had been found out.

Suddenly, about ten o'clock the door burst open, Madame de Guéméné and the Duc de Bouillon stormed in and Anne-Françoise was ordered downstairs. Then the storm broke: as Louise's friend went downstairs she could hear from beyond the closed door, Louise's loud sobs and her mother-in-law's voice, low and calm. Madame de Guéméné probably spoke quietly and carefully since she was talking in front of the girl's father and may have felt she had to choose her words carefully, but she certainly was not Louise's friend, then or later, as she claimed to be. Anne-Françoise said later that Madame spoke sweetly enough to Louise's face, but behind her back she 'reviled her with every kind of horror'.

Madame began to speak, calmly, but surely hardly as a 'friend', as Louise wrote to the Prince. Said Anne-Françoise in a letter describing the bedroom confrontation to Charles:

La belle mere . . . luy parle avec assez de douceur devant elle mais il n'y a sorte d'horeurs quelle n'en dise quand elle n'est pas avec elle.[5]

For an hour and a half they talked – that is to say, Madame de Guéméné and the duke talked while Louise lay on her bed crying hysterically. The *belle-mère* told Louise she had known about the affair for a long time and ignored it, but now it had to end. She had dismissed one of Louise's servants who had acted as intermediary to the Prince and another was being kept on for a few days in order to avoid gossip, but would go soon. She herself would see to it that the business was kept concealed from the entire universe, but Louise must write a letter to the Prince and promise never to write to him again.[6]

Anne-Françoise was summoned back upstairs and found all three – Louise, her mother-in-law and father – in tears. The duke now did the talking, poor Anne-Françoise taking in his words through a haze of dread: he told her what had happened and, no doubt in the expectation that it would be passed on to Charles, added that he hoped the Prince would have enough self-respect not to stop visiting the house during the day because if he didn't keep up an external appearance of normal behaviour, people would be convinced that the rumours were true and Louise would be ruined.

Louise was then made to sit down and write the letter, dictated by her father and *belle-mère*. The 'cher coeur d'amour' with which she would normally have begun had become 'monseigneur':

Monseigneur,
What I had only too well foreseen has come to pass. My mother-in-law knows of all your approaches and has just come with my father. They have both spoken to me like two friends. Thus, Your Highness, I am obliged to inform you of this and you have known for a long time what I told you. And so I owe it to them not only never to see you, but not even to receive news of you. If you will do me the honour of coming to visit from time to time, as I believe you will in order not to ruin me completely – that process is well advanced – you will be received in the usual manner. Farewell, Your Highness. This is a cruel test of my love for you which will only end when my life ends.[7]

Through the tearful days that followed, Louise waited for a response from Prince Charlie. Strangely, there was silence: he neither wrote to acknowledge the letter nor, as Louise hoped in her heart, did he smuggle a love note to her. And he certainly did not appear at one of Madame de Guéméné's after-dinner receptions. Charles Stuart was out of her life, and that was more than Louise could bear.

After five days Louise could wait no longer, and she wrote him a long letter giving her version of what had happened that awful night. She was still in love – 'O Lord how happy I will be if you still think of your sweet mistress. To the end of my life I shall be yours. I swear to you that there will be better times ahead. Promise me that you will share them.'

By then tears were covering the paper and she closed the letter by telling the Prince, 'I am, greatly to be pitied, but if you continue to love me I shall be happy.'[8]

That same day she wrote a second letter as she had been unable to smuggle the first to him. She was about to try to sleep, but she remembered that it was eight days since he had lain with her. Now she had a fever, she could not eat and her hand was too feeble to hold a pen.[9]

On learning that Anne-Françoise de Carteret had been at the Place Royal on the night of the frightful confrontation, Prince Charlie demanded the full story of exactly what had happened and Mlle de Carteret obliged. She put Louise's behaviour in the best possible light, but unfortunately she relayed the Duc de Bouillon's remarks that the Prince had shown neither respect for his uncle or his cousin, nor gratitude for the many proofs of affection the family had shown him since his arrival in France.[10]

This struck home because Charles knew it was true. From that moment his arrogant self-righteousness turned to blind fury against Louise, her father and of course her mother-in-law. The relationship changed dramatically and L.L. Bongie blames that on the tactless remark of Anne-Françoise. In *The Love of a Prince* he writes,

Now that love [for Louise] could be transformed into a kind of abstraction, something that he could turn off at will, just as he had been able to turn off completely his love for Henry after his brother's defection. Louise . . . had been the occasion of his humiliation; because of her, certain authority figures had presumed to be critical of his conduct and to set down rules to govern his behaviour. By playing their game, Louise was as guilty as they were, and she had to be punished. She had wronged him just as the entire Rohan-Bouillon clan had wronged him. Amends had to be made.[11]

Charles punished Louise and all the members of the Rohan-Bouillon family who had been so kind and generous to him. He was incredibly rude to them, he snubbed them when they tried to help and he would not listen to them. Once when they tried to make peace by inviting him to a supper and a ball he accepted but sent a message at the last moment to say he was suffering from colic.

As for Louise, he still retained a vestige of the passion that had built up over the past half-year, but he was determined that she should be punished too. It was just as if she had never meant a thing to him: he refused to send her so much as the scrape of a pen, yet he made sure that little messages filtered to her through intermediaries, shedding tantalizing beams of hope on her miserable existence.

She continued to smuggle notes to him, ever more rambling and longer, affirming that she would love him until she drew her last breath, pleading with him to see her again, even suggesting rendezvous, and begging him to come for the sake of his child who was growing inside her. She was now five months pregnant and had to be bled to save the child, but he still did not respond. When letters sent directly to the Prince failed to elicit a reply, she wrote to his valet and to Chrétien, her own footman, who had been sacked, pouring out her feelings and begging them to intercede.

Nothing could stop Louise: she even laid an elaborate plan to go out on her own and visit the Prince but, with so many spies around, Madame de Guéméné was bound to find out and there ensued another terrible scene. On hearing of this, Charles had the effrontery to blame Louise and tell her she ought to be her own mistress and she had shamed him.

Charles Stuart still could not see anything from someone else's point of view – he was his own master and would have done exactly what he wanted; in fact, that was just what he had been doing ever since he returned from Scotland, and it was getting him nowhere. The French were coming closer to making peace with Britain and part of that peace was going to mean his leaving France, but even that threat could not make him behave more circumspectly towards King Louis. If he could not manage that, it is hardly surprising that he was unable to modify his behaviour towards the woman he had loved so passionately.

Although she had virtually cut herself off from the outside world, Louise forced herself to attend the Opéra and a concert that Easter just to see him, but he did not deign to look her way. If he no longer wishes to hear of me or to give me his news, let him send me a glass of poison, she told the footman.[12]

Charles did not stay at home and mope: his social life blossomed and, whatever the Rohans and Bouillons might think or say, he remained as popular as ever. They crowded to the Tuileries every day to watch him walking with the beau monde of Paris, escorted by a retinue of splendidly dressed Highlanders. He went to suppers, balls and the Opéra, where every appearance brought the entire house to its feet to cheer him. Charles remained as great a hero as ever.

It was inevitable that Louise began to fear that he had taken a new mistress and her letters grew more frantic, with her threatening to kill herself if he continued to ignore her. She continued to go to the Opéra just to catch sight of him, and every time was cut to the quick because he ignored her. Yet she felt impelled to go again, and on 27 April, she wrote to tell him that she would be there to see him the following evening.

Louise took her place at the Opéra in good time to see the Prince arrive. As the entire audience rose to its feet as usual to cheer and applaud, she saw that her worst fears had been realized – her Charles stood there in the royal box with the queen's cousin, Madame de Talmont, at his side.

She held back her tears until she left the Opéra, but she cried afterwards long into the night, as she told the Prince's valet the following day.[13]

Louise was as much in love as ever, and remained determined to be with her lover. Her husband had gone back to his regiment and the *belle-mère* was due to leave soon, so the coast would be clear for a meeting. It was all the more urgent to see him now because gossip had it that he would soon be forced to leave France when peace with Britain was concluded. Professor Bongie believes that Louise had stumbled by accident on the one means of obtaining agreement to a meeting. 'She had managed it, not by appealing to his love, his guilt, or his gratitude, but rather by accidentally goading his sense of vanity. Everyone was indeed talking about his having to leave because of the peace talks, and it infuriated him,' Bongie wrote.[14]

Whatever the reason, and it could hardly be love after all this time, Charles sent a letter in the middle of May agreeing to meet her at his house on 18 May. Louise was delirious with happiness: even their child in her womb would feel her joy, she told him.[15]

Her heart sank as the great day approached, for Madame de Guéméné had not left after all and she had Charles's house in the rue du Chemin du Rempart staked out with her spies. But Louise would not be beaten: she proposed that the Prince should come to the Pont Tournant in a carriage at midnight, muffled up in his great riding coat, and there she would meet him absolutely alone. 'A minuit precise je serai au pont tournant,' she ended the note.[16]

The ruse worked and the pair managed to keep the assignation at the bridge just as Louise planned. She was beside herself with happiness afterwards and confessed that she didn't shut an eye all night and kissed the hands which had touched him. They discussed the peace treaty and how it would affect him, and even alluded to his new mistress. But as they parted both promised to write every day and already she was looking forward to his first letter.

Soon she was writing to him again, this time reminding him that she had suffered three months of martyrdom:

> When I think that it is three months! . . . My head spins, I remember so clearly the happy moments . . . I spend as much of my time as I can shut away in my room, gazing at your portrait, bursting into tears, and kissing a thousand times the lock of your hair which I carry over my heart day and night.[17]

She reminded him of their child who was now growing large in her womb. 'I love only you in all the world, and no moment passes without thinking of you,' she told him. 'I can live no longer. My unhappy child responds to my woes. Have pity on me and remember the time when you told him in my breast that you would love him.'[18]

Even the reminder of his child could not soften Prince Charlie's heart. Louise was left to wait and watch day by day for a letter which failed to come. Yet the meeting at the Pont Tournant had been friendly, and intimate enough for her to remind him that 'I am spending my nights kissing those parts where I have felt so happy. In the carriage I shall allow you as much of your little pleasure as you may wish.'

Of course she continued to worry about the Prince having to leave France and about the new mistress, but she still hoped for his

After Clementine retired to a convent James showed his young sons off on many social occasions such as this fête in the Piazza Navona, Rome, to mark the birth of Dauphin of France in 1729 which was painted by G.P. Panini. Below, left: detail from the painting showing James with Charles and Henry.

Dear Papa

I thank you mightily for your kind letter. I shall strive to obey you in all things. I will be very Dutifull to Mamma, and not jump too near her. I shall be much obliged to the Cardinal for his animals. I long to see you soon and in good health. I am

Dear Papa
your most Dutifull and affectionate
Son   Charles P.

In a letter written to his father when he was seven, Prince Charles promises not to jump too near his mother

The 'bonny Prince' enters Edinburgh in triumph after the battle of Prestonpans; a romantic nineteenth-century engraving

Prince Charles Edward in army uniform about the time of the '45; by an unknown artist

Clementine Walkinshaw; by an unknown artist

The grave of the Finsthwaite Princess in Finsthwaite churchyard, Cumbria

THE JILTMEGANT.

A satirical drawing showing Charles Edward and Jenny Cameron riding together on a horse

The meeting of Flora MacDonald and Prince Charlie at a shieling on South Uist; by A.Johnson

Louise de la Tour, Duchesse de Montbazon, dressed as a shepherdess; after Lancret

A passionate note from Louise to Charles, written when their affair was at its height, recalls their night of love and looks forward to many more of the same

A report from the Paris Police, who tailed Prince Charlie on his nightly journeys to Louise's house, fearing it was some secret plot to assassinate the Prince. Although this report mentions the sighting of Louise with Charles, the police never found out what really was happening

The Princesse de Talmont –
Charles was her last great
love

King Charles III at the age of fifty-five

Princess Louise of Stolberg; by an unknown artist

The Palazzo Guadagni, Charles Edward's home in Florence

Prince Charlie's daughter, Charlotte, the Duchess of Albany; by H.D. Hamilton

promised letter, and he had told her he would never abandon her. 'Goodbye, my love, I await your news tomorrow.' she ended. 'Send me your love if you wish your child and me to live.'

But Louise waited in vain. At the end of May 1748 he told her finally that he would not meet her again in a carriage as he had done at the Pont Tournant, and they never did meet either at a secret rendezvous or at his house. Her last letter to him had a depressing ring to it. Louise had lost her fire: the love still burned bright, but hope was gone. 'Goodbye, my love,' were her last words to him. 'Send me your news. I feel very sick from sorrow today because you have chosen not to write to me.'[19]

There was a strange sequel to the affair between the little duchess and the Prince. Madame de Guéméné and Charles hated one another with an unrelenting intensity, and during June the Marquis d'Argenson reported that very noisy and very public lovers' quarrel between the Prince and the *belle-mère*. He wrote:

> Prince Edouard amuses himself by making love. Madame de Guéméné almost took him by force. They became embroiled in a ridiculous scene.[20]

The simple explanation is that the two sworn enemies met and tempers became heated so that they shouted at each other like fishwives. A much more likely reason for the incident is that Madame saw her opportunity and decided to stage a scene as if it were the *belle-mère* and not the daughter-in-law who was embroiled in the much talked about affair with the Prince. This would save her son's reputation, which she was determined to preserve at all costs.

After d'Argenson had reported the brawl everyone would know that the affair, regardless of whom it involved, was over.

On 28 July 1748 Louise gave birth to a son. Two days later the child was baptized Charles-Godefroi-Sophie-Jules-Marie, second son of Jules, Duc de Montbazon and the Duchesse de Montbazon. Jules's mother, Madame de Guéméné, wrote at once to King James in Rome to tell him that his niece had given the Rohans a second son and heir. She did not pass the good news on to Charles Stuart.

Prince Charlie's love-child was accepted as Jules's son and a member of the Rohan-Guéméné family without a syllable of scandal spoken aloud at court or anywhere in Paris. So far as we know Jules never knew that the child was not his, or if he did, his mother made sure that he did not give away his wife's secret scandal in public. Madame de Guéméné saw to it that the Rohan name was not tarnished by the Stuarts.

As so often happened in those days the child did not survive his first year – he died before he was six months old, on 18 January 1749, and was buried in the traditional Rohan-Guéméné burial place, the crypt of St Louis in the Convent des Feuillants.[21] Today, it is as if the son who was the fruit of Louise's passionate winter with Prince Charlie never existed. Even his burial place has been swept away: it was destroyed in the nineteenth century to make way for the rue de Castiglione and the rue de Rivoli, and his name was eventually blotted from all the official genealogies of the Rohan-Montbazon family. Louise died on 24 September 1781 and was buried alongside her infant son.[22] By that time Charles Edward Stuart had long forgotten his first, and probably his only, long passionate love affair with his cousin. By then he had been abandoned by the woman he did marry and was living out his last, lonely, drunken years, a sick man forgotten by all of Europe.

THIRTEEN

CHERCHEZ LA FEMME

Her attractive face, her affected manners, the nobility of her expression seduce many; but the impression she makes does not last; her moods quickly warn of the danger that lies in wait for anyone who attaches himself seriously to her.

The Marquise du Deffand describing the Princesse de Talmont.[1]

Louise sat in a daze as she watched Prince Charlie that night at the Opéra in April 1748: stunned, not merely because the man she had loved to distraction and whose child she could feel inside her womb stood before her in the royal box with another woman at his side, but because she was a woman who was older, far older, than he was.

Charles Edward was twenty-six at the time and Marie-Anne-Louise Jablonowska, Princesse de Talmont, was forty-seven, old enough to be his mother – in fact she was a year older than Clementina Sobieska. Although her looks were now fading, people had raved about her beauty in her day, and she had had many lovers. Marie was intelligent, witty, emancipated, and since she was a cousin of Louis XV's wife, Queen Marie Leszczynska, she had powerful friends in high places. As Charles Stuart's mistress she was going to need them.

Marie Jablonowska had been the mistress of Queen Marie Leszczynska's father, the deposed King Stanislas of Poland, who lived in exile in Lorraine, and it was he who helped to arrange her marriage to Anne-Charles de la Trémoille, Prince de Talmont, in 1730. Given Marie Jablonowska's reputation this was not easily achieved and Anne-Charles, who was ten years younger than his proposed bride, was only lured to the altar by a large dowry and the dukedom of Châtellrault.[2] The marriage of the Duc and Duchesse de Châtellrault had lasted for

179

eighteen stormy years by the time Marie and Charles met, and had produced a teenaged son. But the Châtellraults' life together was a succession of great scandals and quarrels, not least because he was not greatly interested in women and she was much too interested in men. While her devout husband passed his time on his knees in prayer, she spent hers in bed with a succession of lovers.

By the time Charles Stuart rocketed into her life her marriage was over and ex-King Stanislas was helping to arrange a separation, which was to be brokered on Marie's side by her close friend at court, the Comte de Maurepas. As part of the separation arrangement their house in Paris was to be sold, but pending that, they were to share it[3] – a situation likely to lead to problems, given Charles Edward's behaviour when he was in love.

The big difference between the Prince's liaison with Louise and that with Talmont was that the little Duchesse de Montbazon was truly the victim of love, but Talmont set out to capture the Prince and she succeeded. The Louise affair on both sides began as pure love, but the Talmont liaison was something much more sinister.

The affair pleased both Charles and Talmont. The princess was a highly experienced woman of the world who cut quite a figure at court, and she suited Charles admirably as a means of punishing the perfidious Louise and her family. Talmont, all too willingly fell in with the Prince's plan and became his acknowledged mistress. She had reached that stage in life when her looks were fading and her days as a courtesan in royal circles were numbered. A long-lasting relationship with a dashing young hero-prince would be a very satisfying culmination to her career as a courtesan. And who knows, it might bring her a full sex life and a lasting relationship.

Louise and Marie were as different as two women could possibly be: Louise was young and, in spite of her experiences in the marriage brokerage market in Poland and Germany, innocent alongside the older, wily, experienced Talmont. She had none of Talmont's poise or sophistication, and she certainly lacked her new rival's brain. Talmont was a thoroughbred alongside the plodding Louise and it showed, both in her past and in the way she handled the Prince in the early days of their relationship.

But Talmont had faults of staggering magnitude: the Marquise du Deffand painted a vivid word picture of her[4] – there was nothing easy or natural in her appearance, she carried her chin high and held her elbows well back, and her look was calculating, successively tender and full of disdain. Deffand was scathing about Marie's vanity, her jealousy and her eternal craving to be the centre of attention.

> The hour at which she chooses to make her toilette, meals and visits, all bear the stamp of the bizarre and sudden impulse. Showing no deference to her superiors, neither regard nor politeness to her equals, no gentleness or humanity towards her servants, she is feared and hated by all those who are forced to live with her. It is different for those who see her only in passing and above all for men. Her attractive face, her affected manners, the nobility of her expression seduce many; but the impression she makes does not last; her moods quickly warn of the danger that lies in wait for anyone who attaches himself seriously to her.[5]

In a phrase Talmont was a constant contradiction: in describing her the marquise could have been speaking of the Prince himself! Certainly a woman of such an unconventional nature appealed to the Prince, and it was only later that Marie's character became a handicap to their relationship, for in essence the pair were too alike. As Frank McLynn summed them up:

> The Prince and Madame de Talmont were oil and water. She was a woman used to satisfying her whims, indulging her intellectual, aesthetic or carnal fantasies – a genuine *capriciosa*, in a word. The prince by 1748 had reached the point where he would allow no one to question his authority, where he (or she) who was not with him was against him, where no one could speak a word of even the mildest criticism about him – this was construed as 'giving him laws' – where his will was paramount. The underlying trend in the relationship with La Talmont was thus the collision of the irresistible force with the immovable object.[6]

From the start the affair was stormy.

Talmont was able to feed his desire for revenge against the Bouillons-Guéménés during the early summer months while Louise continued to deluge the Prince with letters, begging him at any price, to come to her or let her come to him. As we have seen Louise's letters became longer, more rambling and less coherent, and only ceased, according to Professor Bongie's date reckoning, at the end of May, after that secret assignation at the Pont Tournant, when Charles refused to meet her again, and broke his promise to continue to write to her. By June Louise was occupied with arrangements for her forthcoming confinement, and after July, when her son was born, she may have had to pass the child off as Jules's, but in her heart the baby was a tangible link to remind her of those months of stolen passionate love.

She made no reference to the Prince again and we do not know what she thought during the months that followed when the name of 'le Prince Edouard' was on everybody's lips and the whole of Paris hung on what would happen to him next, for he was facing yet another great crisis. His handling of this proved more damaging to the Cause than the defeat at Culloden and hurt him personally more than the betrayal of his generals at Derby or the defection of his father and brother from the Cause when Henry accepted a cardinal's hat.

Long before the affair with Louise finished, it was obvious that the long drawn-out War of the Austrian Succession would soon be coming to an end, which was bad news for the Prince. While the French and British were at war there was always hope for the Jacobites, but the peace already under negotiation at Aix-le-Chapelle could mean only one thing so far as the Stuarts were concerned – the British were going to insist on a clause to banish the Stuart Prince of Wales from French territory. Charles found that particularly hard to accept: how could King Louis, whose armies had won such glory on the battlefield, be forced to bow to the Elector of Hanover on this? The truth was that Charles Edward, particularly since his return as a hero greater than any living Frenchman, was a pain in the side of the French king, and it would be a great relief to Louis to see him go.

But Charles Stuart was determined to defy the British and the French and stay. As he saw it, refusal to accept the treaty could only increase his standing as claimant to the throne of Britain by showing the people there that he would not be pushed around by their enemy. And in France it would demonstrate that the hero of the '45 had more fight in him than their own monarch.

First news that an agreement at Aix was close came in April just as his affair with Talmont was burgeoning, and there is no doubt that she encouraged him to kick against it, although both should have known, had either been the type to sit down and think about anything, that this was a battle the Stuarts could not win.

Charles had been thinking out his own plans for the future. With his intensely ardent lover, Louise, whose existence dared not be whispered, out of the way, and a mistresss who was an acknowledged courtesan installed, it would be easier for him to organize his own life in his own way during the summer of 1748.

He was now twenty-seven and realized that it was time he took a wife to ensure the succession, so Charles hit on a plan to solve all his problems – restoration, marriage, and the idiotic treaty which would compel him to leave France. He would marry a Protestant princess: this would show the British that he was no Roman Catholic bigot and it would give him a refuge when the peace was finally signed. And (he must have smiled with smug satisfaction at this) it would show his contempt for the Pope, his father and brother Henry for that treacherous business of Henry's red hat in Rome. It was a neat plan!

He had already brought Sir John Graeme, who had been with him in 1744 and was now in Avignon, back to Paris and now he put his plan into action. Charles aimed high: Graeme was instructed to travel to Berlin incognito and in absolute secrecy with a proposal in his pocket to no less a person than the sister of Frederick the Great.[7] He was to reveal the purpose of his mission to nobody until the had an opportunity to put an offer of marriage directly to the Emperor. Should the proposal be rejected, then he was to ask the Prussian king to help with the arrangement of a marriage with another German Protestant princess.[8]

Sir John set out at the beginning of May and it didn't take long for Charles to have his answer. Frederick soon had wind of the visit and told his minister of state that, in the light of his current good relations with George II, he had no wish to 'mix with this personage'.[9] In a letter written from Frankfurt on 6 June, Graeme told the Prince that the King of Prussia had refused even to see him and ordered him out of Berlin and out of the country forthwith, adding that he was lucky not to have been arrested and thrown into gaol.[10] Graeme tried to advise Charles to abandon hope of a German marriage alliance in view of this, but to concentrate instead on the more urgent problem of relations with France. But of course Charles would not listen to reason.

Still in the greatest secrecy, he now sent Sir John orders to go to the court of the Landgrave of Hesse-Darmstadt and view the Landgrave's daughter, Princess Caroline-Louise – 'If you finde her Fitting and to the Purpose strive to get her picture immediately,' he was told.[11] Somehow this did not have the romantic ring of Wogan's trip to Ohlau to view Clementina Sobieska for his father in 1718.

Sir John was reluctant to approach any princess who came within the powerful orbit of the King of Prussia and protested again, but Charles was adamant. Time was running out and somewhere must be found for him to go before the treaty was signed. By the second week of July he was desperate enough to give Sir John the authority to proceed with the proposal if the princess proved suitable.

'Iff you finde ye Princess fitting and willing . . . I think you should Embrace it on any maner Rathere than Let it slip; Considering ye Difficultys I may have of finding en other one to my Porpose, and ye necessity of my marying immediately. This is of ye Last Consequence,' he told Graeme.[12]

Matters were coming to a head in Paris and even Prince Charlie was beginning to realize that he could not stay on much longer. He would not face up to the inevitable though, and as a result a war of words and wills was waged between the Prince and the French authorities all the summer of 1748, a campaign which grew more frantic as October and final ratification of the treaty neared.

Charles's principal ally was the French people who still adored him:

he felt sure that no one would dare harm him so long as he remained their idol, so he made sure of their continued love by being seen constantly among them – he walked in the Tuileries gardens more frequently than ever with his Highlanders, he appeared at balls, at the Opéra and Comédie-Française, and even his attendance at mass became a public appearance. Despite his distrust of religion and churchmen, Charles was quite happy to let churchgoing become part of his image-making process.

He had enemies at court, however, especially Louis's minister, the Marquis de Puisieux, who hated him heartily. Puisieux suffered the painful experience of having to call on his enemy twice to try to persuade him to abide by the treaty, but Charles's response was a cold refusal to discuss the clause concerning him – since he did not recognize the treaty, he said, he could not be bound by any part of it that referred to him. Puisieux was furious, but could do nothing except bide his time.

Fortunately for the Prince, the king himself was not badly disposed towards him that summer – although his patience was sorely tried. Louis wrote a kindly letter pointing out that Charles's interests could not take precedence over those of the whole of the people of France and indeed of Europe, but he sympathized – if Charles did not wish to return to Italy he would use every influence to try to arrange for him to settle at Fribourg in the Swiss Confederation.

Charles's hopes were still on Germany and marriage to the princess of Hesse-Darmstadt on whom he had never set eyes. Unfortunately the Landgrave was in no hurry to oblige by offering his daughter's hand to Charles.

The Landgrave was away on a hunting expedition and Princess Caroline-Louise was taking the waters at a spa somewhere in Germany, so Sir John had to cool his heels and wait, making the most discreet enquiries about the girl. What he learned was good: she was pleasant, even-tempered and polite, so he was happy to put his master's proposal to the Landgrave on his return.

Caroline-Louise was already promised to someone else as it turned out, but Graeme persevered until the Landgrave gave his permission for Charles's emissary to speak to the princess herself although there were religious doubts in the German's mind because his family was Lutheran and the Prince was Roman Catholic. Graeme assured him that his master was most tolerant on these matters.

When Caroline-Louise returned from taking the waters a week later, the proposal was put to her and she was no doubt shown Prince Charlie's portrait, which the Landgrave had admitted was handsome. Her response was to take to her bedroom, indisposed, and stay there for nearly a fortnight, saying she could not yet see Graeme in her room – although she did manage to receive nearly everybody else of importance in the town. The Landgrave was no doubt sounding out others about the wisdom of allying himself to the Stuarts.

July had turned to August before Graeme was able to see Caroline-Louise and the result was equivocal to say the least: she said she would do what her father wished, and at the same time the Landgrave was telling Sir John that his daughter would make up her own mind. In short, Sir John Graeme was having problems.

At long last Charles realized that the Hesse-Darmstadts were stringing him along and he became very angry. Perhaps he was already out of sorts with the world of women since it was at the end of July that Louise gave birth to their son. In a foul temper he wrote to Graeme, 'I must now tell you Plainly to make this marriage now or not at all, my Circumstances admitting no delay on Ceverall accounts. So Desier you to make a hog or a Dog of them.'[13]

A hog or a dog, the German prospect was over and it was back to arguing with his mistress and with France, his father, his followers or anyone who crossed him. It seemed that Charles would refuse whatever was arranged. When Fribourg offered him its hospitality he rejected it out of hand, so that by October, when the Treaty of Aix-la-Chapelle was signed, he was no nearer to accepting that he should leave France. Puisieux and his friends were furious, Louis was nonplussed and the king in Rome fatuously told his son to issue no more proclamations in his name.

Louis tried gentleness, first sending the Duc de Gesvres, who had been the Prince's neighbour at St Ouën, with a personal letter, but neither the king's letter nor Gesvres's cajoling proved any more successful than Puisieux's threatening noises. Charles was fond of the duke, but would not listen to him. Louis then tried to get James to order his son to leave, but there was even less likelihood of Charles taking notice of that.

All Europe watched to see who would make the first move to relieve this impasse. Louis was in a corner, and kings, especially kings as powerful as Louis XV of France, do not like to be cornered.

The Prince went his loving way, as if unaware of the bomb that was waiting to go off under him. He showed no concern that his mistress had laid her position at court on the line for him, as well as her marriage settlement, and soon her health as well. Madame de Talmont, a woman as wilful as himself and a close friend of the queen, was being blamed for encouraging Prince Charlie. D'Argenson wrote that his mistress 'had taken control of the Prince's mind, and was influencing her with her foolishness and anger, without common sense in regard to the proposals being made to him: mutiny and misplaced pride are all there'.[14]

But Talmont now had to be careful because things had reached such a pitch that the queen's protection might not be enough. The Bastille was a real possibility for her and there were rumours that she might be sent to Lunéville in Lorraine. Her separation settlement still had not been resolved and much could go wrong with that if her enemies at court interfered.

The Talmont house in Paris had not yet been sold, and until it was, the estranged husband and wife used it turn about, so it was hard for Charles to know which of the two was occupying it at any given time. This led to problems as Charles kept calling at the house when the husband was in residence, and making a thorough nuisance of himself. The Prince de Talmont eventually ordered his servants that if the Prince ever arrived while he was in residence he was to be informed that Monsieur de Talmont would not permit him to enter. They did not have long to wait for the first confrontation: when Charles was told there was no one at home, he created a scene on the doorstep. By the following morning he had worked himself up into such a rage that he set out for the Talmont house armed and ready to break the door down. Of course he was refused entry again, and was about to batter the door in when fortunately Francis Bulkley, one of his most loyal supporters, arrived and managed to persuade him to stop.[15]

Even his mistress realized that Charles was going too far and felt compelled to tell him so – a dangerous action in the light of his refusal to have his behaviour questioned by anyone, even his mistress. She emphasized her point neatly by referring to his conduct outside Madame de Guéméné's house: 'I fear you are trying to give me a second chapter to the Mme de Montbazon story,' she told him, 'you dishonoured her by firing two pistols [outside her house].'[16]

The incident with the Prince de Talmont simply made the French authorities the more determined to get rid of Charles. Gesvres was sent to him for the third time, now armed with a letter from his father – a move guaranteed to be counter-productive. Charles would not even receive his old friend.

No wonder the nineteenth-century historian, Andrew Lang, described this and the years that followed as 'the Prince in fairyland':[17] the whole situation had become a tragicomic battle of wits, a trial of wills. When the French let James's letter be known, Charles declared it a forgery, then he asked for time to write to Rome to confirm whether James really had written it.

If Prince Charlie had accepted the inevitable at that point he could have departed with dignity, still a hero, and Louis and his ministers, especially the hated Puisieux, would have been left to look the villains of the piece. But no, Charles could not do that, and so he left himself without even the support of the Paris Jacobites who took their orders from James in Rome and from Louis who footed the bills while they were staying in France.

Charles continued to make noises, threatening to take his own life rather than be expelled. He was still seen by his adoring public in all his usual haunts, but inwardly he must have felt troubled. As Louis grew more angry, Charles baited him further, until he was given a deadline, which he ignored. The French government then decided that he must be arrested and expelled, but where to, how and by whom?

Arresting him at his own house was rejected in case he committed suicide or fired on his attackers; so was arrest in a public place in case it roused the Paris mob; in the end it was decided to execute the order quietly one evening as Charles was on his way to the Opéra.

The day chosen was 10 December, with plans drawn up with meticulous care.[18] The Duc de Biron, a colonel of the grenadiers, was delegated to carry out the arrest in a little cul-de-sac at the entrance to the Opéra, where carriages set down their passengers, an area easily controlled by the army and police. The prisoner was to be taken straight to the Château de Vincennes pending expulsion. Since the Prince had so many friends in Paris more than a thousand soldiers were posted in the streets and houses all round the Opéra in case of trouble, but there was no trouble.

The most controversial detail of the whole operation was an order that the Prince was to be bound in case he might try to commit suicide. Red silk cord was bought specially for the purpose.

Of course rumours were flying around Paris all day on the 10th, but Charles ignored these and set out to drive to the Opéra as usual around five that evening. In the rue St Honoré he heard a shout in the darkness: 'Go home, Prince, they are going to arrest you. The Palais Royal is surrounded.'[19]

Charles ignored that too, and when he arrived at the Opéra cul-de-sac he stepped into the crowded roadway as if everything was normal. In an instant he was surrounded by a group of sergeants, one of whom struck him on the back of the legs to knock him off balance, while two others seized his arms and legs. An officer by the name of Vaudreuil told him, 'I arrest you in the name of the King.'

The brave Biron hid himself away in his carriage while the job was done.

Charles screamed in protest as he was marched into a nearby house, where Vaudreuil took away his weapons. No one but a senior officer of the musketeers could arrest a prince of the royal blood, Charles protested,[20] but the time was over for fine points of court precedence.

Vaudreuil was more concerned about the indignity of tying their prisoner up, but Biron insisted, Charles must be bound for his own safety: so, to more loud protests, the red silk cords were tied. This was the first point at which the Stuarts' royal breeding showed through – as Vaudreuil admitted he was ashamed to be tying the cords, the Prince told him, 'The shame is not yours but your master's.'[21]

Prince Charlie was bundled into a carriage and driven to Vincennes, where the governor, the Marquis de Châtelet received him with great embarrassment and horror. At once he ordered the cords to be untied and Charles was put into a cell, where he was carefully searched again. Charles was permitted to live in the state apartments of Vincennes during the day, but every night he was returned to the cells to sleep.

Two days of cooling his heels in this manner brought Charles at last to the realization that he must capitulate and Louis, generously in the light of the way the Prince had treated him, agreed that he would not force him to go all the way to Civitavecchia, but they would escort him as far as the Pont de Beauvoisin at the border of Savoy and he could go wherever he wished from there so long as it was not back into France. Charles swore agreement in front of Châtelet and all was made ready for the Marquis de Pérussis to accompany him.

Unfortunately, as they prepared to leave on the evening of the 12th, the Prince took ill with coughing and vomiting, a form of illness which recurred when he was under stress. It was the morning of the 15th before he was able to travel and he only got as far as Fontainebleau before he said he was too ill to go further. Professor Bongie suggests that this might have been a ruse to allow his servants, who had now been freed, to catch up, or it could have been a delay to see Madame de Talmont again. If it was the latter it failed, for Madame's request to visit the Prince at Fontainebleau was turned down. Charles's old enemy Puisieux, told her sharply that if she had anything to say to the Jacobite Prince she could put it in writing.[22] Puisieux was cast as villain of the piece by the people of Paris, especially as the Prince behaved in the most light-hearted manner, playing *volant* with his guards and asking for news of the opera and who had sung the leading role. Even the king announced that he was angry with Puisieux.[23] Madame de Pompadour also was blamed by Parisians, who said she ruled as prime minister, interfered, and wanted to change all Louis's ministers.[24]

During these days everyone involved in the expulsion of Charles Edward lived in dread of something going wrong, and they watched out for escape attempts round every corner. By chance, two British travellers arrived at the *Cabaret de la Poste* inn the night Charles stayed there: to the great alarm of Pérussis, they turned out to be General James St Clair, who had led a small British landing in Brittany in 1746 just at the time the Prince was returning from Scotland, and his secretary, David Hume, who was to become Scotland's great philosopher. Pérussis feared that this might be a plot to assassinate the Prince or some other anti-French ploy: in fact, there was nothing in the least sinister about it for the general was simply on his way home from Turin and it was pure chance that brought him to the *Cabaret de la Poste*, and the same chance that had led the landlord to put them in the room immediately above that of the Prince.

St Clair had no idea who slept below him, and told his masters in London later that 'his attendants said he was a Prince, but did not name him. However, as he wore a Star & Garter, he was soon known to every body.'[25]

The timid Pérussis could not get his charge on the road again quickly enough, so they set out at three in the morning of 16 December and reached the Pont de Beauvoisin around mid-morning on the 23rd. There Pérussis took leave of the Prince, with a message from the Stuart Prince to express his respect for their majesties, and assurances that he would neither return to France nor go to Avignon.

Four days later, at seven o'clock in the morning of 27 December, Charles Edward Stuart was in Avignon, 'standing at the bedside of his old tutor, James Murray, Earl of Dunbar, who was staying with his widowed sister, Lady Inverness. The Prince was in the uniform of an Irish officer in French service.'[26]

It would be nice to say that Louis and his ministers were stunned to learn of *le Prince Edouard*'s arrival at Avignon, but they could hardly have been more thunderstruck than they were already at the reaction to his arrest. From the moment the soldiers surrounded

Charles at the entrance to the Opéra the authorities feared an uprising of the people, and with good reason, for this man was probably the best loved man not just in Paris, but throughout Europe. He was a hero even in the heart of enemy territory: the dauphin wept on hearing of his arrest, and people in high places at Versailles were as shocked as the governor of Vincennes on learning that the hero-prince had been trussed up, even if silk cords were used to bind him.

Government reaction was swift and firm. Many people, including those only remotely connected with him, were arrested, *for the Prince's own good*, the authorities insisted. Madame de Talmont's lackey, on his way to deliver a billet- doux from his mistress to the Prince, was seized and thrown into the Bastille. She boldly sent a letter to the authorities, demanding his release – a brave move by Talmont, considering how panicky Louis XV's ministers were, and how unsafe her own position was.[27]

By the 14th, four days after the seizure of her lover, Madame de Talmont was living in fear of being exiled to Lorraine,[28] yet was fighting to stay on in the capital with as much doggedness as her lover had always shown in the past.[29] Her husband left Paris, however, which d'Argenson seemed to think did not matter much since he had 'less authority than her lackey'.[30]

When Madame de Talmont learned of the arrest of her messenger she was so infuriated that she wrote a brave – or foolhardy – letter to Maurepas demanding his release:

Now that so many laurels are heaped on the King, how can the imprisonment of my manservant add more? I beg you, therefore, to send him back to me.[31]

Unaware of the chaos he had left behind Charles was proceeding on his merry way. In Avignon he asked for and received a splendid official welcome, much to the annoyance of the Pope, who knew that both France and Britain would browbeat him to expel his unwelcome visitor. Charles continued to enjoy himself, and even tried to add to the festivities by having bullfights added to the entertainments. Bullfighting was forbidden, so in the end he had to settle for a festivity featuring nothing more exciting than a fountain which ran with wine. His French troubles forgotten, Prince Charlie danced the night away, but retired at 8 a.m., long ahead of the others who did not give up until four the following afternoon.[32]

A concerted effort now was made to get Charles out of Avignon, out of the Pope's jurisdiction and hair. Every effort proved unsuccessful, until suddenly at the end of February it was reported that the Prince was ill and confined to his house. He was not seen for days, then suddenly it was announced that Charles Stuart had left on 25 February, accompanied only by Henry Goring. No one knew where he had gone, but papal spies managed to trace him as far as Orange where he vanished and everyone in Avignon waited with bated breath for him to return, but he didn't. No one knew for sure where he was at any given time throughout the next ten years.

Where was he? First he and Goring went to Lunéville in Lorraine, where the two parted, one for Paris the other for Dijon. By much swopping of carriages, horses and a portmanteau, both were to end up in Paris. Heavily disguised, the Prince arrived in the city at the beginning of April and the French capital was his home for the next two months and from time to time over the years that followed.

Andrew Lang believed the reason why he was anxious to get back to Paris was to organize a system for receiving mail from his supporters in Britain, and one of the first things he did there was to tell the banker Waters that he would call at his house to collect letters.[33]

Equally important, however, was a compulsion to gain revenge over King Louis for the indignities of last December. Charles Edward had grown more paranoid than ever, and saw in every slight or questioning of his demands a personal affront and an attack on his rights. It was now more than sixty years since his grandfather had been deposed, but Charles believed as firmly as ever in his family's right to the crown.

But of course the most compelling reason for returning to Paris was Madame de Talmont: she was equally anxious to see him and was willing to help him find a safe haven in the city. She was still deeply in love with him and absence (or absence plus the need of her help) made Prince Charlie's heart grow fonder, for the relationship warmed up while they were apart. During his stay in Avignon they corresponded and together they plotted his next move.

So within three months of giving his solemn undertaking never to return to France, Charles Stuart arrived back in Paris, heavily disguised, and had taken up his abode at a very secret and most unlikely address – the Convent of St Joseph in the rue Saint-Dominique. The convent idea, undoubtedly Talmont's, was brilliant, quite simply a touch of her genius at its finest. Neither Louis XV, nor his lackeys Puisieux and Madame de Pompadour, would ever think of searching for him in such a place.

St Joseph's had a non-religious retreat attached to it, where ladies of quality could go to enjoy temporary respite from the outside world. The Princesse de Talmont had stayed there herself from time to time – heaven knows she had probably needed it as an escape from the problems of her affair with Prince Charlie. In the convent no one asked questions or compelled residents to attend prayers, so it was a perfect hideaway.

With the help of her friends, Elisabeth Ferrand and the Comtesse de Vassé, Talmont set the Prince up in the convent, where he stayed for two months and often thereafter over the next three years.

A false wall in the countess's room concealed a little *garde-robe*, which provided a cramped and uncomfortable, but secure refuge. In Mlle Ferrand's room there was an alcove, equally safe, and in these the Prince lurked during the day while visitors were liable to call on the countess and Mlle Ferrand. From his hideout Charles enjoyed all the conversation and gossip of the court, sometimes even favourable and unfavourable morsels of news about himself, or speculation as to where he was at that precise moment. It was just the kind of joke Charles Stuart enjoyed, and it was all the more amusing because it was at the expense of the French.

Fortunately Charles did not have to sleep in these cramped spaces since a secret stairway led from the Comtesse de Vassé's *garde-robe* to the Princesse de Talmont's apartment below. After daytime visitors to the convent left, the Prince would slip down the secret stairs to spend the night in his lover's bed.

The pattern of their love was just as it had been in the days before the expulsion: the night began with the tenderest love-making, but sooner or later something would be said to throw Charlie into a wild rage and a violent quarrel would ensue. These were not confined to hurling epithets around the room, but often turned to something much more distressing for the unfortunate Ferrand and Vassé who could overhear it all in their rooms above – full-blown battles in which the bonnie prince battered the woman he had loved so tenderly moments before.

Charles just could not bear to be crossed in any way: he was so insecure that even the most gentle contradiction was interpreted as a personal attack which had to be repelled. Words were not enough and time and again he resorted to physical violence. Poor Mlle Ferrand and the countess, who seem to have been the mildest of women, suffered these scenes until they could stand them no longer, and in the end had to ask the lovers to leave.[34]

The Prince was quite happy to oblige – the place was none too comfortable, but it had served its purpose, and he was bored with its cramped lifestyle. Talmont had enabled him to defy King Louis and set up his system for receiving mail, but Paris could never be a permanent home. He made his decision not a moment too soon, for by now the French had found out he was in Paris and sooner or later they would discover his whereabouts, even in this secret sanctuary of St Joseph's Convent.

Charles had already decided to seek permission to settle in Venice, and had written twice asking the Earl Marischal to meet him there. Marischal, who was in Berlin, was thoroughly disillusioned with the Prince by now, and had no intention of becoming involved with Charles Stuart ever again, so he tactfully pleaded poor health. Early in May 1749 the Prince left the convent and reached Venice by the middle of the month, only to find he was not wanted there either. He accepted the doge's decision and left without demur. The Pope and all the papal states held their breath in case he might turn up in one of them, but to their relief he did not.

Instead he returned to Lunéville, which had two attractions, ex-King Stanislas of Poland was well disposed towards him and the

Princesse de Talmont had a home there. When they did manage to meet in Lunéville they could not share Marie's house for fear of being discovered by the spies who were on the look out for him, so they kept separate houses and Charles crept into Talmont's bedroom furtively as he had done at the Hôtel de Guéméné in Louise's day – creating similar petulant scenes when he felt he had not been admitted quickly enough.

The Prince could have settled in Lorraine, but for some strange reason, Charles Stuart always coveted what he could not have and rejected what was on offer.

He preferred instead to spend the next fifteen years wandering from place to place and of course saw it always as someone else's fault that he had to move on. As he told Bulkley, 'What can a bird do that has not found a right nest? It will always wander and never pitch on a branch.'[35]

Prince Charlie now adopted a lifestyle similar to that he had led in the Highlands and Western Isles after Culloden. For five months he was constantly on the move, his enemies at his heels, restless, and ever with the scent of danger in his nostrils. In Europe during the 1750s he relished the hunt as he eluded both friends and enemies, turning up in unexpected places and disappearing just as quickly. He became more skilled at disguising himself, and at laying more false trails than all the other spies of Europe put together.

It was an admirable achievement to elude the armies, police, spies and court gossips of Britain, France, and every kingdom and petty dukedom in Europe as they hunted for clues, often while he lay low under their very noses. It was rumoured at various times that he was in England, Ireland, Sweden, Spain, Flanders, Germany, Austria, Poland, Russia, Venice and other Italian states, and indeed he was in many of thes at one time or another, but seldom when the spies were sighting him. And much of the time he was simply in Paris or Lunéville, or moving between the two, for the Prince was always restless and 'on the wing.'

Prince Charlie would have made a better spy than any of these secret agents who were on his trail, for he was skilful at disguising himself: he had not made a very good woman when he played Flora

MacDonald's maid on a voyage over the sea to Skye, but now he could pass himself off skilfully as an Irish officer in the French or Spanish service, or as a priest – a surprising choice of persona considering the low esteem in which he held the Church and priesthood – looking authentic enough to have taken in even his cardinal brother.

Pickle the Spy testified to his success. 'Sometimes he wears a long false nose which they call *Nez à la Saxe* because Marshal Saxe used to give such to his spies whom he employed,' Pickle told the Duke of Newcastle. 'At other times he blackens his eyebrows and beard and wears a black wig, by which alteration his most intimate acquaintances would scarce know him, and in these dresses he ahs mixed often in the company of English gentlemen travelling through Flanders without being suspected.'[36]

Aliases helped too, and Charles travelled under many names, but most often as Mr John Douglas. Others he used included Benn, Burton, Cartouche, Mildmay, Smith or even Thompson, and to complete the confus, he encouraged his followers to spread false stories about his movements, or to report that he was ill, married, or even dead! The search turned to farce as secret agents sniffed their way back and forth across Europe, finding many scents but never the right one. To his delight there were many false Charles Stuarts, some genuine lookalikes, but others fraudsters and swindlers cashing in on his name. In 1753 one of these tricked his way through much of northern Italy, leaving behind a string of debts in the Prince's name.[37]

If all this confused Europe's rulers, it left James and Henry totally bemused – they could be certain of only one thing, the wild man that their son and brother had become was not in Rome.

There was only one sure way of tracing Charles – *cherchez la femme*. The Princesse de Talmont was still madly in love with Prince Charlie, so if she was at Lunéville the chances were that Charles was there and if she was in Paris, then he would either be in Paris or on his way. It seems incredible no one thought of that.

During the early autumn of 1749 Marie-Louise was in Paris, but had problems other than the Prince. About the middle of September her son, the fifteen-year-old Comte de Taillebourg, died of smallpox, and her own health began to crumble, probably as a result of the strain. She began to suffer from migraine, accompanied by nausea and vomiting. It is interesting that so far as can be seen from surviving correspondence, she received not a word of sympathy from her lover either over the loss of her son or the deterioration in her own health. The only benefit that came from her son's death was that it allowed her to end her marriage at last.

The relationship between the lovers took on a deeper, darker aspect now: they loved more passionately, but hated with greater ferocity too. Charles wanted Talmont with him, but it was not easy for her to rush to him every time he beckoned because she needed the king's permission to travel to Lunéville, and that was not always forthcoming. But Charles could not comprehend why she simply did not defy Louis and he became jealous and suspicious just as he had been with Louise de Montbazon.

But Marie was too experienced and worldly wise to give in to him: she had the courage to deal with his paranoia and hectoring. At one point she even told him he did not need friends, but victims.[38] As a result, he found himself playing the Louise role in the relationship, and he was the one who was writing the complaining, begging letters. 'I am dying,' he told her once, 'I love you too much and you love me too little . . . I have passed a terrible night.'[39] The words could have been written by Louise.

Talmont was given no secrets to keep because Charles was as close as ever and didn't even tell her when he made his trip to London in the autumn of 1750 – he just disappeared from Lunéville on 2 September and reappeared there on the last day of the month. He had spent nearly a week in London conferring with Jacobite followers, spying out the Tower of London, and had been received into the Anglican Church at the Church of St Mary-le-Strand. And he told his princess nothing of it.

To Talmont, who had had a long and successful career as mistress to better men than Charles Stuart, this was unforgivable. It brought home to her what a disappointment the Prince had been – her liaison with him had not been the satisfying culmination of her career as a courtesan that she had hoped it might be.

When Charles begged her to return to him at Lunéville at the end of 1750, Marie had to go before King Louis to beg another *congé* from court. As she had overstayed the last leave she had been granted to visit Lunéville, the king was furious and flatly refused. Marie eventually won him round and was granted permission to absent herself from court from January to May 1751, but just as she was about to set out from Paris she suddenly was stricken with one of her illnesses, which seemed to be brought on by stress, and had to write to Charles to say she would be delayed. Callously he showed neither compassion nor pity, but simply announced that he was leaving Lunéville to visit Berlin.

Marie became frantic with worry and before she was really sufficiently recovered, she set out on the long journey to Lorraine. She arrived at her house there on 25 January, but found no sympathy awaiting her: the Prince refused to stay at her chateau, complaining that it was too small to hold their two households. Next day he vanished and she didn't see him again for two months.

Eventually she sent him a note at the end of March, when more than half her *congé* had been wasted, and asked him to have the goodness to come and see her since she had made the journey at great personal risk. If he did not come, she said, she would return to the capital and make her peace with the king.[40]

He told her in reply that he wished she had stayed in Paris, but relented enough to spend a single night with her, then left the next day.[41] Talmont had taken enough insults and when he returned she was icily cold towards him, which enraged him again. She listened but said she didn't care any more, which was not true: Charles could still hurt her.

When the time came for her to return to the court in May, Prince Charlie flew into one of his rages and she promised to write to the king to ask for an extension to her *congé* provided he would live with her and be with her all the time.

Charles promised and Marie prepared to enjoy the passionate love they had shared previously, but unfortunately on the very first night they were to be together he arrived at the chateau to find her laid low with one of her attacks of migraine and vomiting. Again he

199

turned all his anger on her, stormed out of the room, and spent the night with one of her maids.[42]

In the morning he came back to her room and told her he was leaving for good. She begged him on her knees at least to stay until she had sent all the servants out of the ante-room, so that the humiliation of their parting would not be witnessed, but he coldly informed her that he was going to take another mistress and would leave when and as he pleased.[43]

As he left, he demanded she return his portrait, which she had in Paris. She was to deliver it to Waters, his banker. When she protested at this further indignity, Charles told her those were his orders, and walked out.

The Princesse de Talmont's final great liaison had reached its humiliating end.

Talmont lived on at court for many years, playing on the fact that she was a cousin of the Queen of France, as Horace Walpole found out when she sent for him during a visit to Paris in 1765. Although she hated Englishmen because of what had happened to Prince Charlie, she summoned Walpole to visit her at the Luxembourg, where she had a state apartment. He was shown into her vast chamber, hung with red damask and portraits of French kings, and lit only by two tapers. As Walpole advanced to greet the princess, who sat on a small bed in the far corner, 'hung around with Polish Saints', he stumbled over her dog, her cat, a footstool and her spitting pot. After twenty minutes of near silence Talmont at last asked Walpole if he could get her a black and white greyhound exactly like her '*pauvre défunte Diane*'.

'I promised', wrote Walpole, 'and took my leave, and thought no more of her and her dog and my promise.' Three months later Talmont's footboy came to Walpole with a picture of a dog and a note from the princess begging him to remember to get her a dog just like this one. Walpole wrote a tart letter in reply, but fortunately he showed it to the Duc de Nivernais – 'He said I must by no means send it,' wrote Walpole, 'for Madame de Talmont was très dévoté, and would be very angry and tell the Queen, who was still more dévoté, and a good deal more sincere – so I tore my note and sent another more grave, but not at all with more intention of trying to execute so impossible a commission.' He met the princess again a couple of years later and she told him with great good humour that she had discovered he had never given a second thought to her request.[44]

Talmont indeed was a mercurial character, proud and vain, but she met her match in Charles Edward Stuart.

Perhaps the Comtesse de Rochefort should have the last word on Marie de Talmont. When someone remarked that Talmont wore a bracelet hung with a picture of Bonnie Prince Charlie on one side and Jesus Christ on the other, and mused on what relation there was between the two pictures, she replied, 'The same text suits both: "My kingdom is not of this world".'

FOURTEEN

DISCARDED BY 'MRS CLEMI'

I quit(e) my dearest prince with the greatest regreat and shalle allways be miserable if I don't hear of his welfair and happiness. May God Almighty bless and preserve him and prospere all his undertakings which is the ernest wish of one how will be till Death, my dearest prince.

Letter from Clementine Walkinshaw to Prince Charlie when she left him on 22 July 1760 at the end of their eight years together.[1]

Charles Stuart was not a man to forgive or forget; nor was he one to accept blame as his father, Louis XV, Louise de Montbazon and now the Princesse de Talmont all discovered. Talmont still loved him after he abandoned her, and dearly wanted to see him again. But, apart from exchanging a few letters, he had nothing more to do with her. When he visited Paris he stayed with Marie's friends Mlle de Ferrand and Madame de Vassé, but never once called on her. He could be very cruel to anyone who crossed him.

In the months after he left Talmont he was busy both with his political life and his private affairs. This was a time of high hopes since George II was ageing and plans were being laid to take advantage of the power vacuum which his death would leave.

Alas for the Cause, George clung to life for another decade and the tide, which might have swept the Stuarts to power in the early 1750s, had receded by the king's death in 1760.

During the years following the '45 Lady Primrose played an active and very risky part in the intrigues leading up to the Elibank Plot of 1752.

In the early autumn of 1750 Charles Edward made his decison to visit London to confer with English leaders about a possible coup to seize the throne and, although we do not know whether this was prearranged or not, it was to Lady Primrose that he came. He reached London on 16 September and stayed there six days, probably at Lady Primrose's house in Essex Street off the Strand.

If he was expected in London the Jacobites did not know when to expect him for his arrival took Lady Primrose by surprise: she was playing cards with friends when he simply walked into the room unannounced. She quickly regained her composure and carried on as if nothing unusual had happened, then sent for Dr King as quickly as she could. King talked Charles out of the scheme he had brought over from the Continent, but out of the visit grew another plot which took two years to hatch. This was the Elibank Plot.

The objective of the Elibank Plot, named after one of its instigators, Alexander Murray of Elibank, was to seize the royal family in London and stage another uprising in the Highlands while Charles went to London to 'remain incognito in the house of Viscountess Primrose'.[2] During his stay in London he converted from Roman Catholicism to the Church of England in the expectation that it would help his chances when the coup took place.

Unfortunately for the Jacobites there was a spy at the heart of their plotting, Young Glengarry, known as 'Pickle the Spy', who betrayed the plan, and as a result the plotters were exposed and Archie Cameron, Lochiel's brother, was executed.

Lady Primrose was deeply involved in the organizing of the Elibank Plot and visited Europe in 1752 to finalize details. Unfortunately Charles chose that very moment to sack the man she trusted most, and who knew all the English Jacobites' secrets. In those days, when money bought information very easily, this was the most alarming thing that could happen, and it certainly played an important part in Lady Primrose's disillusionment with Prince Charlie.

After he returned to France the Prince was as concerned about the succession as he was about the plot. It seemed more urgent than ever for him to find a wife, and since he was now a Protestant his marital thoughts revolved round Germany again and a dowry of troops and armaments to support an invasion rather than money. He offered his hand to the daughter of the Duke of Daremberg in return for a dowry of twelve thousand men,[3] but when that came to nothing his thoughts turned again to Frederick the Great's daughter.

This time Frederick met him and, while still resisting the Prince as a son-in-law, he did promise to give thought to supporting another Jacobite rising.[4] Charles was very satisfied: help for the Cause was every bit as acceptable as the promise of a bride. Getting back to St James's was the hard part of his plan, and finding a wife would be easy once he was there.

Women had their place in the longer-term political scheme of things, but Prince Charlie needed immediate sexual satisfaction. He still required mistresses, and in the wake of the Talmont affair, there were new mistresses, all unnamed and none of any lasting interest to him except one. He confessed that he was beside himself and dying for this particular unknown amour.[5] He needed these women, but realized, as political intrigues moved faster and his own paranoia grew, that the women he bedded might prove to be dangerous Hanoverian spies or in the hire of would-be assassins.

He racked his brains and out of the past came one name – a girl who had promised to come to him if ever he needed her. She was Clementine Walkinshaw, whom he had met six years before at Bannockburn House at the beginning of 1746. He had not exchanged so much as the scrape of a pen with her since then, but that did not stop Charles.

It would be nice to feel able to say that he remembered her with affection and longed to have her with him again, but knowing Charles Stuart, it is much more likely that his decision to send for Clementine at that juncture was a matter of pure expediency and love had little to do with it. He heard she was on the Continent and he wanted her: and when Charles wanted something he had to have it now, and it had to be his totally.

Clementine had been in France or the Low Countries for many months at the time the Prince started to search for her. Much against the wishes of her family she had decided to enter one of those religious houses for the daughters of nobility on the Continent and had prepared a long detailed birthbrief to confirm that her pedigree was suitably genteel.[6] Thanks to that and the influence of a friend, she was promised entry into a religious house in the Low Countries. She left Scotland sometime in 1751, and possibly stayed at a convent in Boulogne, but it is important to note that she did not enter the religious order immediately.

Early the following year Charles moved from Lunéville to Ghent, now pretending to be the Chevalier William Johnson, and there he took 'a preti house and a room in it for a friend'.[7] He had heard that Clementine was in this part of the world and at once began to search for her.

If anyone could lead him to her, John William O'Sullivan, one of his loyal followers in the '45, could. O'Sullivan had been at Bannockburn in 1746 and knew Clementine well: he was now living in this region, too, and knew all the Jacobites of north-east France and Flanders. So Charles wrote to O'Sullivan asking him to help find 'Mrs. Clemi'.[8]

With typical Stuart obsessiveness that secrecy must be paramount, O'Sullivan was only to give the task of approaching Clementine to 'en absolute trusty Cervant' and she was to be ordered never to mention the matter to anybody. 'Burn this immediately,' he ordered O'Sullivan, but O'Sullivan did not – Louise de Montbazon would have smiled at that!

From Cambrai O'Sullivan replied on 29 May:

I can assure your Hs upon my word of honor I dont know what directions to glve to the bearer about her . . . Her lettre to me was from Dunkerque, where she gave me to understand, that if she had no account from you, y^t her intention was to go into a Convente.

O'Sullivan strongly advised against Charles's bringing Clementine to him in Ghent:

As to have her with you, I am afraid it wou'd be too dengereouse, as well for your Hs safety, as glory, in the present jouncture.[9]

That was a deliberate lie because, within two days of professing ignorance as to Clementine's whereabouts, O'Sullivan was able to pass on the Prince's demand to her in a letter. He may not have seen her in the very recent past, but obviously he had been in close touch with her not long before. As Clementine had decided not to enter the Convent of the Poor Clares at Gravelines or another she had talked about at Arras, he told her, 'It is now a question of your going to him, as the Person in question absolutely desires.'

He warned her darkly not to say too much to the messenger. 'You must not under any pretext whatever, confide in him as to the past nor talk to him abut the Person in question. You know, moreover, of what consequence it is both for you and for the Person you are going to see to keep as an inviolate secret everything that he may tell you,' The letter was long, rambling and, reading between the lines, far from enthusiastic about her joining Charles.[10]

Surely O'Sullivan was holding back. Another three days on – on 3 June – he was still telling the Prince he did not know where Clementine was, but said he was sure she would abandon the convent for him even if she had taken her first vows.[11]

The ever-devious Charles could not simply bring his new mistress the forty miles or so to Ghent from Douai where she was, but ordered her to travel to Paris from where she would be brought to him. Obediently, Clementine agreed and Charles began to make arrangements.

First he asked Madame de Vassé to escort her, but the strait-laced Vassé flatly refused, much to the Prince's annoyance. 'In spite of your repugnance I command you to carry out what I have ordered, taking every precaution possible,' he hectored.[12] But Madame was adamant and the request cost him his friendship with the woman who had given him a hideout in Paris for so long. She would have nothing more to do with him thereafter.

His next choice of escort brought equally disastrous results: when he ordered Henry Goring to bring Clementine to him, Goring resigned rather than become involved. Such commissions, he told the Prince, 'are for the worst of men,' then added contemptuously, 'but if you are determined to have her, let Mr Sullivan bring her to you'.[13] In a subsequent letter he spoke out even more forcefully. He told

Charles in it that 'the man who keeps a mistress is indeed not so much liable to censure, but surely he that procures her for him . . . is no better than a pimp'.[14]

Strong language, but no stronger than that used by other leading followers of the Cause. Goring's abandoning of Charles was just the first of a trickle that became a stream of defections in the wake of Clementine's arrival. Almost every Jacobite hated her with astonishing vehemence: because her sister, Catherine, was employed by the Dowager Princess of Wales, they were all certain that she was a Hanoverian spy. When the Elibank Plot failed soon after she joined him they needed no more proof – Clementine Walkinshaw was passing on information to London. It took more than a century and painstaking work by Andrew Lang to discover that the real spy was not Clementine at all, but young MacDonald of Glengarry, the notorious Pickle the Spy.

The Jacobites' distrust of Clementine hardened to hatred, whose intensity is difficult to explain unless the theories, which follow, on subsequent events are right.[15]

Lady Primrose became especially bitter about Clementine, but gradually her anger turned on Charles for defying his English Jacobite friends for this woman who, she was convinced, had caused the Elibank Plot to fail and Archie Cameron to be executed. The years did not calm her anger: Alexander Murray wrote to the Prince in September 1758:

I learn that that infamous creature Lady Primrose has propagated over the whole kingdom that you are a drunkard. The only and most effectual way to convince your friends of the falsity and malice of her villainous lyes is to drink very little while these gentlemen are with you. In case any of them should propose drinking for God's sake evite it yourself, because your character and success depend upon the report of these gentlemen upon their return to London.[16]

In only a few years Charles managed to destroy the deep loyalty and generous support of one of the women who had most admired him when he was the bonnie prince at the head of the Jacobite army.

To the end of her life in 1773, Lady Primrose gave the Cause no further support.

Unaware of the effect her joining the Prince was having on the Cause, Clementine obediently made her way to Paris and there was handed a letter, which was a cold command rather than an invitation from a lover, demonstrating that from its first day the relationship was devoid of the beautiful passion that illuminated the affair with Louise de Montbazon. His instructions stated starkly:

I hereby absolutely forbid you, from this instant forward, never to put pen to Paiper for anything whatsoever, and neither Sr John (O'Sullivan) or anybody whatsoever must know ye Least thing about you or what passes betwixt us, under pain of incurring for ever my displeasure.[17]

The letter was unsigned. Against that unpromising background, around midsummer of 1752, Charles received Clementine into a house he had taken to share with her in the rue des Vernopele in Ghent. In spite of endless financial worries she brought him happiness there for a while although there was no real love between them, but he did show her kindness at times. Pickle the Spy – no friend of either Charles or Clementine – wrote the following spring that 'the Pretender keeps her well and seems very fond of her'.[18]

By the time Pickle passed that judgement, Clementine was pregnant and the relationship was changing. They moved to a house in Liège during the summer of 1753, presumably to provide more space to live as a family when the baby arrived, but their existence together continued to be a succession of moans and threats from the leaders of the Cause on both sides of the English Channel.

They still feared that Clementine was a spy, or that her presence might betray his whereabouts to Hanoverian assassins, so they urged him to send her to a convent, where she could remain his mistress if he still wished to have her. But they wanted rid of her at all costs and said so more stridently week by week.

Charles was as determined as they were – no, more so. No one would dictate to him, so Clementine stayed. The only concession he made to their fears for his safety was to be constantly on the move, between Flanders, France and Germany, still in disguise and still under false names.

Sometime in October 1753 Clementine gave birth to a daughter, who was baptized in the Church of Sainte Marie des Fonts, Liège, on 29 October, but the baptism was not entered in the parish register until some years later when it was added as a note on a flyleaf:

The year of our Lord 1753 was baptized in our parish church of the Blessed Virgin Marie des Fonts in the town of Liège, daughter of the noble Seigneur William Johnson and the noble lady Charlotte Pitt. The godfather was the noble Seigneur Georges Frimenten, proxy for the noble Seigneur Andrew Giffard.[19]

Charlotte later claimed in a petition to Louis XVI that her birth gave the greatest joy to her father, but it is doubtful whether he was actually present at the baptism: in view of the fact that he had abjured the Catholic faith only the year before it seems extremely unlikely that he approved of the ceremony at all. Compton Mackenzie suggests that the first serious quarrel between the couple seems to have been over the baptism of Charlotte,[20] but the two were quarrelling almost from the day they came together again.

The quarrel over the baptism was serious, and displayed Prince Charlie at his most despicable and meanest. Within weeks of Charlotte's birth he issued instructions that all his Catholic servants were to be dismissed, then he issued the incredible order:

My mistress had behaved so onworthely that she had put me quit(e) out of all patience, and as she is a Papist to, I discard her also.[21]

Charles knew that, unlike Talmont, Clementine hadn't two pennies to rub together, so he added a postscript to the letter just to rub in her dependence on him:

She told me she had friends that would maintain her, so that, after such a declaration, and other impertinences, makes me abandon her, I hereby desire you to find out who her friends are, that she may be delivered into their hands. Daniel [O'Brien who had been so useful during the Louise affair] is to conduct her to Paris.[22]

This was Charles Stuart beyond his most callous and meanest and it requires some explanation. One must ask, did the Jacobites know some dark secret related to her life before she came to live with Charlie in Ghent?

There were persistent rumours about other children about the time she joined the Prince and later: it was said that Lady Primrose, when she visited the Continent in 1752 in connection with the Elibank Plot, took a child of Charles's back to England with her and arranged for her education. Did the Prince have children other than Louise's son and Clementine's daughter around this time, and was there even an earlier one, perhaps the Finsthwaite Princess?

Daft stories abounded about children Charles begat by Clementine, just like those myths about those he was supposed to have fathered in Scotland during the '45. One of his daughters was even supposed to have been marooned on a desert island called Campbell Island far to the south of the southern tip of South Island in New Zealand. This weaves together threads of truth and fiction to add up to a total nonsense, which would not take in anyone. It names the mother as Meg Wilkinshaw whom he met during the 'memorable festivities' at Holyrood, and was thought to be an English spy:

The suspicions which attached to the mother now fell upon the daughter, and the Jacobites entered into a plot to carry her out of the country. In order to attain this they entered into a compact with a seaman named Stewart, after whom Stewart Island was called. The story goes that she was carried on board Stewart's vessel, and he, sailing with her, marooned her upon Campbell Island, where she was left for years to drag out a miserable existence.

Another version of the same tale has the girl of Scottish extraction but born in France, who unwisely claimed the throne of

England. To get rid of her, 'she was smuggled on board a Dundee whaler with an attendant, and banished to some unknown island, being heard of no more by the world'.[23]

The stories have all the hallmarks of tales told by the Dundee whalers during the long southern winter nights!

Charles swore on oath at Florence in March 1785 that he never had a child other than Charlotte – a declaration which must be taken with a large pinch of salt in the light of the Montbazon son and the child, supposedly born in 1752, documented by Leo Berry in *The Young Pretender's Mistress*, who was taken in by Lady Primrose and brought up in England.[24]

Charles remained very touchy on this point – touchy enough to make the Florence declaration years later. And, as if to ensure that nobody else's child would be foisted off on to him, he demanded at the time of his daughter's birth that 'a marque be put on ye Child if I part with it – I am pushed to ye last point and so wont be cagioled any more'.[25]

Did Charles discover that his new mistress had had an earlier liaison in Britain or on the Continent before she joined him? And was it that liaison that Jacobites on the British side of the English Channel feared?

If the earlier relationship theory is true, this would be a reason why her family were so silent about the meeting with Charles at Bannockburn and reacted so strongly to her leaving Scotland. She was beautiful, eligible, yet had not married, and now she said she was going to take up a life of meditation in a religious house. Her family could have disliked the idea of Clementine withdrawing from the world, or perhaps they feared that she would take up with Charles Stuart or someone else. Whatever their reason – and it must have been a strong one – they cut her off from that moment, and for as long as her mother lived none of them communicated with her.

A number of hints nudge us towards the name of the man she took up with when she went to France in 1751. When Charles asked Goring to escort Clementine from Paris, Goring cuttingly replied, 'if you are determined to have her, let Mr Sullivan bring her to you.'[26] Yet O'Sullivan told the Prince he didn't know where Clementine was even after he had sent her a letter in which he told her, '*You must not under any pretext whatever, confide in him as to the past.*'[27] Was the secret she had to keep that she had been O'Sullivan's lover?

Further circumstantial evidence of this may be found in the fact that the Irishman who had followed so loyally all the way from Rome in 1744, suddenly was pushed out of favour by the Prince. He was then listed among the Prince's bitterest enemies.

Apart from Lord Elcho, who said in so many words that Clementine became the Prince's mistress at Bannockburn, the only person who actually accused O'Sullivan of being Clementine's lover before the Prince sent for her is the double-agent, Oliver MacAllester, and he is an unreliable witness. MacAllester said, 'Sullivan had been the person who had introduced Miss Walkinshaw to the young pretender when in Scotland, after having first had a previous intimacy and acquaintance with her himself: and that he had since been the cause of her being brought over to France to be his companion. This was the accusation privately whispered about against Sullivan, with this addition, that he himself had boasted of it in private to some of his intimates.' However, O'Sullivan always denied the charge.[28]

But, all the evidence is circumstantial and, as Frank McLynn points out, 'It is important to be clear that this is a judgement on the basis of probability rather than on the stronger criterions of "beyond all reasonable doubt". Cast-iron evidence on this point simply does not exist.'[29]

Perhaps not, but Charles never contacted O'Sullivan again after the '45 until he sought Clementine, and the Irishman was the person Charles thought might know her whereabouts.

From that moment the Prince's treatment of Clementine (never princely) was nothing short of disgraceful. He could have sent her away, but he didn't, because that was what the Jacobites, especially the English followers, wanted, and he would not give in to their threats or demands. No one 'gave him laws', and if he wanted to keep a mistress he would do so.

The years that followed were particularly difficult for Charles in his affairs of state: he was perennially short of money, he always had great difficulties with his followers, and relations with his father sank to a new low as Charles manoeuvred for power and James denied it to him. As for the French, they were as fickle as ever, promising an invasion when the Seven Years War broke out, but in the end failing to deliver that promise because the British Navy destroyed the French fleet at Quiberon Bay on 20 November 1759.

The British became more active than ever in trying to track him down to his hideouts and as a result Charles was constantly on the move. What should have been stable years devoted to a settled family life turned into a nomadic existence, without roots, without friends and without money.

For Clementine, constant partings had to be endured, as well as new homes in places where she felt unwanted, and in the background all the time both had to face the failure of all Prince Charlie's hopes and plans. Sometimes he took Clementine with him on his travels, sometimes Charlotte went as well, but as often as not he left them behind.

Such a situation would have tested any family relationship, but in the case of Charles and Clementine, where he already had no respect for his partner, it proved a disastrous culmination of ten years of frustrated hopes.

Charles lost control of his life and of the Cause as well, as he descended into a blurred abyss of alcoholism. Every day started badly and went downhill from there until he slid in a drunken stupor in which he flew into fits of rage with Clementine. In this state he could not even have been the sexually satisfying partner he had been with Louise or Madame de Talmont – the Walkinshaw relationship became a cruel charade.

When the Prince took to solitary drinking the English Jacobites blamed his mistress for not stopping him and when she joined him they carped that she was as bad as he was. Clementine just couldn't win. The two had battles royal in private and in public and the whole Jacobite world eavesdropped with disgust, but it is hard to tell which of the stories they reported are false and which true since many were spread by people like Lord Elcho who was no friend of the Prince.

It was Elcho, for example, who reported that Charles gave his mistress as many as fifty beatings a day.[30] Elcho, too, recounted the often-told tale of how Charlie became so jealous that he surrounded her bed with chairs hung with little bells which were set ringing if anyone approached her bed during the night.

Charles's cruelty to Clementine was bad enough and did not need such stories.

The only thread of happiness in all that dark cheerless tapestry was the child, Charlotte: Charles loved her very dearly and constantly spoiled her and worried when she was unwell. He called her *Pouponne* and described her as 'my only comfort in my misfortunes'.[31] Clementine loved the child too, yet the sad fact is that loving her did nothing to bring them more closely together.

The year 1754 was to be a terrible one for the Prince: he was chronically short of money and spent much time quarrelling with his supporters, particularly the Earl Marischal who finally abandoned the Prince. In the spring the Hanoverians were on his trail at Liège, so he took Clementine and Charlotte to Paris, where he quarrelled with his mistress in front of their hosts, and publicly in the Bois de Boulogne as well.[32] Naturally, Paris soon discovered the identity of this strange couple and they had to move on. In September 1754 Mr and Mrs Thompson and their child arrived in Basle and settled in at the *Auberge des Trois Rois* while they sought find somewhere permanent to stay. Apart from finding Switzerland expensive, he liked the place well enough.

Here he met – and lost – another long-standing supporter, Macpherson of Cluny, a Highland chief who had sheltered him for a week in a hideout known as Cluny's Cage during his flight after Culloden. Charlie had commanded Cluny to come to him because he believed the chief had some of the gold that was hidden at Loch Arkaig during the '45, and Charles needed money. Unfortunately, Macpherson had none of the treasure and the Prince took umbrage when the chief gave him some good advice on how he should behave especially where drink was concerned.

On top of all this trouble, the Paris banker, Waters, unfortunately stirred up trouble in Rome, by telling James about Clementine. 'There is a woman with the Prince who is the author of all this mischief,' Waters told the king, 'and unless she be got away from him without loss of time, it is only too apparent that HRH's reputation will be made very black over all Great Britain.'[33]

James, who knew only vaguely about Clementine until then, at once demanded to be told whether the woman's name was Walkinshaw and if it was true that there was a child. He also demanded to be told where they were living, for the court at Rome had no idea that the Prince was now in Basle.

Waters realized he had betrayed his master's confidence and apologized to Charles. But he did not give away the Prince's whereabouts. Fortunately James took ill at that juncture, so was unable to follow the matter up any further, and Charles was able to move on, back to Liège, which at least had the merit of being less costly to live in than Basle.

But James did not give up: he spent several years trying to persuade his son to abandon Clementine and marry. To his credit (and probably for all the wrong reasons) Charles refused. The upshot was simply a greater rift than ever between Charles and Rome – indeed it was the end of their relationship.

Soon Charles had a new will o' the wisp to chase, and he was on the road to Paris again. With the Seven Years War raging, he heard tales of a French expedition to England and was determined to be sure it would not suffer the same fate as previous French efforts on behalf of the Cause. The French did not want him involved and went their own way without him – to the naval disaster at Quiberon Bay, which ended that particular hope for the Cause.

It was time to move again and this time Charles and Clementine settled in the last home they had together: the Château de Carlsbourg, near Sedan, a house rented from his uncle, the Duc de Bouillon, father of Louise of the raging passion a decade before. One can only marvel at the audacity of Charlie to bring his current mistress to a house owned by the Bouillons: it is impossible even to try to understand how he could face the uncle, who had treated him like a father when he needed comfort in 1745, and whom he reviled when the Louise affair burst into the open.

Charles and Clementine found no more happiness at Carlsbourg than there had been at any of the other places where they had lived

– one hesitates to call them homes. Clementine's life continued to be the hell it always was, and her only relief came when he was away, which was often since Charles continued to flit from place to place, vainly trying to promote his Cause. But all his efforts in that direction merely tore it further apart.

His father continued to worry and sent Andrew Lumisden from Rome to try to sort things out. On the subject of Clementine his instructions were clear:

> You will explain to the Prince the comfort and satisfaction it has been to me to hope, from some accounts I have received that Mrs Walkinshaw is, or will be soon, separated from him. This is an article on which I had thought myself obliged to have writ to the Prince long since, had I thought my writing would have had any effect; but that particular for some time past was become so public and was of so much prejudice to his honour and interest as well as to his conscience that it cannot but be extremely satisfactory to me on all accounts to have reason to hope that he may have at last taken on that head a resolution becoming himself.[34]

The idea that his son was about to get rid of his mistress was wishful thinking on the king's part, as was the belief that Lumisden would have the slightest success in persuading the Prince to abandon his mistress. When Lumisden returned to Rome to report failure James took to his bed, too ill even to protest.

When he did recover sufficiently to reply on 29 May 1759, it was clear that he still did not understand his son. 'It is really time to finish this scene, which does you little honour about her and does still more prejudice to your honour,' he hectored, going on to add, 'If you approve it, I will undertake to place her in some country convent in France, where I will maintain her and her child decently, and where I will answer that she shall not go to any parlour, much less out of the house, and you will be no more troubled about her.'[35]

Charles did not even bother to reply.

He was now drinking more heavily than ever and the arguments with his mistress turned more and more to blows and beatings. Every disappointment, every wrong perpetrated by anyone, was blamed on Clementine and she was punished. At times she began to fear for her life, not that he might deliberately murder her, but that one of his drunken attacks might end in death.

At last she decided she must get out of the terrible web in which she was trapped. But how? She remembered Lumisden's visit and no doubt knew of James's suggestion that she should be put into a convent and, as things now stood, that appeared to be an acceptable solution since it would give her a refuge and provide an education for her daughter.

Clementine contacted the king in Rome, McLynn claims, through the notorious and unreliable Father Kelly who was no longer a friend of the Prince and was motivated by revenge.[36] James was delighted to help get rid of the mistress who had caused so much trouble so, after suggesting that it should be done with the Prince's assent if possible, proposed that Clementine and her daughter should go into 'one of the better convents in Paris'.[37]

On the night of 22 July 1760, while Charles was away from Bouillon, she took her child and fled. On his return Charles found a note, clearly written under terrible stress, telling him she had gone, but not where:

Your Royalle Highness cannot be surprised at my having taken my partty when you consider the repeated bad treatment I have matte with these eight years past, and the dealy risque of loosing life, not been able to bear any longer such hardships, my health been altered by them has obliged me at last to take this Desperate step of removing from your Royalle Highness with my child, which nothing but the fear of my life would ever have made me undertake any thing without your knowledge. Your Royalle Highness is to great and just when you reflect, not to think that you have push'd me to the greatest extremitie and that there is no one women in the world that would have suffer'd so long as what I have done, however it shall never hinder me from having for your Royalle persone all the attachment and respect and I hope in time coming by my conduct to merit your protection and friendship for me and my child, I put myself under the care of providence, which I hope wont abbandone me as my intentions are honest and that I never will doe a dirty action for the wholle world. I quite my dearest prince with the greatest regreat and shall allways be miserable if I don't hear of his welfair and happiness. May God Almighty bless and preserve him and prospere all his undertakings which is the ernest wish of one how will be till Death, my dearest prince.

your most faithfull and most
obedient Humble Servant

Clementina Walkinshaw

P.S: There is one thing I most assure your R.H. that you may not put the blame on innocent people, that there is not one soul, either in the house or out of it that knew or has given me the smalest help in this undertaking, nor anybody that ever you knew or saw. [38]

Clementine had been careful to absolve all staff at Bouillon from blame and made only a passing reference to Charlotte, who, she knew, was the apple of her father's eye – no regret at taking his *Pouponne* away, no acknowledgement of the loss the child would be.

Charles was beside himself with anger and would see no one at Bouillon. His fury was not because his mistress had left him, but at the loss of his six-year-old daughter whom he loved, and at the fact that here was someone 'giving him laws.' He sent his faithful servant John Stewart at once with a letter to Abbé John Gordon, Principal of the Scots College in Paris, threatening to burn down every convent in Paris to find his daughter. Although he was too upset to write the letter himself, he added a postscript in his own hand. 'I take this affaire so much to heart that I wass not able to write what is here above. Shall be in ye greatest affliction untill I greet back ye childe, which was my only comfort in my misfortunes.'[39]

Gordon replied at once to tell the Prince he had seen 'the young Miss with her mother'; he had found them somewhere to stay and had 'expostulated with her [Clementine] about her elopement', but was told flatly that she would not be returning. She had no money and asked the Abbé for some, but 'by the greatest good luck I had none in my pocket'. He refused to help her to find a place in a convent on the grounds the father's authorization would be necessary.[40] As Clementine's biographer, Leo Berry, comments, 'It was really an unscrupulous untruth. Charlotte was an illegitimate child, not even formally acknowledged as his by the Prince – as both Clementine and Charlotte were to complain in later years – and thus Clementine alone stood *in loco parentis*.'[41]

When Gordon returned to Clementine's lodgings next day he discovered she had gone – she was astute enough to know that Gordon was likely to side with the Prince. At Charles's request the Abbé instituted a search through the Duc de Belle-Isle and the Paris police and Charles issued a description of the mother and daughter, which give us an excellent idea of their appearance at this time:

> The mother is about 40 years of age, fair, of normal height, freckled, her face thin. The child, aged 7 or 8, very fair, with round, full face, large eyes, a rather snub, plump and strong for her age. They took the road to Paris, but it is believed they may have gone on to Flanders.[42]

He was wrong about the departure for Flanders: Clementine was still in Paris and the Prince's valet, John Stewart, actually found her, but she told him she would rather make away with herself than go back. As for the child, she 'would be cut to pieces sooner than give her up'. At 10.30 on the night of 30 July, she sent for a coach and made no objection when Stewart asked if he might accompany her. They drove for a bit, but suddenly the coach stopped alongside a coach and four, and two other men appeared; Clementine changed to the other coach, but when Stewart tried to join her he was told roughly, 'Go about your business if you have any.' Clementine and Charlotte were driven off and Stewart tried to follow but lost sight of them. The following day he reported all this to the Prince.[43]

Day after day the search continued, wanted posters were put up, the police made enquiries everywhere, but Clementine was not to be found. Charles was still beside himself with rage, and compiled lists of everybody he could think of who might help: then he drew up lists of places his daughter might be. He even winkled out O'Sullivan, who professed to know no more than anyone else about the fugitives, and Charles railed even more.

Everybody in the Jacobite circle was drawn into the hunt and every possible place searched – Nice, Venice, Flanders, to no avail. Lord Elcho, who later had the effrontery to pretend to be Clementine's friend, was cruelly offhand and advised the Prince. 'Why bother about the woman, take another.'[44]

Suddenly the hunt was over: Clementine and Charlotte were still in Paris, in the Convent of the Visitation de Sainte Marie in the rue du Bac. And she was under the protection of Charles's father.

Then it all came out; James had known all about the planned flight from Bouillon for months before it happened and had not only assisted in the arrangements, but had taken over financial responsibility for the mother and child. The French also had obviously been aware of what was happening before it became known to the Prince, but had done nothing since it was what the Jacobite sovereign wanted and his wish was paramount.

On learning this Charles collapsed completely, with a total physical and mental breakdown: he caught a severe cold, then an attack of fever, haemorrhoids, and 'une plénitude de bile' followed.[45] He could not sleep, he hardly touched food, and he even sobered up for a while. He brooded alone at Bouillon, refusing to answer letters, and he would see only a few of his very closest associates.

The humiliation of Clementine's leaving him and the loss of his beloved Charlotte was as devastating as those other great traumas of his life – the decision to retreat at Derby, Culloden, the duplicity of his father and brother over Henry's acceptance of a cardinal's hat, and his own arrest and expulsion from France in 1748. It was also the end of any hope of reconciliation with his father.

Charles did not care about Clementine – it was the manner of her going, in her own time and taking their child, that hurt. Charles was Prince of Wales, Clementine was merely a mistress, and it was princes who decided when their mistresses were to be thrown aside, not the other way round. He had ended the liaison with Louise de

Montbazon and Marie de Talmont, and he could not accept the humiliation of being rejected by Clementine Walkinshaw.

Clementine was a name that rang like a knell through the Stuart family: his father had been abandoned by a Clementina, and now he was repudiated by one. It was all too much.

Alongside humiliation ran sorrow at the loss of his daughter: Charlie genuinely grieved for her and would have liked her back, but he knew that without the backing of his father and the French that was unlikely. He soon resumed his drinking and lived on alone at the Château de Carlsbourg, virtually a recluse and wallowing in his sorrow. He was no longer any threat and even his most ardent followers must have found it hard to believe the story that when George III came to the throne, Charles travelled to London and secretly sat through the coronation service in Westminster Abbey. Charles Stuart hardly ever left his 'prison' at Carlsbourg for more than five years after Clementine Walkinshaw left him.

He never saw his mistress again although he did communicate with her during the dying days of his life. She took the title, Countess of Albestroff, and with her daughter lived in near penury for twenty-four years in various convents in or near Paris, subsisting on the charity of 10,000 livres a year from King James in Rome, and after he died, the lesser generosity of Cardinal Henry, who paid them 5,000 livres annually. Charles not only gave them nothing, but prevented them from obtaining a pension from France by flatly refusing to write a letter in their favour when he was told that with such a letter the French would come to their aid.

FIFTEEN

A WIFE OR A MISTRESS?

A rumour has been started by enemies of the family . . . that the King, my brother, was actually married to a certain lady, and which he believes when she hears of it, she will schiver to imagine that any body could think her capable of such an intrigue, and of such a supposition, the falsehood of which no body can know better than herself.

Letter from Henry, Duke of York, to Abbé Gordon, written on 16 February 1767.[1]

Clementine Walkinshaw and her daughter, Charlotte, settled into a life of genteel poverty in the Paris convent where they lived as pensioners of the King over the Water.

Towards the end of the 1760s Clementine began to call herself the Countess of Albestroff, a title which Sir John Coxe Hippesley said had been conferred on her by the Holy Roman Emperor. It seems a reasonable thing to have happened in the light of the fact that Albestroff, which is actually in the Moselle area of France, then belonged to the Empire, and Clementine's father had been ambassador to Vienna at the time James's fiancée, Clementina Sobieska, was imprisoned there on her way to Italy to marry the Pretender. It is a good story, but, alas, no reference is to be found in the archives in Vienna to such a title being conferred on her.

Charlotte, in one of several *mémoires* to the French King during the early 1770s,[2] refers to her mother as *actuellement connue à Paris sous le nom de Comtesse d'Albestroff* – note she was not the *Countess d'Albestroff*, but was *known as the Countess*.

At this time Clementine had already been using the title for some six years and her daughter had explained to her father in a letter dated 8

October 1769 that they had been forced to use a foreign name in the convent where they were residing.

'In the convent where we are living we have been obliged to take a foreign name. Mama goes under that of Madame d'Albestroff,' she told her father.

Surely Clementine could not just have 'taken' a title just at her own whim. Leo Berry in *The Young Pretender's Mistress* offers a very plausible explanation. Some religious houses had authority to confer titles, he explains, and Albestroff, which had recently passed into French ownership, was subject to the Bishop of Metz.

'It is not impossible,' Berry explains, 'that the authority for the revival of this title (Comte d'Albestroff) lay with the bishopric of Metz, possibly on the representation of Clementine's good friend the Archbishop of Paris.' But he adds carefully, 'This, however, is nothing more than conjecture.'[3]

Conjecture or not, Clementine took the title to pursue her claim for financial help from France at a time when she was desperately short of money. It was not merely to add gentility to the penury under which she and Charlotte were living, but actually as part of the plan to relieve that poverty. The title was accepted by everyone in her circle throughout her life, but there was doubt about it right up to the end of her life. When she died at Fribourg on 27 November 1802, she was described in the burials register as 'Lady Clementine Walkinshaw' who had resided in the city under the title of Countess of Albestroff.

The title was part of Clementine Walkinshaw's constant fight for the financial support due to her and her daughter. She and Charlotte had managed to make ends meet, but not more, thanks to the allowance which James Stuart gave them.

Then the year 1766 changed everything: James III was dead, Charles III was king (even if the Pope refused to recognize him as anything other than Count of Albany), but he was unmarried and his heir to the crowns of Great Britain was his brother Henry – unless of course it could be proved that Prince Charlie and Clementine Walkinshaw had been married and their daughter, Charlotte was the legitimate heir to all the Stuart and Sobieski inheritance including the Stuart thrones.

The Stuarts all approached the problem differently: for old King James it was an unfortunate blot on the family and the respect which it had enjoyed from its supporters. Charles simply didn't care whether Clementine and Charlotte lived or died except that they were an impediment to his matrimonial prospects, for how could he take a wife if he already had a woman claiming to be his lawful wife? He approached the problem as he did all situations that were beyond his power to alter – he just pretended Clementine and Charlotte did not exist and would not have their names mentioned in his presence. Waters, the family banker in Paris, was instructed by Henry to mention Clementine only when necessary and in letters addressed to him, marked 'X', 'for she must never be named to his majesty'.[4]

As for Henry, his problem was prudery: he could not bear the shame of the very existence of his brother's mistress and daughter – it was not seemly for an eminent cardinal of the Roman Catholic Church to have such a skeleton threatening to be brought out of the family cupboard. Yet he could not bring himself to cut the mother and daughter off completely as his brother had done.

When the old king died the allowance he had paid to Clementine died with him, for Charles had no intention of contributing a penny piece to mistress or daughter. That left Henry to provide a pension of 5,000 livres a year, half the amount his father had given them, and just about enough to enable them to go on living very modestly in their convent. But there his generosity stopped, and there was a price to be paid for it.

Gossip had started among enemies – and friends of the Cause too – who were curious to know what would happen when the new King over the Water died, leaving only his celibate brother as his heir. It was a perfectly fair question, but soon it began to turn on the question of whether Charlotte might be able to inherit if it could be proved that her parents had in fact been married.

Clementine herself was blamed for spreading the story and indeed she may well have genuinely believed that she was Charles Stuart's wife under Scottish law.

Henry 'schivered' at such a thought. Apart from losing his inheritance and the right to his British kingdoms, it would be a dreadful embarrassment to him as a cardinal, so he took immediate steps to scotch the rumours.

The king's secretary, Andrew Lumisden, was instructed to order John Waters, the family banker in Paris, to go to Clementine and make her sign a declaration stating that she had never been married to Charles Stuart. On 9 March, Clementine duly signed:

> Whereas I, Clementine Walkinshaw, a native of Scotland, has heard a report spread about that Charles, heretofore Prince of Wales and now the Third of that name King of Great Britain, etc. is married to me, grounded on the connection the public think the said Prince now King had formerly with me: I, the before mentioned Clementine Walkinshaw, do voluntarily and on my oath declare before God my Creator and before the here subscribing witness, Mr John Waters, standing so at my request, that such a report of marriage, or anything relative to the least tendency of that kind, is void of foundation: and that I never gave the least room, either by word or writing to such a falsehood, spread abroad by enemies to me, I suppose, as likewise to the said King Charles the Third, my sovereign. And I do likewise further declare, by the most solemn oath here already taken, that I will if necessary, or if required, do everything, sign any public instrument, or give whatever authentic proofs possible, to confirm this my hearty and voluntary declaration, in order to wipe away any injury to me, formed by a report, impossible however to gain the least credit to any reflecting mind. All of which I write in my own hand, and here sign at Paris, March the 9th 1767.
>
> Clementine Walkinshaw.

Waters added confirmation that Clementine had written the document in her own hand and put her name to it:

> The above declaration was wrote and signed by Mrs Walkinshaw in my presence March the 9th 1767
>
> Jn Waters[5]

The declaration was mean, offensive and there is no evidence that Clementine ever claimed publicly to be Charles's wife. The affidavit of March 1767 was certainly not 'wrote and signed' voluntarily and Waters was putting before her the cardinal's pompous words. It must have embarrassed him to stand there blackmailing the poor woman with the threat of losing the only income she and her daughter had if she did not do as was ordered from Rome.

Even the opening words, describing her as a native of Scotland, were carefully designed to take away all the standing she possessed as a member of a family of quality. The document was a nonsense: Clementine might never have been married to Prince Charlie, but neither he nor she could say (as she had to admit in that document) that they had not been involved in 'anything relative to the least tendency of that kind'. Little Charlotte was proof of intimacy if not of marriage.

As if Clementine's humiliation in having to put her name to such a declaration were not enough, she was then compelled to grovel and offer *to sign any public instrument* or provide whatever other 'authentic proofs' might be required in the future.

Henry's affidavit was a disgraceful piece of blackmail by a man who professed to be a Christian, and it was as shameful as anything his brother ever did. Henry Stuart could be every bit as unpleasant as his brother when he chose to.

Before the ink was properly dry on the paper, Clementine realized the enormity of the Cardinal's arrogance and she sat down and wrote to tell him that she had only signed it under threat and that she now repudiated it.[6] Fortunately Lumisden, who sympathized secretly with her, managed to smooth things over and she kept her small allowance, but with a firm warning that she must never leave the convent or try to bring herself to the notice of the king in Rome. Lumisden knew the risk he ran with regard to his own position by writing to her for he added to one of his letters, 'Did the King know that I had wrote to you, he would never pardon me.'[7]

Henry kept a close watch on Clementine and on 12 May told Waters it was useful to know what 'scames' she was up to and threatened to foil any attempts to get in touch with Charles. If she tried, he said, 'she would be left as to everything in the lurche, since I do not care one figue for all she can say or doe.'[8]

Why did Clementine try to rescind her declaration to Waters in 1767? She never explained that it was because she resented the cardinal's blackmail; on the other hand neither did she say it was from a genuine belief that in law she might be Charles Stuart's wife.

Clementine obviously considered she had some claim on Prince Charlie and, according to Lord Elcho and Sir John Coxe Hippesley she never hid the fact that she believed she was his wife. Hippesley wrote:

> I visited the Countess d'Albestrof . . . at Paris in a Convent, accompanied by Mr Andrew Stewart, a few days after the demolition of the Bastile, 1789. She then produced many letter of Prince Charles, evidently denoting their connection as man and wife.[9]

In the petitions which Charlotte sent to Louis XV and XVI pleading for financial support in the early 1770s, she suggested that her parents had been husband and wife, but it must be remembered that she was trying to put the strongest case possible to the French kings.

In the first of these *mémoires* she merely said that her mother 'belonged to one of the powerful families of Scotland' and had been 'treated by the Prince as his wife'.[10] In another she was bold enough to write that her mother 'had contracted a marriage with him [the Prince] in its regular forms', and that her father announced her birth 'as the fruit of a marriage which for important reasons he was obliged to keep concealed'.[11]

Yet another of her *mémoires* to the French king in 1774 – documents largely drafted by Clementine herself – she did refer to her mother as having 'well founded hopes of becoming wife of the Prince, having even always been treated by him in public as such, and realizing how advantageous this would be to Charlotte, his daughter, who according to the laws of Scotland ought to be considered by that alone as having the rights of a legitimate daughter.'[12]

Under the law of Scotland . . . were the key words of the first of those memoranda and the law of Scotland is quite clear on the question of irregular marriage.

Before the Reformation Scots law recognized the validity of three forms of irregular marriage, none of which involved any ecclesiastical formalities. These were:

Marriage *per verba de praesenti*, which took the form of a declaration by the parties that they took each other as husband and wife. The consent of the parties was sufficient to constitute the marriage, and the presence of an ordained priest or witnesses was not required.

The second was marriage *per verba de futuro subsequente copula*. This was a promise to marry at some future date followed by sexual intercourse on the faith of that promise. The intercourse was deemed to be the agreement to marry. Understandably the presence of a priest or witnesses was not required!

The third form was marriage by cohabitation with habit and repute. In this case the marriage was constituted by the tacit agreement of the parties to marry, that being presumed from a period of cohabitation with habit and repute that they were husband and wife.

All these forms continued to be recognized after the Reformation and the first two forms were only abolished by the Marriage (Scotland) Act of 1939. Marriage by cohabitation and repute still remains a valid method of constituting a marriage in Scotland.

Clementine and Charles certainly never made any declaration; nor was there likely to have been a promise to marry followed by sexual intercourse. The nearest they came to this latter form was Clementine's promise to come to him if he ever needed her. So the relationship did not fall within the first two forms.

What of the third?

Marriage by cohabitation and repute infers that because of their living together with habit and repute, there is a presumption in law that they have tacitly agreed to be married. As a result, they are married unless there is evidence that they never intended to be husband and wife. Normally in such a case an action would be raised for declarator of marriage in the Court of Session, but such an action is not needed to establish the marriage for the couple are married by virtue of the doctrine.

However, a number of requirements have to be satisfied:

They must live together – having sexual intercourse is not enough; cohabitation must be as husband and wife – mistress or housekeeper would not be enough, nor would Prince's loyal subject;
cohabitation must take place in Scotland;
it must be for long enough for the Court to infer that the parties had tacitly agreed to marry;
they must be generally reputed to be husband and wife;
they must be legally free to marry.

Charles and Clementine were both free to marry. They lived together as man and wife for eight years, they certainly had sexual intercourse which resulted in the birth of their daughter, Charlotte (accepted by the Prince as his), and he generally presented Clementine in public as his wife. The great impediment was the point that cohabitation had to take place in Scotland.

This was tested in law even at the very time when they were living together. In the case of *MacCullock* v. *MacCullock* (1759), cohabitation in the Isle of Man was held not to qualify, and again in 1801 in *Napier* v. *Napier*, cohabitation in Gibraltar was not accepted. In the Dysart Peerage Case in 1881 the House of Lords held that cohabitation had to be within 'the realm of Scotland'.

Their brief weeks – days even – together at Bannockburn could hardly have counted in Scots law as cohabitation within the realm. It would seem that the acceptable period has become briefer today than it used to be, and while ten months was not held to be long enough in 1909, six months was accepted in 1991. Charles and Clementine were together only for a matter of days, so even if they had satisfied all the other criteria it is unlikely that they could have been accepted as legally man and wife in 1746.[13]

The Prince made no promise of marriage and probably had no intention of taking Clementine Walkinshaw as his wife. He merely promised that if successful, she would have a place at court. In return she gave an undertaking that if Charles Stuart ever needed her she would come to him. There was not promise of marriage, or thought of it, on either side.

There was one further impediment to an irregular marriage: Clementine was a devout Roman Catholic and Charles, apart from his brief flirtation with the Church of England, lived and died within the Catholic Church as well. Whatever civil law said prior to the Reformation, the Church in the eighteenth century would not have countenanced such a marriage, Scottish fashion. It would not have been considered valid and Clementine would never have been accepted as Queen Clementine, nor Charlotte as a princess and heir to the throne.

The very fact that rumours of the marriage were rife was largely Prince Charlie's own fault: Charlotte was right in her *mémoires* to King Louis – he did treat Clementine as his wife. While they were together in Ghent and Liège they called themselves the Count and Countess de Johnson, and in Switzerland and at Bouillon, he presented her to everyone as his wife. Their daughter was even baptized as if she were a legitimate child of a wedded couple. When it suited him, Clementine was his wife – when it didn't, she was his mistress, or even just 'a woman who lived with me'.[14] And as regards Charlotte, when it pleased him she was 'my only comfort in my misfortunes',[15] but for more than twenty years he ignored her.

When her daughter was declared legitimate by her father and came to live with him during the last years of his life. Clementine was satisfied to forget whether Charles had ever been her legal husband or not, and to live quietly as the Countess of Albestroff. But the marriage was too important for Charlotte to let it go. She wanted more than to be declared legitimate by decree of the king; for her it was a matter of honour that she had been born legitimate.

Right up to 28 February 1788, a month after her father's death, she was still petitioning France to have the marriage confirmed. Her last plea stated categorically that a marriage took place in Scotland, 'according to the custom of the country', but since it had not followed the rites of the Roman Catholic Church the Prince believed he could then disregard it and he married the Princess of Stolberg in Italy.[16]

From then on, Charlotte became too ill to pursue her cause, which is a pity, for she had her father's fiery determination and, unlike him, was victorious in most of the causes for which she fought. She survived her father by less than two years, so never saw her parents' marriage recognized. Had she lived longer she might well have persuaded the world that she was the child of a legitimate union between the heir to the House of Stuart and the daughter of an old and distinguished family who had sacrificed her honour as well as her life for the bonnie prince.

When Charlotte joined her father in Florence in 1784 she lost no time in persuading her father to make some provision for Clementine, and the letter acknowledging receipt of the first six-monthly payment of 2,612 livres was dated 23 November – barely a month after Charlotte reached Florence.[17]

Charlotte was a faithful daughter and wrote regularly to her mother, more than a hundred letters in a single year. These told Clementine about her father, her cardinal uncle, life in Rome and always asking for reassurance that all was well with her. She always asked about the three children of her own liaison with the Archbishop of Bordeaux, whom she had left behind in Paris in the care of her mother.

After Charles's death, Charlotte's consuming interest was to obtain sufficient money to allow her mother to live comfortably, and she found a house for her which enabled her to leave the convent. But by that time the French Revolution had begun and Charlotte's last great effort was to get her mother safely out of Paris.

Clementine may not have had a virtuous life worthy of the genteel but reputable families of Barrowfield or Bannockburn; she may have been the mistress to another, or others, as well as Prince Charlie, and simply by her presence in his bed, she may have compromised herself and the Cause to which she was so devoted. Clementine lived on for fourteen years after Charles. Her daughter left her an annual pension of 15,000 francs for life and 50,000 francs to dispose of 'in favour of her necessitous relations' at her death. Henry, the executor of his niece's will duly paid the moneys, but that stopped at the French Revolution. For safety Clementine moved to Switzerland as her daughter had begged her to, and there she lived in poverty until her death at Fribourg towards the end of 1802.

Clementine's will, which can still be seen in the archives of Fribourg, testifies to her generous, pious character as well as to the sad loneliness of her later life, without her daughter and cut off from her roots in Scotland. She made small bequests to her physician, neighbour, servants and to the Capuchin fathers, her confessor and the poor of the town to pray for her, and bequeathed to Thomas Coutts, the London banker, 'my gold box, on which there is a medallion, on which is a woman under a weeping willow near a tower, as a token of his bounties to me.' Before assigning the residue of her estate to her servant, Pierre Couppey, she made one pathetic small bequest; 'To each of my relations, if I still have any alive at my death, in order to find them out: 1 louis.'[18] She had paid a high price for all she had given to Charles Stuart, suffering abuse when she was with him and lonely years without him, without the company of the daughter she loved, and cut off from her Scottish roots. Charles broke his long silence only towards the end of his life. On 6 January 1787, a year before his death he sent her a letter to which he added his last words to his Clementine in his own weak hand after it had been transcribed:

Soyer assurer que . . . je suis et serai votre bon ami.
Charles R[19]

Somehow it seems an inadequate epitaph to the eight hard-fought years Clementine Walkinshaw endured with him and the lifetime she spent in his shadow.

SIXTEEN

TRUMPING THE QUEEN OF HEARTS

The mould for any more casts of the Royal Stuarts has been broken, or what is equivalent to it, is now shut up in a convent of nuns under double lock and key of the Pope and the Cardinal York, out of reach of any dabbler who might foister in a spurious copy. Historians may now close the lives of that family, unless the Cardinal should become pope and that would only produce a short scene of ridicule.

Sir Horace Mann on the final phase of Prince Charlie's marriage to Louise of Stolberg.[1]

King Charles III drove into Rome on the evening of Thursday 23 January 1766 and as he alighted from the coach outside the Muti Palace in the Piazza di Santi Apostoli a small crowd shouted, '*Viva il rè.*' Alas, this was not a spontaneous welcome of the kind he had been accustomed to in Paris or even in Rome twenty-two years previously, before he last rode away from the *palazzo*. This was a mock welcome from a little claque organized by his brother for a mock king. Charles Stuart reigned as Charles III, by divine right sovereign of Scotland, England, and Ireland, only in his own mind: neither the man nor the title carried the authentic stamp of royalty any more.

Charles certainly was not in the mould of either of the two Charleses who had reigned before him, although people saw in him what they wanted to see. Sir William Hamilton passed on a not unflattering picture of the king in middle age given him by a female admirer:

As for his person, it is rather handsome, his face ruddy and full of pimples. He looks good-natured, and was overjoyed to see me – nothing could be more affectionately gracious . . . He appeared to me to be absorbed in melancholy thoughts, a good deal of distraction in his conversation and frequent brown studies.[2]

A supporter of the House of Hanover was less complimentary, but even she found something to admire in the new king:

The Pretender is naturally above middle size, but stoops excessively; he appears bloated and red in the face; his countenance is heavy and sleepy, which is attributed to his having given in to excess of drinking, but when a young man he must have been esteemed handsome. His complexion is of the fair tint, his eyes blue, his hair light brown, and the contour of his face a long oval; he is by no means thin, has a noble person, and a graceful manner . . . Upon the whole he has a melancholy mortified appearance.[3]

Charles wrote off to the kings of France and Spain and to the princes of Italy informing them of his accession, but none took any notice. As king he sought an audience of the Pope, but all that happened was His Holiness one night removed the royal Stuart arms from above the door of the Muti. His brother tried hard to lobby on his behalf, but it was useless: the papal authorities would no longer recognize the Stuarts as sovereigns of Britain.

It hardly mattered any more, but Charles's ascension to the throne was welcomed by Jacobites in Scotland, and some strange followers re-emerged out of his past, some of them probably unwelcome. Even the famous Jenny Cameron turned up in Rome to pay her compliments to her bonnie prince. Horace Mann heard of her visit and (prepared to think the worst of any friend of Prince Charlie) suggested that it was to ask for her pension to be continued by the new king. As she had no pension in the first place and she was perfectly well off, this is as unlikely as many of Mann's tales sent home from Florence.

Mann wrote, 'I forgot to acquaitng you that Miss Jenny Cameron with a female companion only has been lately at Rome to make a visit and to solicit (they say) the continuance of her pension from her hero, but it is said she did not meet with so kind a reception as at Holyrood House. She returned again to Leghorne a few weeks ago, and embarked on board a merchant ship (Captain Mangle) for England.'[4]

Charles was showing his usual often-irrational bluster at this time and if Jenny did try to see him, he probably would have shown her the door. However, he may not even have been in Rome at the date of her alleged visit for, piqued by the Pope's snub, he was spending as much time as he could away from the city. When he was at the Muti Palace he attended social events incognito so that no one could humble him by failing to treat him as a king.

Pope Clement XIII at his most petty could be just as childish as Charles and seized one of the king's carriages which displayed the Royal Stuart colours. Charles's response was to comment tartly that he thought he would go and live in Venice, where there were no horses but only boats.

At long last a truce came in May 1767 when the Pope received Charles, not as king but as a private citizen. He was kept waiting in an ante-room while his brother, in accordance with his right as a cardinal, was shown into His Holiness's presence, then Charles was summoned in as 'brother of the Cardinal of York', and was forced to stand throughout the fifteen minute interview, while Henry was seated.

From a religious point of view, Charles did not really care whether he met the Pope or not. He had said that in Rome they looked on him as a Protestant and in Britain as a rank papist, and he only intended to stay on in Rome to gain recognition as king. He had already drifted back into the Catholic Church, but said that if he married a Catholic and had children their mother would have nothing to do with their education.

Hopes rose when Clement XIII died and was succeeded by Clement XIV in 1769, but the new Pope also refused to recognize Charles as king. Charles ignored this new snub and now took a greater part in the social life of the city, visiting the Pope and hunting in the Albano hills where he had been so happy as a boy. He dressed as the king he

235

believed himself to be, in a scarlet coat edged with a broad band of gold lace and a large antique cameo pinned to it. And on his breast were the Orders of the Garter and St Andrew.

He was still drinking heavily, but not as openly or as regularly: for days he would remain sober, then off he would go on a great binge with disastrous effects similar to his earlier drinking bouts in France. Towards the end of 1768 he was so drunk one evening that members of his staff and his secretary, Andrew Lumisden, who had wanted to retire but only stayed on at Charles's request, refused to accompany him to the oratorio. He dismissed them all, but when he sobered up, he asked them to stay on, but they refused. In the letter giving the news of his departure to Lord Dunbar, Lumisden was generous to the drunken king who must have tried his patience many, many times:

> May he ever judge wisely for his own advantage, may his conduct be such as to acquire him the esteem and love of mankind and may he yet enjoy the crowns that are due to him and transmit his royal blood to latest posterity.[5]

Charles was now nearly fifty, but had recently shown little sign of marrying let alone 'transmitting his royal blood to the latest posterity'. In his last efforts at finding a wife he had been seeking one who would bring a dowry of soldiers to invade Britain: now he needed a dowry in hard cash, and sought the hand of the daughter of the Duc d'Orleans only to find she was already taken. Next he tried the daughter of the Prince Frédéric des Deux Parts, but she dithered and Charles gave up.

By 1771 the question of finding a wife for the King over the Water became urgent. Charles was now past fifty and, apart from his illegitimate daughter by Clementine, he and his cardinal brother were the last of the Stuart line. Jacobites in Britain and the French king were both anxious to see an heir, but for a different reason. While the motives of the Jacobites were straightforward, the French were up to their old tricks. The Seven Years War was not going at all well for them, and Louis XV saw the threat of a new invasion in support of the Stuarts as a means of distracting Britain: besides if the marriage did produce an heir this would perpetuate the Jacobite threat for generations to come.

When Charles sent his new secretary, Lord Caryll, to Paris to negotiate, he found that the whole political climate had warmed up – Charles's enemy Choiseul was out and in his place in charge of France's foreign affairs was the Duc d'Aiguillon, who was well disposed to the Stuarts.

Charles rushed off to Paris to ask formally for French approval for his marriage, not to any girl in particular, but simply Louis's blessing on any marriage the Stuart king might make. Having received French agreement, Charles sent Edmund Ryan, a colonel in Berwick's Regiment, in search of a bride, and he himself set out for Rome well pleased with his success.

Ryan's mission had none of the dash and romance of Wogan's journey of 1719. For one thing the prospective bridegroom he had to offer was a man of fifty, a heavy drinker, and eighty-three years removed from the Palace of St James's, whereas Wogan was seeking a bride for a 34-year-old James Stuart, who was still dashing and was actually on his way to dislodge the German lairdie from the throne the Stuarts had lost a mere thirty years before.

The first princess Ryan visited was Marie Louise, daughter of the Prince of Salm-Kymburg, a girl of eighteen, who burst into tears on hearing of Charles's proposal. Next he called on Louise of Stolberg, one of four daughters of Prince Gustav Adolf of Stolberg-Gedern, who had been killed fighting for the Empress Maria Theresa at the Battle of Leuthen in 1757, when Louise was only five. Although the Stolbergs were poor, their blood was as richly royal as any in the whole of Europe and, prize of prizes for the waiting Jacobites, Louise's mother was a daughter of the Earl of Elgin, a family which could trace its descent from Robert the Bruce, King of Scots. With such a pedigree, Louise appeared to be a perfect consort for Charles Stuart in spite of the fact that she was just thirteen months older than his own daughter, Charlotte.

Louise was born at Mons on 20 September 1752, and was living in the Chapter of St Wandru at Mons at this time, a well-endowed order which was devoted to educating the daughters of noble, but impoverished families. Quickly, before the Stolbergs could change their minds or the British object, a dowry was offered and accepted, and a proxy marriage was arranged in Paris.

Louise's mother was an ambitious woman, and enough of a realist to be relieved to have the oldest of her four daughters taken off her hands. One of the four daughters was already married to a member of the Fitzjames family, who were descended from the Duke of Berwick, a half-brother of Charles's father, and that was very probably how the Stuarts came to hear of the Stolbergs in the first place. Louise was now nearly twenty and, with one sister married already, ran a grave risk of being left on the shelf as suitors came round and were liable to choose the younger ones.

Louise herself was happy with the idea of becoming a queen, even without a throne. Clementina Sobieska had felt the same about marrying Charles's father, but there the resemblance ended. Louise was a poised, self-assured girl, able to turn on great charm; she was intelligent and read French novels, played the guitar, harp and mandolin, and sang, and danced well. She was witty, but sometimes had an over-sharp tongue.

Louise was pretty enough, if not exactly beautiful, but the Duke of Fitzjames reported that she had 'a pleasant face' with a fine skin, vermilion lips and excellent teeth.[6] What was left unsaid was that she did not hesitate to make use of her attractiveness to men to get her way.

In Scotland the loyal little Jacobite clique watched the marriage quest with fascination. Bishop Forbes and the Oliphants of Gask followed it all with great impatience in a correspondence in which they referred to the king by the clumsy codename Cousin Peggie. From the autumn of 1769 until 1773 they speculated on progress until Forbes received confirmation from Bishop Gordon that Charlie had taken a wife. Forbes could scarcely believe it:

Ten thousand thanks for your most comfortable intelligence. Tho' I believed the interesting event in part, I suspended my firm belief of it till I should hear from you.[7]

Forbes did not even know the chosen girl's name, and begged to be told it not only for his own sake but for the sake of 'others who are desirous to give the name to daughters when they appear'.[8] At last on 4 June, more than six weeks after the wedding took place, Gordon was able to write, 'Within these two hours I have been enabled to inform you that the Lady's name is Louisa, and a most amiable princess by all accounts she is.'

While the Jacobite world speculated, the process of bringing Louise to the altar ground on slowly. Louise's mother was not an easy woman to please and quibbled about the details, but she finally agreed to the marriage arrangements and the proxy wedding took place in Paris towards the end of March 1771. Immediately the Stolberg party set off to meet the bridegroom by a route which took them through Innsbruck to Venice and then by sea to Ancona and on to Viterbo.

To travel by way of Innsbruck was tempting fate in the light of what had happened to Charles's mother there, but in the event all went well and the Stolbergs had nothing more to overcome than the discomfort of bad roads and petty officialdom. The final destination in Italy was changed to Macerata, twenty miles inland from Ancona, where Cardinal Campagnoni-Marefoschi had put his house at their disposal. The couple met on Good Friday, 17 April 1772, and there and then the marriage was solemnized by the cardinal.

Charles and Louise met, married and (in the words of Andrew Lang) he 'bedded the bride' all within a single day – at least we assume that Charles consummated the marriage that day since Louise's mother had laid down that the ceremony and consummation had to take place on the day the couple met, and Louise was such a gossip that she would certainly have told the world if Charles had failed in any respect. Charles himself wrote that 'ye marriage was made in all ye forms'.[9] As for Louise, all she said afterwards was that her marriage was 'solemnised on the lamentation day of Christendom' – but that comment came later![10]

Although it took place on the most solemn day of the holy year, the marriage was a splendid affair with both bride and bridegroom gorgeously dressed and a great celebration that extended over the following two days. Charles gave his bride a turquoise ring and a poem written by his own royal hand:

This Crown is due to you by me,
And none can love you more than me.

Given by C. yᵉ 3rd to his Queen, yᵉ 17th Aprill, 1772.[11]

After a couple of days at Macerata the royal honeymooners spent a few days at Terni, where Louise, rather pertly, recommended that her hostess (a woman renowned for the freshness of her complexion) would look better if she rouged her cheeks. Then it was back to Rome and reality.

Charles had hoped his marriage might persuade the Pope to recognize him as King Charles III and he and Louise travelled back to the eternal city confident that a royal welcome awaited them. Henry had done his best to force the Pope's hand by arranging a fine procession from the Porta del Popolo to the Muti with the bride and bridegroom riding in a carriage drawn by six horses, escorted by four state coaches and outriders in scarlet liveries and with white cockades in their hats. It was as near to a royal procession as Queen Louise was ever to come, and she enjoyed the experience in spite of the fact that her husband sulked gloomily in a corner of the carriage because he had just learned that the Pope still would not recognize him as Charles III.

Henry did his best: he received them formally at the *palazzo* and presented Louise with a diamond-studded snuffbox containing a draft for 40,000 crowns.

Charles rather stupidly tried to force the Pope's hand, by writing at once to inform His Holiness officially of the arrival of the King and Queen of England. But the response simply informed him that the Pope had been told of the arrival of 'Baron Renfrew and his wife', and 'assured them that he will be very glad to receive them, but as he is now very busy he wishes to defer it till he is less engaged than at present'[12], and he refused to accept the letter.

The Pope did not want Charles around at this time because he was busy receiving the Hanoverian Duke of Gloucester, who was then in Italy, in order to try to gain greater tolerance for British Catholics. The only gesture Clement made to the Jacobites was to suggest the duke should leave the city when Charles and Louise were due to return.

To add to his miseries the French failed to pay the monies they had promised, and Charles realized his marriage had achieved none of the political objectives he had hoped for.

Far away in Scotland details of the marriage filtered through to a ready audience. John Farquharson of Aldlerg's comment on the Good Friday marriage was very different from Louise's. 'The better the day the better the deed,' he said.[13] And he recounted the magnificence of Cardinal York's gift: 'The outside, beautiful as it was, was nothing in comparison of the beauty within, 'he said. 'Oh! My dear Lord! it contained an order upon his bank to pay her down 40,000 Roman crowns.'[14]

The Scots saw through the cynical French manipulation of their Cause, for Farquharson finished this letter with the wish that 'they may produce a race of pretenders that never will finish, which the French will be always playing upon every quarrel'.

How they all hoped for an heir – a hope that was expressed in a coarse toast: 'God bless Louisa Horne [a corruption of her mother's maiden surname] and Jock in the ham cellar.'[15]

The Hanoverians waited with equal impatience for news of Louise, but their method of discovering what was happening was somewhat different. Horace Mann had his spies hard at work and they missed nothing: 'I have the most authentic means of being informed of everything that goes on in the Pretender's house,' he said. That was true, for his spies were bribing staff in the Muti Palace to let them examine Louise's soiled linen so that they could see whether her menstrual cycle had been broken. It had not, or we should have heard about it.

As usual the Jacobites saw what they wanted to see at the Stuart court. Forbes reported on 28 July 1772 that 'a gentleman lately arrived from Rome declares he had the honour not only to see, but likewise to talk with the amiable Louisa, and that it is his opinion she is pregnant. All glory be to God for all his mercies. Amen.'[16]

But Louise was not pregnant. It has been customary for writers in the past to blame Charles for this, claiming that he was so worn out by his dissipated life that be could not have satisfied a twenty-year-old girl, let alone sire an heir. But gossipy little Louise would have reported such a failure back to her mother, and we know that Charles was neither impotent nor infertile. Louise on the other hand led a long life of infidelity to her husband and to her lovers, yet she did not bear a child. One can only conclude that in all probability Louise was infertile.

That first year at Charles's little court was reasonably happy; the only blemish was that Clementine Walkinshaw burst into his life again to remind him of his daughter and to try to put pressure on him to support Charlotte. She even turned up in Rome with the girl at the beginning of 1773, but Charles was furious and would not see her. She was ordered to leave the city and went home with nothing.

Louise ignored this 'other woman' and continued to charm Roman society, especially the men. For a young woman interested in the arts the court at the Muti was boring in the extreme, since her husband would not allow her to mix freely with Roman society so long as the Pope refused to recognize her as queen. The Jacobites around the palazzo were an ageing, boring collection of sycophants compared with the many intellectuals who lived in the city or visited it. It was not an environment to appeal to a young, outgoing girl like Louise.

They had little in common and as she drifted towards reading and intellectual pastimes, he returned to the bottle. It was inevitable that she should begin to develop intellectual friendships – and equally inevitable that these should soon turn into something more lustful. The first of these was revealed in a denunciation by one Giorgio Ghalt of the king's first lackey, Bernardo Rotolo, who admitted that the queen had told him that she loved him.[17] The odd thing is that Charles, normally so jealous, does not appear to have taken any action.

The following year, at a masked ball, Louise met a young Englishman on the Grand Tour and the two became infatuated. Thomas Coke, later the famous agriculturist Coke of Norfolk and Earl of Leicester, was a Whig, but like so many enemies of the Jacobite Cause on the Grand Tour, he became ensnared by the romance of the King over the Water when he arrived in Rome. It was the Queen over the Water who caught the imagination of Coke, and a rather innocent romantic flirtation followed. The only memory of their meeting is a splendidly romantic portrait, which Louise commissioned from Pompeo Batoni, showing Coke as Theseus with a statue of Ariadne abandoned on the island of Naxos in the background – Ariadne to whom Batoni had given Louise's features. Coke took the picture back to England.

The flirtation caused sufficient stir in Whig circles at the time for the ever observant Sir Horace Mann to remark, 'The young Mr Coke is returned from his travels in love with the Pretender's Queen.'[18] The only reminder left of Coke's brief little 'amour' with Louise is Batoni's portrait which still hangs at Holkham Hall in Norfolk.

From Coke, Louise turned to Charles-Victor von Bonstetten, a young Swiss who was in the course of a kind of literary Grand Tour of his own, which took in eminent people rather than places, among them such giants as Rousseau, Voltaire and the English poet, Thomas Gray. Bonstetten, an earnest but rather irresponsible character, amused Louise and shed a shaft of literary light into the Muti gloom. Bonstetten's philosophy – even his republican views – appealed to Louise, and brought out her opinions on human relationships, which pointed the way to her future behaviour. She told him once that she approved of men's polygamous instincts, but that they ought to apply to women as well. Women should be allowed an intellectual companion by day and a carnal one at night.[19]

It was Bonstetten who put the name 'the Queen of Hearts' on Louise: he imagined he was in love with her and handed out sweet compliments to her dark blue eyes, her slightly uptilted nose and her happy, pert, perceptive look, whose grace and youth adorned the Prince's court.[20]

She flirted with him when she was with him and no sooner had he left than she was sending him coquettish, amorous notes:

The refrain is always the same after I have been talking with you for two hours, you are charming, enchanting, lovable. And what joy to be able to tell you on paper what it would not be possible to say if you were here. Then I could only think it. I have thought so a hundred times and sometimes I am driven to rage that you have not divined my thoughts. It makes me wrathful. But I blush to make such confessions: you also feel, Monsieur, that it is propriety which suffers.[21]

For several years in Rome and Florence, and later by correspondence, the two enjoyed each other's company. Louise certainly was close to being in love with him, but it is hard to say how deeply in love he was with her. He certainly adored her and James Lees-Milne hits the mark in his assessment:

It is probably near the truth that he was more in love with her image than reality. Immature, naive lion hunter, he was about as captivated by his quarry of the moment as the stalker is enamoured of the game he is about to shoot. The moment the kill is over and done with he embarks upon the pursuit of another victim.[22]

To be fair to Bonstetten, it must be said that he remained faithful to Louise for a considerable time, and remembered her with great affection. Years later, in 1807, when he found himself once again in Rome he wrote to her, 'I never pass through the Piazza dei Apostoli without gazing at the balcony and the house where I first saw you. It seems that I have a whole lifetime to recount to you.'[23]

Sir William Hamilton, the British envoy in Naples, saw the royal couple in Rome, and was told that Charles's temper had 'grown so violent as to make his wife and every one about him unhappy', yet he never gave her a moment's peace. Hamilton thought the Prince's mind was going:

He says that his wife is six months gone with Child which she constantly denies (neither indeed is there the least appearance of it). He tells her that he understands these matters better than she can; in short, he is universally looked upon as in a great degree out of his Senses, and would be deserted if a few people did not go to him out of compassion for his Wife, whom he never quits a moment.[24]

Bonstetten was still mooning around Louise and moved to Florence when Charles decided it was time to leave the eternal city. The overt reason was that Tuscany would be better for his health and less expensive, but the main motivation was to avoid being in Rome, unrecognized as king, while the Pope was celebrating the fifth anniversary of his pontificate. Charles also needed a change of scene because he was out of sorts with France: Louis XV had died suddenly and his successor showed no signs of treating the Jacobites any more kindly than his predecessor had done.

For Louise there was only one reason to move and it was a good one – Rome was deadly dull.

After a while in Siena and Pisa the Stuart King and Queen arrived in Florence during the autumn of 1774 and leased the Villa Corsinsi, where they stayed for eighteen months, during which time they were known in the city as the Count and Countess of Albany. Louise might have been happy here had she been left to share her life with her literary friends, but Charles was bored stiff and soon increased his dependence on the bottle and on his wife's company. He was suffering considerable pain and discomfort during this period and through all his ill health, he was also engaged in a constant running battle against the Florentine aristocracy who would not recognize him any more than would those of Rome. As Mann lived in Florence, London was kept well informed of every ache, every pain and every slight.

During the summer of 1776 the king found a new home in the city, the beautiful Palazzo Guadagni in the via San Sebastiano – now the Palazzo San Clemente in the via Gino Capponi. The Guadagni was a *palazzo* fit for Charles's little court: it was a fine, solid late Renaissance building with a garden shaded from the Tuscan sun by cypress and ilex trees. The three-storey building comprised two projecting wings and a recessed central portion, all shaded by wide projecting eaves. There was a portico through which carriages could drive in, leading to spacious entrance hall and stairway up to beautifully decorated rooms on the first floor. Charles added his own royal touches, the arms of Great Britain painted on a ceiling and a weather-vane with the initials C.R. to make it his very own *palazzo*, where he could hold court and Louise was able to receive her intellectual friends.[25]

The sad thing was that, having found this little palace, Charles had at last given up real hope of ever being restored to his throne, and he was now known simply as the Count of Albany. Only two years earlier, Sir William Hamilton had said that the Prince still talked of 'his return to England as being in hand'.[26] But no longer.

He and Louise were both bored stiff and Mann reported their joint discontent and the king's ill health faithfully: Charles received British visitors to the city and in the scalding heat of the Florence afternoon he tottered round the city's public gardens, hardly able to put one swollen, ulcerated, suppurating leg past the other – his legs had always given him trouble ever since his wanderings in the Highlands and Western Isles of Scotland in 1746. He cut a pathetic figure on these walks, and when he grew unable to walk he drove in an open carriage, accompanied by liveried servants and his wife who clearly hated every moment of it.

In the evenings he would arrive at the opera, drunk, where he lay huddled in a corner of his box, drowsing and then waking up to abuse his staff or to leave hurriedly to be sick. All Europe savoured gossip about the sight of the king being carried out by his servants at the end of the performance more drunk than ever, cursing every inch of the way to his carriage.

It is easy to blame every one of Charles Edward Stuart's many troubles on drink, but in the heat of the Tuscan summer he suffered constantly from asthma and high blood pressure and his legs were ulcerated and particularly painful. Bleedings and emetics were prescribed by his doctors, and the cure was often worse than the ailment. The King over the Water was a poor, miserable, unkingly character, despised by everybody – especially his wife.

Louise escaped to books and beaux for she turned herself into quite a blue stocking, seeking consolation from her awful marriage in chatter and flirtations with Bonstetten and others. Lees-Milne quotes an extraordinary letter sent home by Dr Moore. He was escorting the nineteen-year-old Duke of Hamilton on the Grand Tour, when the duke fell under Louise's spell in Florence:

Though the Duke's mind is preoccupied this does not make him blind to the Countess of Albany's charms, and if there was a possibility of his forming an acquaintance with her without making an acquaintance with her husband, I imagine he would be glad of such an opportunity. I have not omitted to hint the Impropriety of such an Intimacy, and if it could be supposed possible that it might be carried a certain length I have represented with equal zeal and loyalty how very ungraceful it would be to His Majesty [George III] you run the risk of begeting Pretenders to his Crown, at the very time when he was fixing honours upon your Grace and the Duke's family. I hope your Grace will put my zeal on this occasion in a proper point of view to their Majesties, that in case the Stewart line should be continued by the Duke's means, I may not incur their disapprobation . . . for the reanimation of the cruel, tyrannical, bloody, papistical race of Stewart when it seemed to be expiring.[27]

The duke's honour – and Louise's too – appears to have remained intact: whether from lack of opportunity or from Louise's barrenness, we don't know, but the young Duke of Hamilton did not manage to perpetuate the Stuart line.

Louise had plenty to complain about: Florence society, at first welcoming and friendly, suddenly cut her off and wherever she went with her husband she was snubbed or ignored. The child she had hoped for failed to appear, and she turned more and more to books and other interests.

If appearing in public with her husband was demeaning, sharing a house with him was worse. After they moved into the Palazzo Guadagni, what should have been the happiest years of their time together turned into a nightmare leading to the break-up of the marriage. Jealousy took command as it had done in every previous relationship Charlie had ever been involved in and, as in the cases of Madame de Talmont and Clementine Walkinshaw, it turned to violence. He railed against Louise, he beat her, yet he still insisted that she should share his bed – for what, one wonders, since he usually fell into bed drunk and coughed and wheezed all night from asthmatic attacks or was sick from time to time.

247

Sir Horace Mann followed it all, since everyone – even the royal physician – passed on the most intimate details of what went on behind the ornate doors of the *palazzo*. The doctor told Mann that Charles had 'a declared fistula, great sores in his legs, and is insupportable in stench and temper; neither of which he takes the least pains to disguise to his wife – whose beauty is vastly faded of late'.

Sharing a house and a bed with various women over the years had taught Prince Charlie nothing; when Louise was allowed to go to her own bed he reverted to the old trick he used with Clementine of piling chairs round the room and hanging them with little bells to warn if an intruder approached.

In Rome and through the early days in Florence Louise was fortunate to have two people she could trust, her lady-in-waiting, Madame de Maltzam, and Lord Caryll, her husband's secretary, who had escorted her to meet Charles for the first time when she arrived in Italy. They knew all that was going between the king and his wife in public and in the privacy of their bedroom, and they were sympathetic. Unfortunately, Caryll resigned early in 1775 leaving her without the sympathetic ear into which she could pour her troubles. That marked an important change, for Louise now had to turn to her admirers and, while they were more than willing to listen and sympathize, they were much less discreet than Caryll had been.

The king and queen were barely on speaking terms by now, and Louise took to writing notes to her husband, listing her complaints and even threatening to circulate them publicly. The royal antics in Florence were well enough known all round Europe not to need such publicity as is proved by a shattering letter the king received from the Jacobites in London in May 1777, blaming him for everything from drinking to failure to father an heir. He was attacked especially for the manner in which he treated his wife, 'a princess who is in every way your equal, descended from our ancient kings of Scotland and allied to all the great families of Europe. From these claims you derive your pride and fancy they give you authority to be wicked unpunished.'[28]

On hand to listen to Louise's miseries was a 27-year-old poet and playwright from Piedmont, Count Vittorio Alfieri, a man in a very different mould from all his predecessors, even the ardent Bonstetten.

Alfieri had enormous talent as a poet, but he was rich, irresponsible, immoral, mercurial and totally unpredictable. Before he met Louise he had already led a restless life roaming Europe, a rebel against almost everyone and everything he encountered. His childhood was lonely and unhappy: he was born at Asti in 1749, but his father died when he was very young and his mother remarried. Young Alfieri was sent off to the Turin Academy to be educated, and after eight lonely years there, he set out into the world against which he was already a rebel.

By the time he fell at Louise's feet in Florence he had a reputation that resounded from London, where he fought a duel between acts of the opera at the Haymarket Theatre, to Cadiz, where he contracted venereal disease. Alfieri was as immoral as he was rich and he enjoyed both qualities to the full.

The story was that he first saw Louise admiring a portrait of Charles XII of Sweden in the Uffizi Gallery and was so taken by her beauty and intelligent comments about the picture that he fell in love. He tried to resist, but soon found himself visiting her at the Palazzo Guadagni. For four years the affair was Louise's solace for the life of hell she endured with her husband, but eventually Louise decided she needed more than comforting words – she had to escape.

And so a plan was laid for her to abscond with Alfieri. The Grand Duke of Tuscany was consulted and willingly gave his approval, since he hated Charles Stuart. A group of loyal friends was then let into the secret – these included Louise's faithful lady-in-waiting, Madame de Maltzam, one of the king's Italian staff, Count Spada, and a Madame Orlandini and her lover, an Irish adventurer named Charles Geoghegan. If it seemed wrong for Louise to trick her husband in this way, the event that triggered Louise's departure provided her with ample justification.

It happened on St Andrew's Night, 1780, a date which always brought back memories to Charlie of his deep affection for Scotland and the Highlanders especially, and of course it reminded him of how close he came to victory only to see it all snatched away at Culloden. Charles drank more heavily than usual on St Andrew's Night and this one was no exception: by the time he joined Louise in bed he was in a drunken rage, which only needed the spark of a remark with which he did not agree. What the spark was we do not know, but its effects were well recorded. Charles went into an apoplectic fury, struck her, tore at her hair, dragged her out of bed, then chased after her and tried to strangle her. Her screams brought the servants running and it was only their intervention that saved her from serious injury or murder.

Louise's mind was made up – she was going. On the morning of 9 December Madame Orlandini breakfasted with Louise and it was proposed that, instead of the usual drive in the park, they should visit the Convent delle Bianchette to see some lace the nuns had made. Charles agreed, but insisted on accompanying them as they knew he would. At the convent the ladies hurried up to the door while Charles limped after them some way behind, assisted by Charles Geoghegan.

As soon as the women passed into the convent the door was slammed in Charles's face, leaving him hammering futilely with his stick and thundering that he wanted to speak to his wife. Eventually the mother superior told him through the grille that his wife had sought sanctuary in her convent and that it had been granted.

Charles went home in a rage, which became greater than ever as the true story of what had happened that morning began to emerge. It took him a considerable time to discover Spada's involvement, but he threatened to have Geoghegan shot and accused Alfieri of being a seducer. The Irishman in turn, as Alfieri's friend, challenged the king to a duel, but that never came off.

While Charles raged, Louise craftily set about securing sympathy for her cause, convincing everyone that all the wrong was on her husband's side of the story, while she herself was continuing to plan to be with her lover. One may have sympathy for Louise, but she can hardly be called innocent.

On the very day she entered the Florence convent she sent a letter to Charles's brother to tell him of her ill-treatment and how she could no longer bear to live under the same roof as her husband. Needless to say Alfieri stayed well in the shadows while Henry hurried to consult the Pope and the two invited Louise to come to Rome, where they would help her.

And so, on 27 December, Louise drove out of Florence in great secrecy, with Alfieri and Geoghegan in disguise and armed accompanying the coach part of the way. In order to preserve every appearance of decency, when Louise arrived in Rome they returned to Florence and they left her to tell her sorry story herself.

Henry told his sister-in-law he was not at all surprised to learn what had happened: he had seen it coming for years. He naïvely showered sympathy and money on her and accepted her story as that of a wronged innocent, which she certainly was not. It was not self-deception on Henry's part: 'He did not shut his eyes to scandal. His eyes were closed to it. They were only opened when his nose was rudely rubbed in it.'[29]

Henry was as naïve as Louise was crafty and she manipulated him to her great advantage. The Pope also was taken in and handed over half of Charles's papal pension to her, which, as Mann remarked, 'will affect him more than the loss of his wife'. Even the Queen of France, Marie Antoinette, agreed to grant her a pension.

At Henry's suggestion Louise agreed to stay in the Convent of St Cecilia – shades of 1727 – the place to which Charlie's mother had fled from his father. But Louise had no intention of living here or in any other religious house for her sole aim was to be reunited with her poet. Her great triumph was to persuade Henry to allow her to leave the convent within a month of her arrival at it and he even gave her a floor of his own official residence, the Palazzo Cancelleria.

Before 1781 was very old the panting lover was back on the scene: from Florence Alfieri headed south to Naples, a convenient destination since the route lay via Rome which gave him a chance to see his beloved Louise again for a brief agonized meeting:

I saw her: my heart is yet lacerated when I reflect on it. I saw her behind a gate, less tormented it is true than she had been at Florence, but in other respects more unhappy. We were separated, and who could say for how long a time.[30]

The affair raged on as passionately as ever, by correspondence in which they addressed one another as Psipsio and Psipsia – names to suggest the sound of kissing – but they longed to be together, and soon Alfieri was settled in Rome, but ever so discreetly so that the innocent eyes and ears of the cardinal would see or hear nothing. The poet rented the Villa Storzzi where he settled down to write a series of tragedies by day and to hurry to Louise every evening to read plays and make love to her. Behind Henry's back she joked about her brother-in-law's naïvety, and once she had the effrontery to arrange for Alfieri to deliver a copy of Virgil to the innocent but grateful Henry.

Charles was astounded and furiously angry – everything seemed to enrage him now. While his pensions were being cut, his wife was having money – his money – heaped on to her, and as for his brother, he had proved once again that blood ties counted for nothing. Charles stormed and raged at the injustice of it, but no one would listen. 'How can a brother be so blind?' he asked in 1782.[31]

Charles, with considerable right on his side, felt humiliated and impoverished – and a laughing stock in Florence. He sent Count Corsini to the Vatican to put his case to the Pope, demanding that Louise be sent back to him, that his pension should be restored, and that Alfieri should be banished from Rome, but the Pope merely called in Henry, who confirmed Louise's tale.

While she accepted everything Henry showered on her, Louise continued her affair with Alfieri under his unseeing eyes, but this could not continue forever, especially in the light of Alfieri's wild temperament. Eventually it surfaced in Rome in April 1783 when Louise arranged a glittering performance of her lover's tragedy *Antigone*, which set all Rome talking. Soon after this Charles fell dangerously ill and Henry had to rush to his bedside, certain that his brother was going to die. In such a situation with death at the bedside, the brothers talked – at least Charles talked and Henry listened. For the first time he heard a version of the story to which he had refused to listen hitherto, and he realized that Charles was speaking the truth. Now he heard the other side of the break-up of the marriage and realized he had been cruelly duped.

As Mann reported this back to London:

I have formerly given you an account of the *fracas* in the Pretender's family by the elopement of his wife, whom everybody then pitied and applauded. The tables are now turned. The cat at last is out of the bag. The Cardinal's visit to his brother gave the latter an opportunity to undeceive him, proving to him that the complaints laid to his charge of ill-using her were invented to cover the plot formed by Count Alfieri.[32]

Henry was angry and rushed back to Rome, where he demanded that the Pope should order Alfieri out of papal territory. Pope Pius VI was equally appalled at being taken in by the lovers, and told Alfieri he must leave within fifteen days.

One feels that the response of both Henry and the Pope did not emanate from the moral issue of the Louise–Alfieri love affair so much as from a sense of having been duped by the couple's lies, which made them look foolish. Mann certainly thought so: 'a more silly mortal never existed', he wrote in his despatch to London.

Alfieri did not wait for the deadline: he left Rome for Siena on 4 May, 'like one stupid and deprived of sense, leaving my only love, books, town, peace, my very self at Rome'.[33] He and his Psipsia continued to correspond, for she did not dare follow him for fear of losing her income. Fortunately Gustav III of Sweden arrived on the scene at this moment and he was able to put the choice to Louise – she could either stay married to Charles Stuart and be sent back to a convent in Florence as Henry wanted to happen, or she could be free of him and leave Italy to live wherever she chose with her beloved Alfieri. Louise wisely chose the latter, and Gustav masterminded the detail of a separation, which gave Charles back his papal pension and the Sobieski jewels and provided Louise with an income financed by France. It was the end of Charles's marriage, which had lasted just the same length of time as his 'marriage' to Clementine Walkinshaw.

Louise and Alfieri were reunited at the Two Keys Inn at Colmar, as one of Louise's naïve Victorian biographers described it, to enjoy 'platonic ecstasies', a risky business since, if it had become known, she might have lost her pensions from the Pope and her husband. They parted again, Louise to Bologna and Alfieri to Pisa, and by the time Charlotte began her campaign, she was living in Paris, which remained the lovers' base until the French Revolution. Part of Louise's enjoyment was irritating Charles through savage complaining letters to Cardinal York and everyone else who was prepared to listen on the subject of her husband's misdeeds.

Louise was wrong: her former husband was on the brink of enjoying a period of contentment such as he had not known for nearly forty years and Louise of Stolberg was no part of it.

Where does the elusive Louise come in Prince Charlie's love league? She did not have the passion of Louise de Montbazon, who was prepared to abandon everything for love; she lacked the maturity of the ageing courtesan, Marie de Talmont; and she could not match the devotion to what Charles Stuart stood for, which Clementine Walkinshaw brought to him when he sent for her in 1752. The relationship with Louise of Stolberg contained less love than any of the others. It was not built on a foundation stone of love as the others were, but was simply a dynastic union to perpetuate the Stuart line. Many royal marriages in those days had no better a basis, yet they were often perfectly viable relationships – after all, Charles's adversary, Louis XV managed to keep his queen, Marie Leszynska, content alongside his mistresses, Châteauroux and Pompadour. Unfortunately, the Stuart King and Queen exchanged roles – it was Charles who sat by while Louise had her amours, but finally his great sin of jealousy, which always spoiled Prince Charlie's love, seeped into the relationship and eventually flooded it and swept it away. Louise of Stolberg was a calculating young woman, who miscalculated with Prince Charlie.

But still there is one question to be answered – was she the clever, emancipated, liberated woman in advance of her time who was beaten by a brutish husband, or was she a cunning, calculating little vixen who richly deserved what she got in the way of marital desserts?

She was neither and yet she was both. Louise was intelligent, but her sharp wit and acid tongue gave the impression of a more incisive brain than she really possessed. Alone she amounted to very little, but with Alfieri, or even Bonstetten's ability behind her, she became a woman of considerable intellectual capacity. Unfortunately her talents were not of a kind that Charles Stuart could understand or appreciate, and neither he nor she was prepared or able to make allowance for the other. Their marriage was a sham, contracted solely to perpetuate the Stuart dynasty and when one (or both) proved barren, there was nothing left. The thirty-year age difference between them soon became an intellectual chasm.

On the minus side of Louise's character, was her willingness to commit adultery; she was not an innocent girl seduced from the straight and narrow path, but went halfway to meet her lovers, and her ability to lie to cover up her faithlessness was quite shameless. The way in which she deceived the innocent Henry and the Pope over her relationship with Alfieri and at the same time wrung allowances from them (at the expense of her husband) was blatant. Louise of Stolberg suffered dreadful humiliation during her years with Charles Stuart, but in the final analysis one is left feeling less sorry for her than one might. Louise made her own disaster of her marriage.

SEVENTEEN

THE WILFUL LASS OF ALBANY

The other event is the arrival of Lady Charlotte Stuart, Duchess of Albany, which has occasioned some little bustle in the town. A French lady who for thirty years has been totally neglected, but on a sudden transformed into a Duchess, was an object that excited the curiosity of both sexes, the men to see her figure, the ladies scrupulously to examine that and the new modes she has brought from Paris, the result of all which she is allowed to be a good figure, tall, and well-made, but that the features of the face resemble too much those of her father to be handsome.

Sir Horace Mann's description of Charlotte, Duchess of Albany, after her arrival in Florence to join her father.[1]

Among those to whom Louise of Stolberg poured out her complaints about how badly her husband had treated her, was Alfieri's mother. There was malicious pleasure in every word Louise set down on paper: 'He drags out a miserable life, abandoned by all the world, without relatives or friends, given over to his servants.'[2]

Unfortunately, Louise was right about her former husband's life: Charles stayed on in Florence after the marriage settlement was completed, ignored by the Grand Duke and most of Florentine society, and visited only by the curious and those with enduring loyalty to the Cause. He visited the baths at Pisa, but otherwise his whole existence was wrapped up in the Palazzo Guadagni, where he drank more than ever, and in his cups, bemoaned past misfortunes and the selfishness of those who had deserted him. He would sit in a depressed silence for days on end, then suddenly talk of the time when he would be restored to his throne at St James's. Whatever else he may have lost, Charlie retained his deep love for music and spent many evenings playing duets with Domenico Corri on the cello and harpsichord. Sometimes he played old Scottish melodies alone on his cello or the French horn, and such evenings would end with 'Lochaber No More', which reduced Charles to tears.

If Louise was right in her claim that her former husband was leading a lonely existence, she was wrong in thinking that he was condemned to such misery for the rest of his life.

No sooner was he free of his wife than he sent word to Clementine in the convent in Paris, offering, in return for Charlotte's company with him in Florence, to acknowledge her as his own daughter, to treat her with all kindness, to create her Duchess of Albany and make her heir to all he possessed.

Why did he want the daughter he had ignored for more than twenty years? It is doubtful whether Prince Charlie himself could have answered that any more than he could have explained why he had sent for Charlotte's mother out of the blue all those years ago at the start of their eight troubled years together. Prince Charlie was not a thinking man, but made decisions on impulse and always within the limits of his own belief that he was a prince (and now a king) by divine right. He did not have to give reasons to himself or to anyone else, and he never did. It was sufficient that he remembered his daughter and could think of no one else – at least that is how it looked on the surface.

Delving behind that impulsive, unexpected decision, however, innumerable reasons are there to be discovered: he was getting old, his health was failing, he had no legitimate child and would never have one now, his hated brother would inherit and he was determined that should never happen. Above all, he was lonely and needed a woman's comfort around him. Sex no longer entered into it, so he had no thought of taking another mistress or wife, especially not a wife!

While he mulled all those points over in his drink-befuddled, self-pitying mind in his empty *palazzo* a solution came to him – he would send for Charlotte. Without giving a thought to the callous way in which he had treated her in the intervening years, he simply made up his mind that he needed her and would send for her. This was what Charles Stuart desired, so it was what he had to have.

Both Clementine and Charlotte had wanted recognition more than anything during all the years since that night they fled from Bouillon in 1760. But he had denied them it up to now. Yet they never gave up the struggle to make him acknowledge his child publicly and provide for her: over the years Clementine had kept reminding the Prince of Charlotte's existence, but he refused to answer her letters even though he had always professed to love his *Pouponne* and moved heaven and earth to get her back when she was first taken from him.

He didn't give a rap about Clementine, he only wanted his daughter, and when he could not have her he refused to do anything for the child. Again we see Charles Stuart's lifelong method of dealing with refusal – he just told himself he didn't want whatever was denied to him.

Over these years it had been as if the child and her mother no longer existed, and had it not been for his father, whom he despised and hated for helping Clementine, both would have been in total penury. Even with the help of the king in Rome, life in the convent at Meaux-en-Brie, where they settled to save money, was hard.

Clementine looked after her daughter as best she could and in the harsh and unfair words of Walkinshaw's biographer, Leo Berry, Charlotte 'was as devoted to her mother as her character allowed. She had not yet developed the calculating selfishness which marked her later life.'[3]

Clementine inculcated into her daughter the righteousness of her case, and as she grew up, Charlotte became even more determined than her mother to be acknowledged by her father. After all he had claimed time and again that she was his child even when he treated her as though she had ceased to exist.

The two never abandoned the fight for recognition. Charlotte sent her first letter to her father, 'Mon très chère et honoré Seigneur et Père', on 15 August 1764, a long appeal probably drafted by her mother and copied out by Charlotte in her beautiful young hand. Even if her father had opened it, which he did not, it would not have won him over. The letter was long and spoke warmly of her mother – 'la plus tendre de mères' – and reminded him of how much he had loved his *Pouponne* and begged him to accept her as his daughter now. She signed it *Pouponne*.[4]

Like all little Charlotte's letters it was long, pathetic, pleading and repetitive, not the kind of approach to win Prince Charlie's heart, but even if it had contained the most compelling arguments, it would still have failed for the simple reason that he never read her letters. This one and others from her were found unopened among the Stuart Papers at Windsor Castle.[5]

Undaunted, Charlotte wrote again to congratulate him on his birthday at the end of the year. Again, silence.

When James died early in 1766, Charles had no intention of continuing his father's payments to Clementine and Charlotte and it was left to Henry to fork out a reduced allowance. As a result, Clementine had to move to the convent at Meaux-en-Brie, outside Paris, where it was less expensive to live.

It was at this time that Henry extracted from Clementine a declaration that she had never been married to Charles Stuart, and he made it clear in a most unchristian way that he would fight any contact between Clementine and his brother.

Charlotte, a girl of fifteen now and with a mind of her own, wrote several times during 1768, reminding, reminding, reminding . . . and always pleading pathetically for his love and recognition. She even had her portrait painted, specially for him she told him in the letter she wrote on 16 May. But he ignored that too, which is a pity, since no other likeness of Charlotte as a girl survives.[6]

Clementine also did what she could to win Charles over, but she was wasting her time: she was the last person from whom he wanted to hear. In 1768 Clementine sent a long letter telling the Prince how the girl was maturing, admired by the whole world: like her father she was a good musician, sang well and had begun to play the harpsichord. She was studying geography and history and had learnt to dance gracefully.[7] Charlotte was growing up and, what Clementine did not point out, was that her daughter was developing a burning determination of her own to win her father's recognition.

A couple of years later came the first mention of marriage, and it

was Lord Elcho of all people who tried to arrange a suitor. Henrietta
Tayler quotes from his diary of 1770:

Miss Walkinshaw proposed to me to find a husband for her
daughter and shortly afterwards i brought to them a rich
Englishman, who having seen the girl, was willing to settle on her
at his death a 'dot' of ten thousand pounds sterling; but, when all
was settled the Englishman quarrelled with Miss Walkinshaw over
a discussion in which she took the part of the Jesuits with too
great zeal. The Englishman said to her that he would have no
friends of Jesuits in his house and never came back again.[8]

Then Charlotte fell seriously ill: Clementine wrote in great distress,
describing how she had developed a swelling in her right side, which
caused appalling pain and left her in a high fever. Doctors gave it as
their opinion that it was an inflammation caused by her developing
constitution, but soon it became clear that it was something much
more serious. This was the first stage of the cancer of the liver from
which she was to die at the age of thirty-six. Even the anguished
letter describing his daughter's suffering brought no response, only a
callous silence as deep and hurtful as ever.[9]

In 1771 Charles visited Paris while plans were afoot to find a wife
for him, but needless to say he did not even attempt to see his wife or
daughter. That and his marriage to Louise of Stolberg the following
year hurt Clementina and Charlotte badly. But Charlotte was her
father's daughter – with his dogged determination she continued to
fight for her rights and threatened to come to Rome with her mother
if they were refused.[10]

It was not the best of times to bring her existence to his attention,
but at least the letters brought a response from the king's secretary,
Lord Caryll, who was a good friend to Clementine and her daughter.
He told Abbé Gordon that he might be able to obtain a place for the
girl in the royal household, but only if she agreed to cut herself off
from her mother. Above all he strongly counselled, Clementine must
never come to Rome.[11]

How strange that suddenly there was a place at Charles's court for the daughter he had ignored for years. Leo Berry offers the theory that Louise of Stolberg may have been responsible for the change of heart since she was young and lonely in a dull and aged court and needed youthful company. Charlotte would have been ideal.[12] The plan to bring Charlotte to Rome alone came to nothing, but it would be interesting to speculate on how different relations between the two women might have been had it come off.

Charlotte now turned to the King of France, presenting him with the first of a number of *mémoires* submitted during the next four years in the hope that France might provide for them. Charlotte was now of marriageable age and it was critical that she should have the financial and social standing necessary to attract a suitable husband. Very likely it was with this same reason in mind that they continued to write to Charles and Henry, but if so, they were disappointed.

Disappointed, but not defeated. With rash impulse worthy of Prince Charlie in 1745 the two women suddenly packed their bags in the late spring of 1773 and travelled to Rome to knock on the door of the Muti. It was a mad decision for which Clementine is usually blamed, but it bears the hallmarks of Charlie's daughter rather than his mistress. Now nearly twenty-one, she was developing a determination as forceful as her father's and, since it was more in her interest than in her mother's, it is much more likely the she was the driving force behind the madcap plan. Certainly it was she who drafted most of the letters involved in the visit, few of which referred to her mother's wishes or problems.

All along the line it was I . . . I . . . I. Charlotte appeared to be turning into as egocentric and selfish a person as her father. She was undeniably his daughter even if he did try to ignore her existence.

In Rome, Charles ignored her. Henry too. So she addressed her plea directly to the Vatican, but the only response that brought was for His Holiness to order Clementine to leave the city, which she and Charlotte did after much protesting and blustering.[13] Back at Meaux in July she wrote to her father again, 'the sad sound of my dying voice from the door of the tomb'.[14] The plea was still the same; 'O, my august father, O my king remember the rights of blood and nature. Do not deny to the one or the other the rights which are their due. Your soul is not cruel or barbaric, how can it not soften or show interest in the destiny of the most loving of daughters.'

The mother and daughter received nothing in return, except that they did not have much longer to suffer in that particular tomb, for the one good thing that came out of the trip to Rome was permission to move to a convent in Paris.

During the years 1772 to 1776 Clementine continued to bombard Louis XV, and when he died in May 1774, Louis XVI, with *mémoires*, all of which fell on ears as deaf as her father's. This must have discouraged the girl because, for the next decade, she and her mother switched roles, with Charlotte doing nothing while Clementine continued to work with new-found vigour to seek security for both of them.

Abbé John Gordon of the Scots College was the king's intermediary to relay messages sent via Secretary of State, Lord Caryll, to spell out his callous determination to do nothing for her and, coming at a time when Charlotte was in pain and despair already, it triggered her to open her heart to Gordon. The Abbé was greatly disturbed by the dreadful physical and mental state in which he found the girl, and relayed this back to Caryll in a letter on 27 February 1775:

I communicated to the young lady in question the contents of your letter of the 10th. It tucht her to such a degree that I was sorry that I had spoken to her so freely. She seems, since she can have no word of consolation from you, inclined either to marry the first who will seek her and has enuff to make her live, since she is at present of a proper age, and if she were to wait much longer it is probable she would find none. The treatment [income] she has at present, is so precarious that, in case no match offers, she is resolved to go into a begging order where she will trouble nobody afterwards, if she lives any time, which she does not believe will be the case as her spirits are intirly brock and the Doctor says that her grief has given her an obstruction on the Liver. All she desired was to be acknowledged as a natural daughter that as she was only six years old when carried off, that she ought not to be intirly ruined for a fault of which her age hindered her to be anyways [anyone's] partner. I am heartily sorry for her misfortunate situation and think she deserves better, being esteemed by all who know her as being one of the most accomplished women in this town. Her health at present is not in a good way and I believe my conference with her will make it worse. I beg therefor you will give me no more such commissions as it hurts me much to be anyways, tho' innocently, the occasion of the death of a person I esteem and respect much.[15]

Elcho gives proof of the high regard in which Charlotte was held. In July 1776 he was present when she was received as an Honorary Canoness of the Noble Chapter of Migette at Bcsançon, where she was visited by many dignitaries. 'In all these houses she was treated as a Princess, and much civility was shown to her mother, Mademoiselle Walkinshaw.'[16]

After this Charlotte vanished from view until the separation of Charles and Louise took place and the king suddenly decided to declare his daughter legitimate and send for her in 1784. But he would not bring her to him in Florence until her legitimacy was confirmed by the French and he could confer on her the title, Duchess of Albany.

Impatient as Charlotte was to claim her inheritance, she was not free come to her father at once. Charles was never given a reason for the delay, and it is doubtful whether he ever discovered it, but Charlotte had a great secret – for some years she had been dividing her life between the convent and the bed of the Archbishop of Bordeaux.

And at the very moment when the summons arrived from Florence, she was recovering from the birth of a son, the third child she had borne the archbishop. Touchingly, she named the boy Charles Edward.

Charlotte Stuart had not found a husband, but she had found love with none other than Prince Ferdinand de Rohan-Guéméné, Archbishop of Bordeaux and later Archbishop of Cambrai, youngest brother of the Duc de Montbazon, the husband of Louise with whom Charlie had that intense first passionate affair in Paris just after the

'45. Ferdinand was a child of less than ten at the time when Charlie was slipping in and out of the Hôtel Guéméné each night to make a cuckold of his brother.

It is not clear when the liaison began, but the first child, a girl named Aglae, was born prior to 1780. A second daughter, Marie, followed and then Charles Edward followed in July 1784, and this doubly illegitimate family took the name Roehenstart, an amalgam of the names Rohan and Stuart. Charlotte's son became Count Roehenstart and lived on past the middle of the next century, when Bonnie Prince Charlie and the '45 lay under the shroud of a century of history.

How the secret of Charlotte's family never leaked out is hard to tell for ever-vigilant Mann had wind of it and reported to Sir Horace Walpole on 24 July 1784 that Charlotte was living with her mother in a convent in Paris, but 'often quits the convent to visit Prince Rohan, Archbishop of Bordeaux, whose society . . . she prefers much to that of Les Dames de Ste Marie'.[17]

At one point she almost thought of confessing to her father about her liaison and her young family when she told him in a letter on 16 August 1784 that she owed much to the Rohans, a family whose members have always been 'fort attachés a votre Majesté'.[18]

Someone must have advised her against saying more – probably her mother who would know all about Louise de Montbazon – and Charlotte dropped the subject. Had either her father or her uncle discovered Charlotte's secret, it could well have wrecked the whole plan to bring her to Florence.

Each would have reacted in the same way, but for a different reason – Henry from prudishness and Charles because it would have been an affront to his dignity for his daughter to be mistress to one of the hated Guéménés. Had they discovered her secret, it is doubtful whether Charlotte would ever have crossed the threshold of the Palazzo Guadagni.

John Stewart, his faithful member of staff who had stuck with the Prince through all the troubled years, was sent off to Paris to fetch Charlotte, and he must have known the reason for her delay but wisely said nothing and warned her to do likewise. Mann unwittingly helped to allay suspicion by writing that 'the retardure is owing to the preparations necessary to equip her out properly to appear, first at Paris, and then here, under the new title her father has given her'.[19]

At last she set off on 18 September on the long journey to Florence and her new life as legitimate daughter of the King of Great Britain. Mann watched and passed on every detail he could to London. Charles had brought furniture from the Muti Palace in Rome and much more, including a large quantity of plate and his share of his mother's jewels.

When the new Duchess of Albany arrived, her father, showing touching and unaccustomed excitement, wanted to present her to the whole of society, but the Grand Duke refused to recognize her title. His wife would not receive the new duchess because she had brought no letter of introduction from the French Queen. However, many of the ladies of the city made up for those rebuffs by rushing to the Palazzo Guadagni to meet her and Jacobites visiting the city all were anxious to see 'the Lass of Albany' as she became known.

Henry's behaviour was even worse than that of the Grand Duke, for he took the greatest exception to Charlotte's invitation to Florence, although he had supported her financially during all those years when his brother would not. She wrote to him at once, but gave tremendous offence by being so familiar as to address him as 'very dear uncle'. He did not answer her letter, but wrote petulantly to Charles and even complained to the Pope about the whole business of the 'legitimation' of this young woman. To add insult to injury she had signed herself, *Duchess of Albany*, a title that was his by rights since it was usually held by the younger sons of the royal family. And as if that were not enough she had the audacity to style herself *Her Royal Highness*.

Henry was so outraged that he started to correspond with Louise again, and to listen to her carping jibes against Charles and his daughter – jibes motivated not so much by jealousy as by fear that Charlotte might inherit what she still hoped would become hers when the ailing king died. Charlotte for her part, disliked Louise, not merely because of the patronizing way in which she was treated by her, but because she saw Louise as a threat to her inheritance also.

In this circle of hatred, cunning and distrust the genuine affection between father and daughter was the only edifying element. Charles worked up a fine anger against his brother for being so stupid as to restore relations with his ex-wife. And soon he was proved right for Louise, dishonest as ever, allowed Henry to believe that she was no longer living with Alfieri. At the end of the year 1784, when Charlotte had been three months in Florence, Louise told Henry:

The king continues to do a thousand absurdities in Florence, although he can scarcely move from one room to another by means of his swollen legs. His illness does not, however, prevent him bestowing the order of St Andrew at the end of a banquet on his daughter and on a certain lord who attends him. It is all very ridiculous.[20]

Charlotte herself was to deal with both the mischiefmakers in her own way and in her own time, but for now she concentrated on building bridges of friendship to her uncle by sending him courteous letters and making her father's life more bearable in the Palazzo Guadagni.

When she arrived in Florence she was horrified to find the king in such poor physical condition that she immediately set about re-organizing his life as well as improving the running of his household. She even persuaded him to lift himself out of the rut of Florence and accompany her on a visit to Lucca to see the opera there. Within weeks Charlotte had added a new dimension to Prince Charlie's life and he loved it. She improved her mother's lot too by persuading him to start to pay her a pension within a month of joining him.

Charles also made a new will and sent off to Liège for an authenticated copy of the record of Charlotte's baptism, and when it arrived he made a declaration confirming her as his child:

That Charlotte Stuart, created by him Duchess of Albany and legitimated with the approval of the Most Christian King, now

266

living in his palace at Florence, was the same as the child of himself and Clementine Walkingshaw, born at Liège and baptized there under the name of Charlotte Johnson, she being his only daughter. He further declares that he never had any other child and in particulare by the Princess of Stolberg.[21]

The people of Florence and visitors to the city were astonished and delighted at the change Charlotte brought about in her father, and so was the Pope, who accepted her new title, Duchess of Albany, to the embarrassment of Cardinal York.

Thanks to Robert Burns, Charlotte has gone into history as a bonnie, sweet, wronged lass who was full of goodness:

> My heart is wae and unco wae,
>   To think upon the raging sea,
> That roars between her gardens green,
>   And the bonie lass of Albanie.
>
> This lovely maid's of royal blood,
>   That ruled Albion's kingdoms three;
> But Oh, Alas! for her bonie face!
>   They hae wrang'd the lass of Albanie.[22]

Prince Charlie's daughter was wronged, there can be no denying that, but the injury was done her by her own family rather than by the British nation or Hanoverian kings as Burns suggests. She was also a hard-headed woman, who had fought tenaciously all her life for what should have been hers as a daughter and as heir to the Stuarts and now that her opportunity came, she seized it. Nobody – neither Charles Stuart himself nor Henry, and certainly not Louise of Stolberg – would stop her. And whether she was fighting her fight with sweet words and deeds or acidic verbal attacks, she showed no quarter.

Nothing would put Charlotte Stuart off: in one letter to her mother she complained that her father would not allow her to go and meet the cardinal, thus spoiling everything she had worked so hard to bring about. 'I shall return to the charge again,' she added with Stuart grit.[23]

A visitor who met Charlotte during her 'campaign', described her as having 'more masculine boldness than feminine modesty'.[24] That was a shrewd judgement: the 'Lass of Albany' was as tough as she was clever.

With the turn of the year she set out, quite coldly and deliberately to win Henry over and to make peace between the brothers, using as her weapon more of those sweet ingratiating letters and appealing to his better nature by telling him about her liver trouble. She stopped at nothing and Henry was as easily taken in by his niece as he had been by his sister-in-law. Eventually he melted sufficiently to tell her, 'Since you appear so anxious for my friendship and my confidence, which greatly pleases me, I can assure you sincerely that you have both.'[25]

She was cock-a-hoop and couldn't wait to tell her mother of her triumph:

You will have learned from my friends the miracle that had been performed in Rome. My word, it is a great victory.[26]

She even seems to have mediated between her father and her mother, and a kind of half-reconciliation took place between them – another minor miracle! From then on the two corresponded spasmodically.

Through all her machinations and organizing she still found time to write to her mother a couple of times a week, telling her all the news of Florence, reporting on Charles's health and her own, ordering clothes, and constantly asking after her archbishop and their children, whom she refers to as her 'amis'.[27] She missed all four very much and constantly wished she could be with them. Once she told her mother she would like to be a little bird and fly to join them. Another time she asked her mother to kiss her 'amies' – Charlotte was never too good on her genders – 'It's for you, it's for them that I work (to get money).'

Charlotte was extravagant and had her mother send dresses, material, lace, hats, gloves, rouge, and even tobacco. Once she ordered two dozen pairs of shoes, asking for them to be made a little wider because the heat shrinks the leather. As Henrietta Tayler points out it was more likely that Charlotte's feet swelled in the hot Florence summer.

Charlotte had not finished yet. Her next objective was to humble Louise of Stolberg and oust her from the Stuart circle forever. By bringing to Henry's notice the way in which Charles's former wife had been living with Alfieri while pretending she was leading a blameless life, Charlotte set in train a sequence of events that threatened Louise's future financial comfort and cut her out of the king's will.

Charlotte became bolder and began to include barbed remarks about Louise in her letters, and again Henry was taken in. She referred to her father's former wife as 'madame' and actually went so far as to call Alfieri 'Alfi'. Eventually she came more into the open and began to spell out to her uncle what the pair were up to:

I am sure, Monseigneur, you must be greatly distressed at the conduct of M. Alfieri and his influence over Madame; your feelings of delicacy, and your principles must be shocked at the neglect of what is due to your house.[28]

Henry realized that he had been taken in by Louise once more and Charlotte had won the last battle of her campaign. It was a triumph worthy of Charles himself and it left Charlotte totally secure; what's more it was done without a breath of the Duchess of Albany's own liaison with the Archbishop of Bordeaux reaching the ears of the king or the cardinal.

At long last, in October 1785, all three met – Charles, Henry and Charlotte – at Monte Freddo near Perugia. They made a strange trio, the elderly ailing king, the pompous cardinal and the composed young woman oozing sweetness and virtue, but their coming together was a success far beyond anything that even they could have hoped for. Charles and Henry at last were realistic about one another, and Henry fell under his niece's spell. For the sake of his health, Charles agreed to give up his house in Florence and return to Rome.

It was a fairy-tale ending with arch-enemies reunited, the lost princess returned to her family, and all agreeing to live together happily ever after. And by and large that is exactly the way it turned out.

The Palazzo Muti was cleaned up and dusted down and by the end of October 1785 all was ready for Charles and Charlotte to return to Rome. Prince Charlie was not a man to hide his feelings and, when he wrote of his delight and affection for his brother, he clearly meant it. He even accepted that he would be known as the Count of Albany and expressed his homage to the Pope. Considering what a thorn Charles Stuart had been in the side of Popes over thirty years and the contempt in which he held the Catholic Church, it was clear that Charlotte's spell was transforming the rebel.

A delighted Henry travelled to Viterbo to meet his brother and niece and the trio drove into Rome on 8 December – home to the Muti. Henry gave Charlotte presents and introduced her to the best of Roman society and he frequently visited the Muti, where he was delighted to find so much affection and care being lavished on his brother by Charlotte.

Charlotte made up for all the royal years she had lost by dressing in the finest clothes and setting them off with Sobieski jewels at the lavish receptions she and her father gave at the Muti. She loved her title and the attention everyone gave her, and above all she basked in the adoration of her now doting father. The only problem was that her father began to display his old sin of jealousy because of the affection Charlotte was showing towards Henry – Charles Stuart could never share love, even the love of his daughter, with anyone.

With such similar iron wills, it was inevitable that Charles and his daughter should spark at one another from time to time, but there was no great lovers' passion involved, so differences were quickly passed over. Charlotte was brave enough even to check him when he drank too much, and it must be said that after Charlotte came into his life there was not a breath of scandalous drunkenness.[29]

One evening she tried to stop him from seeing a visitor named Greathead, but her father turned on her and said in his loud, cracked voice. 'I will speak to my own subjects in my own way.' To Greathead he added. 'Ay, and I will soon speak to you, Sir, in Westminster Hall.' Charlotte merely shrugged her shoulders.

When Greathead tactlessly raised memories of the '45 the effect was dramatic. 'Gradually the panorama of the past ran vividly before the dull brain,' one of his early biographers, Charles Ewald, wrote:

. . . for a brief moment the Prince was no longer the ruin of himself, but again the hero of the '45. His eyes brightened, he half rose from his chair, his face became lit up with unwonted animation, and he began the narrative of the campaign. He spoke with fiery energy of his marches, his victories, the loyalty of his Highland followers, his retreat from Derby, the defeat at Culloden, his escape, and then passionately dwelt upon the awful penalties so many had been called upon to pay for their devotion to his cause. But the recollection of so much bitter suffering – the butchery around Inverness, the executions at Carlisle and London, the scenes on Kennington Common and Tower Hill – was stronger than his strength could bear. His voice died in his throat, his eyes became fixed, and he sank upon the floor in convulsions. Alarmed at the noise, his daughter rushed into the room. 'Oh, Sir,' she cried to Mr Greathead, 'What is this? You must have been speaking to my father about Scotland and the Highlanders! No one dares to mention those subjects in his presence.'[30]

Charlotte's willpower had won her a great victory in her fight for her inheritance, but she still had one battle to face. Her health was poor and she genuinely feared that her father might outlive her: he kept approaching death's door only to see it close as he was about to pass through, and although it was clear that death was approaching, he still lived on. She knew that if she died before him her secret family would lose all their security, so she quietly determined to outlive him.

During the spring of 1786, when Charles had just passed his sixty-fifth birthday, his earlier illness recurred; his mind became clouded, he had alarming heart palpitations, limbs became swollen, there was difficulty with his breathing and bouts of nausea overwhelmed him.

Charlotte too was troubled by the 'obstruction' in her side and her illness was taking a great toll for someone who saw her at this time believed her to be 'on the verge of forty', whereas she was only thirty-three. This same person took away a rather uncomplimentary picture of her:

She was a tall robust woman of a very dark complexion and coarse-grained skin with more masculine boldness than feminine modesty or elegance, but easy and unassuming in her manners and amply possessed of that volubility of tongue and that spirit of coquetry for which the women of the country where she was educated have at all times been particularly distinguished.[31]

The Roman summer of 1786 became unbearably hot, so Charlotte tried to take Charles to Albano, where the air was more agreeable, but she could not prise him away from the fêtes and festivals, which he insisted on attending even though he had to be carried to them. At last he agreed to go and they spent the remainder of the summer and the autumn there together until he recovered a little. She saw something of her uncle at Albano, too, and was delighted that he was 'amoureux fou de moi'.[32]

Mann reported that during his stay at Albano, Charles even indulged in 'the folly practised by his father and grandfather to touch people who are affected with scrofulous disorders'.[33] It was one of Mann's last reports for in November the same year, soon after Charles returned to Rome for the winter, the British envoy in Florence died. He had been a voyeur at the keyhole of the Jacobite Cause for forty years and his demise must have brought some gratification to Prince Charlie's fading mind even if he was aware that he could not outlive his old enemy for long.

Through 1787 Charles lingered on and Charlotte, who was also suffering considerable pain from her recurring liver complaint, caught smallpox. Although she recovered she became less certain that she would live to inherit her father's fortune, but she struggled on to humour and nurse him and Charles was determined to get as much out of life as his sick body would allow, attending the opera, theatre, dinners and balls regularly. Again she could not drag him away to Albano until the beginning of July.

Clementine wanted to find a new lady-in-waiting in France, and boldly proposed that her former lover and the Duchesse de Montbazon (daughter-in-law of Louise of the passionate affair of 1746–7) should help to select someone. Charles agreed meekly.

By the time they returned to Rome from Albano the king was failing badly. Just a week after his sixty-seventh birthday a paralytic stroke struck him down on 7 January 1788, and his brother hurried to his bedside to give him the last rites, but Charles lingered on, lying on a bed under a canopy, eyes open but unseeing, haunted by the '45 and his expulsion from France in 1748.

For three weeks he clung to life, suffering more strokes from which he never regained consciousness. Charlotte was distressed that she herself was ill and could not go to his room until 23 January, but Charles Edward Stuart was now so close to death that it scarcely mattered whether she was with him or not – she had been there to comfort the last four years of his life.

At nine o'clock on the morning of 30 January 1788 Charles III, King over the Water, died. Charlotte, Henry and his staff kept silent until the following day because 30 January was the anniversary of the execution of his great-grandfather, King Charles I in 1649 and too painful a day for the death of another Stuart monarch to be announced.

That iron will had won Charlotte her final wish: she had lived to inherit everything her father possessed apart from a piece of plate which was bequeathed to his brother and a few annuities to his servants. As his legitimate daughter she was also entitled to style herself Queen of Great Britain and Ireland, but Charlotte had no interest in that century-old claim. She left it to her uncle to proclaim himself king, and have medals struck bearing his portrait and the legend: 'Henry Ninth, King of England.'

Charlotte kept in touch with her mother and hoped fervently that she would be able to make Clementine's life easier and to help her children. 'Have courage, mother,' she wrote. 'One day we shall be happy together. The day when I can come to you will surely be the most beautiful of my life.'[34]

But they were never to see one another again. Charlotte continued to write, always asking after her children, and obsessed with money to give all of them the comfort for which she had fought for so long. But among all this she still found energy to order clothes, to complain if a dress was too short or too tight, and to order more and more shoes – not too tight though!

The new year brought new worries – 1789 was not a good time to be of aristocratic blood and in Paris, and Charlotte worried herself sick about the safety of her mother and the children in the Revolution. She begged Clementine to go to Switzerland, where it was peaceful.

Charlotte herself was not at all well, her liver complaint had worsened after her father's death and she was suffering great pain. Towards the end of the summer she went to Nocera to take the waters to help her condition and for a time she did feel better – well enough to ask her mother to go out and buy her some lace because she believed prices would be low following the storming of the Bastille.

On 22 August 1789 she wrote to her mother from Nocera saying that she had a pain in the place where she had formerly had an obstruction, and a month later she referred to the swelling which was rather like the one she had before. Soon it became clear that her only hope lay in surgery and on 14 October she made her will and received the last rites. The operation was performed and she bore it with enormous fortitude – *incusionem forti animo sustimuit*, they wrote – but it was too late, the cancer was advanced and gangrene had set in. She died on 17 November 1789.

The Lass of Albany had enjoyed a mere five years of contentment.

It is easy to dismiss Charlotte as hard and self-seeking, but that accusation must be set against the years of neglect and rejection which she suffered. She lived the life of an unwanted illegitimate daughter and then of a princess whose royalty was only conferred by a king without a crown – royal status which many around her denied her.

Charlotte grew up in poverty, a state which sharpens the mind to spot opportunities, and seize them. One must admire her single-minded determination and her systematic, cold plan to gain what should have been hers anyway, was fully justified. She fought her fight and won it round by round against her father's cruel neglect, against her uncle's empty prudery, and against Louise of Stolberg's determination to take it all away from her. The only fight she could not win was against the cruel cancer which claimed her life.

She gave much in return to her father and uncle: to Charles she brought the comfort and peace which enabled him to enjoy the closing years of his life, and to Henry she proved by friendship and sweetness that she truly belonged to the Stuart family.

The Lass of Albany was loved by Prince Charlie, both when she lived with him as a child and when she was his comfort during the twilight of his life: in between he loved her too, but because he could not have her with him on his terms, he denied that love even to himself. His deep affection for his daughter highlights that great flaw in Charles Stuart's character which cost him so much.

He would never have rediscovered her love, but for her own strength of character. Charlotte was the only woman in Charles Stuart's life who ever got the better of him.

EIGHTEEN

LOVE LOST AND LOVE FOUND

Follow thee! Follow thee! wha wadna follow thee?
Lang hast thou loved and trusted us fairly!
Charlie, Charlie, wha wadna follow thee,
King o' the Highland hearts, bonny Prince Charlie?

'Bonnie Prince Charlie', song by James Hogg.

By the time Bonnie Prince Charlie died his Cause had long since gone to its rest also, and his brother's decision to proclaim himself Henry IX was easily ignored in Rome, London or Edinburgh. The Cause was history.

Most of the women who had been Charles Edward's admirers, friends or lovers had gone by 1788 too.

Dear, faithful old Lady Bruce, who had done so much to ensure the Jacobites would be remembered in history, died in 1752, only six years after the end of the '45 and at the exact moment when Clementine Walkinshaw joined the Prince at Ghent to begin her eight-year penance as his partner and mother of his child.

Lady Primrose, that other great benefactress of the Cause, was long dead too: she had fallen out with the Prince after Clementine Walkinshaw joined him and gave him no further support to the end of her days in 1773.

Prince Charlie's little Louise de Montbazon, for whom he faced the canonfire of Madame de Guéméné's wrath, appeared to come to terms with the loss of the man she had loved so passionately and who had rejected her so cruelly. She lived out her life quietly as wife of the limp Jules de Rohan, and when she died in 1781, was interred at the side of the love-child Prince Charlie had given her in the family tomb at the Convent of the Feuillants in Paris. It is not possible to make a pilgrimage to the grave of Prince Charlie's son and the woman he loved more passionately than any other, because the church of the Feuillants was swept away in the nineteenth century to make way for the rue de Castiglione and the rue de Rivoli.[1]

Madame de Talmont, too, had died long before – in 1773 – the aged, witty courtesan to the last. The Marquise du Deffand told Sir Horace Walpole that on her deathbed she summoned her doctor, her priest and her steward and spoke to each in turn. She told the doctor he had killed her, but had done so in conformity with his rules and principles: the father confessor had caused her great fear; and the steward was present only because her staff wanted her to make her will. To all of them she said, 'You are all of you playing your parts very well, but you must grant I am not playing mine badly either.'[2] And so the most sexually experienced of Prince Charlie's women made her exit.

One wonders what she might have had to say to Charles Stuart had be been at her bedside – perhaps she would have repeated what she had already told him in a letter: 'It is not friends you need, but victims.'

One tends to forget that Jenny Cameron was a victim of the Prince and his Cause. All her life she suffered from vicious Hanoverian propaganda, and yet she maintained a dignified silence which brought her great respect. Important people came to visit her at Blacklaw, East Kilbride, where she settled and she talked politics knowledgably with them. It was said that her interest extended beyond her own country, which indicates that she kept in touch with what was happening to the Prince over the Water. John Lindsay, who saw her only a month before she died, said she lay in bed, perfectly clear in her mind, but her body was wasted away and her hand too weak to sign the receipt for some rent money he had brought. She held the pen, kissed it, and handed it to her niece and asked her to sign on her behalf.[3]

Jenny died on 27 June 1773, and in her will she bequeathed £1,500 to be divided among her four nieces. To her spendthrift brother she left only £68 'to put on and wear mournings' for her, and she left £100 to pay for interment at the family burial place at Kilcolmkil in her native Morvern, with another £50 to erect a tomb in the churchyard.

Jenny was given the nearest thing possible to a Highland funeral with plenty to eat and to drink, and family and friends from the north in attendance, but her remains were not taken to Morvern. Whether from spite due to the meanness of the bequest to her brother, or because he simply hadn't the money, she was buried just beside the house in which she had lived, and her body rests there to this day.

Blacklaw house was sold towards the end of the eighteenth century and in the course of time the land around it was turned into a golf-course. The building was demolished in 1958 and houses were built on its site as part of East Kilbride's development as a new town. However, the site of Jenny's grave was left undisturbed and, in a small enclosure, a tree and a plaque mark her resting place. In her lifetime Jenny had few compliments paid to her by Prince Charlie or anyone else, Jacobite or Whig, but the names Mount Cameron and Glen Dessary are still to be found in the area of East Kilbride where she lived.

Four of the most important women in Prince Charlie's life outlived him – the woman who saved his life, his wife, his mistress and mother of his daughter, and of course his daughter.

Flora MacDonald learned of the Prince's death while she was living out her own last years in Skye. In spite of the fact that Lady Primrose and her friends in London gathered a fortune of £1,500 for Flora, life for the heroine had not been easy since she was released from custody in 1747. Flora returned to the Hebrides and married Allan MacDonald, son of Kingsburgh, who had sheltered the Prince in his house on Skye.

She and her husband lost virtually all their money through bad luck, bad weather, bad economic conditions on the island, and bad decisions of their own. They were as poor as church mice when Dr Johnson and James Boswell visited them during their tour of the Western Isles in 1773, but the travellers were greatly taken by Allan's fine Highland presence and Flora's gentle manners and elegant appearance. Seated at her fireside they heard the story of the Prince's rescue from her own lips, then the doctor commanded Boswell to write it all down.

To escape the poverty and misery of the islands, Flora and her husband emigrated to North Carolina in 1774, just in time to be caught up in the American Revolutionary wars there.[4] Again, Flora chose the wrong side, and her husband, who raised an army of Highlanders for King George, was defeated at Moore's Creek Bridge early in 1776, and was taken prisoner. While her husband was held in gaols in the north, Flora suffered terrible hardship and ill treatment and lost everything of value that she owned. She was allowed eventually to join her husband in New York after his release, and they spent a bitterly cold winter in Nova Scotia before returning separately to Skye. Flora died there in 1790 and Allan died two years later. To the end of her life – and ever since – Flora MacDonald has been a heroine, worthy of Dr Johnson's epitaph, written after he met her in 1773:

Her name will be mentioned in history, and if courage and fidelity be virtues, mentioned with honour.[5]

There was no love between Prince Charlie and Flora, and one must question how much real love there was between the Prince and the woman he married. Louise of Stolberg did not grieve for her husband after they parted. She held her little court with the poet, Alfieri, in Florence until her lover's death, after which she poured out her shallow soul in letters to all who were prepared to read them. Chateaubriand found Louise 'commonplace' and wrote of her: 'If Rubens' women grew old they would look like Madam d'Albany at the age when I mew her.'[6]

Compton Mackenzie was harsher still in his epitaph for this last Stuart queen, who died in 1824:

She began life as a chatterbox with good teeth and a pretty complexion. She ended it as a dowdy, interminable old bore, in a large red shawl.[7]

How much real love existed between Clementine Walkinshaw and Charles Stuart is a matter of doubt, and Clementine certainly received little reward for the years of her life that she gave to the Prince and the decades of effort she put into ensuring that the child she bore him received her due as Prince Charlie's daughter.

Had Charlotte of Albany lived longer, things might have been different, but after her daughter's death, Clementine was left without money or powerful friends to protect her in revolutionary France. She was lucky to escape with her life and died in genteel poverty at Fribourg in Switzerland in 1802.

The death of the Bonnie Lass of Albany was not the end of the saga of Prince Charlie's children, in or out of marriage. Charlotte left three illegitimate children behind, all fathered by her lover, Prince Ferdinand of Rohan, Archbishop of Bordeaux, who could all claim to be children of the royal Stuart blood – even if it was on the wrong side of the blanket twice over.

Virtually nothing is known of Prince Charlie's two female grandchildren, but his grandson, Charles, grew up to serve in the Russian army and at court there, before travelling to America and then to Britain to petition the Prince Regent for support, which he was never given.

Charles used the title Count of Roehenstart and lived the life of an adventurer, always seeking to prove his right as a legitimate child of Charlotte and grandchild of Prince Charlie. He married twice, but had no family, and he died from injuries received when a coach on which he was travelling as an outside passenger overturned at Dunkeld in Perthshire in October 1854. He was buried in Dunkeld Cathedral and on his memorial are carved the words, 'Sic transit gloria mundi', the end of a once glorious house.

But Count Roehenstart was not the last to claim to be heir to the 'once glorious' royal house of Stuart. While the official royal line rather boringly sought a new identity by reaching back to Charles I's daughter, Princess Henrietta, who married the Duc d'Orleans, other claimants hove into view. Claimants as colourful as they were improbable.

In 1847 a book was published in Edinburgh under the title, *Tales of the Century of Sketches of the Romance of History Between the Years*

1746 and 1846. The authors called themselves John Sobieski Stuart and Charles Edward Stuart, and their work, a novel copiously augmented with historical notes, contained three tales concerning the birth, youth and marriage of a man known by the Gaelic name of *Iolair dhearg* or *Red Eagle.*[8]

Briefly, the book begins with a tale told by an aged Jacobite, called Dr Beaton, who was called to attend a young woman in Tuscany in 1773, and arrives to find she has just been delivered of a son. In the room he sees a portrait of James Stuart and 'an exquisite miniature of my noble, my unfortunate, my exiled Prince'. When he has treated the patient he is told to leave Tuscany at once, but at the coast a little later he sees a woman and baby being taken aboard the British warship HMS *Albina.*

The second tale takes the story to the Scottish Highlands years later and to a mysterious young man, known as the *Red Eagle,* who is said to be the son of the man who had commanded the *Albina.* A stranger in full Highland dress and accompanied by a piper and attendants in brilliant red tartan steps ashore from another warship, and in the course of a chain of adventures, an old man, who claims to have been present at Culloden, addresses the *Red Eagle* as *Your Royal Highness* – an understandable mistake in the confused old mind since *Iolair* bears a very close resemblance to the Prince.

The last of the tales is set in Derbyshire, where *Iolair* is in love with Catharine Bruce, daughter of a local landowner. Of course, the mysterious guide from Tuscany is also there and addresses the *Red Eagle* as *My Prince. Iolair* rescues Catharine and wins her hand.

The story is a veiled claim of John Sobieski Stuart and Charles Edward Stuart to be the sons of a child of Charles and Louise, and consequently legitimate claimants to Queen Victoria's throne. Behind the fiction are factual characters: old Admiral O'Haleran was Admiral John Carter, grandfather of the authors, who at the time of his death in 1800, was described as related to the Marquesses of Salisbury and Downshire and the *de jure* Earl of Erroll. Young O'Haleran, the *Red Eagle,* is his son, Thomas, who was the father of the Sobieski Stuart brothers.

Thomas was the child alleged to be the son of Charles and Louise and in the book the reason given for smuggling him out of Italy is fear of kidnapping by British secret agents. And yet he was entrusted to a Hanoverian sea captain aboard a British warship and taken to Britain to be brought up by the captain!

What reason could Charles Stuart have had for wanting to conceal the birth of an heir – the heir he married expressly to beget? And how could Louise's pregnancy and confinement have been concealed from all the Jacobite household, let alone from prying British spies? Louise, too, would not have remained silent. During the Napoleonic wars the Emperor sent for her, hoping that she might admit to having borne a son whom he could make King of Scotland in return for Scottish help against England.

'Have you never had a child?' he asked.

'No, sir. Never,' Louise replied.

'What a pity, madame,' answered the Emperor and left her abruptly.

The Sobieski Stuarts produced other works whose literary veracity was questioned with good reason. John Sobieski called himself Count of Albany and his brother adopted the title after his death. Some of the Scottish nobility accepted the pair as Prince Charlie's heirs and, although the brothers never proclaimed themselves king, they lived as decayed royalty, accepting the hospitality of those who believed them and ignoring with great dignity those who did not. They bore some physical resemblance to the Stuarts and this they cultivated carefully to support their claim.

John Sobieski married rather late in life and died without issue in 1872. His younger brother, Charles Edward, married Anne Beresford, a member of the Marquess of Waterford's family, and they had four children. Their only son, another Charles Edward, married into the Erroll family to which the Allens had had pretensions generations before. He died without issue in 1882.

After the death of his wife, the elder Charles Edward lived in poverty in lodgings in the Pimlico district of London, but kept up the Stuart pretence, walking through the streets dressed in Royal Stuart tartan or in some foreign uniform bedecked with medals he had not won, but purchased. He died in France in 1880 and is buried beside his brother at Eskadale in Ross-shire under a Celtic cross which proclaims their pretensions to be the wronged kings of Scotland.

How well the Sobieski Stuarts would have fitted into the unreal world of Bonnie Prince Charlie: their very existence keeps alive the question of his relationships with the opposite sex and adds to the romance which history has built around him. When Charles Stuart was no longer the bonnie prince, legend took over – legend which grew as the pain of the '45 receded and only its glories were remembered.

Even when the Cause was in its death throes on the Continent, there were many in Scotland who were still prepared to drink toasts to the King over the Water and sing songs in praise of the Cause.

The Laird of Gask, who had been out in the '45 rising would never permit King George to be mentioned by name, but insisted when the newspapers were read to him that the king and queen be referred to as 'K' and 'Q'. When his daughter was born in 1766 he named her Carolina after the Prince. Carolina Oliphant grew up to be a true Jacobite like her father, and married into another Jacobite family, the Nairnes. As Lady Nairne she became a prolific writer of Jacobite songs, full of that haunting heartache for the lost cause. Sorrow, loyalty and hope are all to be found in Lady Nairne's Jacobite songs, 'Charlie He's My Darling', 'The Hundred Pipers', 'Will Ye No' Come Back Again?', and a host of others, which paint a very different portrait from the real Prince Charlie who claimed to be King Charles III. But no one cared about historical accuracy when they sang about the Cause or its hero.

Charlie had enormous personal charisma, which ensnared every woman who came within his orbit, but his misfortune was that he was incapable of returning the love they offered him so generously. To discover the root of this failure one has to delve into his childhood in what was virtually a broken home, with parents who could not cope with each other let alone with their children. The Muti Palace was a miserable place for a boy to grow up in: it was not a home, nor were the Stuarts a family in any real sense of the word. Charles and Henry each coped with boyhood in this strange environment in his own way – Charles by becoming difficult and despising authority and Henry by retreating into religion.

James Stuart was a sad, ineffectual, dithering, dull, uninspiring, but well-meaning man, who tried so hard to rear Charles to be a good man and a good monarch when the time came. Unfortunately from Prince Charlie's early youth it became clear that James accepted that he would never be restored. Neither he nor his son would ever inherit.

As the Prince came to realize this he began to question his father's decisions and advice, then he came to despise them. When his brother, Henry, became a cardinal of the Roman Catholic Church and it was clear that James was openly accepting defeat, Prince Charlie cut himself off from both of them. The loss of affection for his brother hardly mattered, but he needed his father's support, steadying hand – and love. Cutting himself off from that was the worst and most stupid mistake Bonnie Prince Charlie ever made.

His mother's influence affected Prince Charlie to his dying day. Clementina Sobieska arrived in Italy a little Polish princess with a fantasy that one day she would become Queen of England. As the truth dawned that she would never achieve her dream she turned from a volatile, vivacious young woman into neurotic, bigot, who ruined her health and her relationship with her husband and sons by spending all her time fasting and praying day after day and far into the night. Yet she was unable to stop herself from continuing along this self-destructive way. Charles needed his mother; he missed her, and yet when she was there he feared her neurotic rages. Worse, having poured out her love to him, she would go off to church or into a convent without warning, withdrawing her affection for long periods. To a child these unexplained disappearances of the woman he adored and the withdrawal of love, must have caused great traumas in the child's mind and her early death left a void which no woman was ever able to fill. Clementina had a devastating affect on her son's ability to love.

Prince Charlie has been accused of being undersexed, but that charge does not stand up when it is viewed against the all-engulfing passion with which he fell in love with his cousin, Louise. He was monogamous by nature, however, and never took more than one lover at a time: even when he was leading a wild life in Paris with young Glengarry in 1744, there was little mention of whoring. The Bouillons were noted womanizers, yet there is no evidence that Charles was promiscuous when he was with them.

His late development as a lover was probably a defence against the fear of losing love as had happened so often during his childhood. But when Prince Charlie did discover love, he delighted in it, and relished the sexual side of the relationship as much as any man. He knew deep passion, although he had no idea how to handle it sensibly, and his mistresses never had to fear so long as the liaison was working smoothly that he might abandon them for some other woman.

As a lover, Prince Charlie could be a gentleman, but a gentleman with a sinister, dark side.

Margaret Forster put her finger on the truth of his relationship with the female sex. Harking back to Clementina Sobieska's influence on her son, she wrote:

> His attitude towards women as a species was romantic. His mother had been a lady one treated with respect, who disliked noise or violence of any sort, whom one felt privileged to serve. She had at all times to be handled gently, as though she might break. When Charles grew up he began by treating all women like this. He was polite, full of small, meaningless attentions, gravely concerned for their welfare. He never flirted, was never vulgar or lewd, sought rather to keep them at a distance rather than touch them.[9]

This solicitude and attentiveness was evident in his contact with Lady Anne Mackintosh and Flora MacDonald; it was even present throughout the first part of his liaison with his cousin Louise, and he showed it towards Clementine Walkinshaw and Louise of Stolberg when they first came to him. Unfortunately, as soon as a relationship proceeded to become a continuing one, this gentle approach was overwhelmed by such jealousy that he could not prevent himself from picking quarrels which often ended in beatings. Charles Edward never had his father's self-control.

Drink has often been blamed for these fights and beatings, but that is only part of the story. He drank heavily and by night-time was often the worse for wear, but the loss of self-control derived from something deeply embedded in the Prince's psyche from an early age. Charles Stuart could not bear to be ordered about or contradicted – by women, by his father, by the King of France, or by life itself. His immediate response was to lash out with his sharp tongue, or, in the case of his women, with his fists. Every woman he cared for carried the bruises of his brutality.

Nothing was ever Charles Stuart's fault: how could it be when he was Prince by Divine Right, chosen by God and responsible only to God? When a liaison foundered – for whatever reason – he always had to blame someone other than himself. And when he could not get his way he had to demonstrate arrogantly that he did not want whatever it was that he had been denied. This attitude did not apply just to love, but to everything in life, and he paid dearly for this uncompromising approach to life.

Prince Charlie fell in love for many reasons – in the case of his cousin, Louise de Montbazon, it began with the joy of being part of a family and the relationship simply drifted into love, which grew more passionate by the day, or rather by the night, since this was a stolen liaison conducted while his lover's husband and mother-in-law were asleep in the same house.

With Talmont, the experienced courtesan, it was not a conquest by the Prince, but a case of Charles being stalked and snatched by her. The Princess was ageing, but was determined to win the most talked about man in Europe as the crowning conquest of her career. She caught her prey, but regretted it – why else would she tell Charlie he needed victims, not friends?

He chose Clementine Walkinshaw because she was kind to him when he felt low and betrayed as the '45 uprising collapsed, and she proved a pliable, obedient subject: he was her Prince and she promised to come to him if he ever wanted her. When he was alone and at a low ebb again in 1752, he sent for her, and she rushed to his side just as she had said she would. She discovered too late that he may have been her Prince, but he was not her Prince Charming.

Louise of Stolberg was chosen for him just as Clementina Sobieska had been chosen for his father. And the result was even more disastrous. Soon the glamour of being consort to the King over the Water wore off for both of them: no heir appeared and the marriage held nothing else for either of them. Louise soon turned to flirting and then to more serious affairs, but by then, Charles was a drunken cuckold, who could hardly have fathered an heir had his wife been the most fertile woman in all Italy. Dynastic marriages did not suit the later Stuarts.

Although his liaison with Clementine Walkinshaw quickly turned sour, it did provide him with love, and later with comfort through the daughter she bore him. Charles adored Charlotte from the day she was born and felt her loss deeply when Clementine walked out with the child and sought sanctuary in a convent. He didn't care about losing his mistress, but was greatly upset to have his beloved child taken from him.

And how did he respond? When he discovered he could not get Charlotte back, he simply acted in his usual way, as if he did not want her anyway. What Charles Stuart could not have, he didn't want. And so for twenty years he refused to contribute to his daughter's upbringing or even to admit she existed. Then, when he had lost any chance of love from Louise of Stolberg, he suddenly offered Charlotte a home and the inheritance he had denied her for so long. She came to him, he adored her and showered all the love he had left on her. And in return she brought comfort to his last years.

For a man who had destroyed every love he had ever known, Charles Stuart was fortunate at last to find in Charlotte a form of love with which he could cope.

Bonnie Prince Charlie was attractive to women, and women attracted him: with them he had even been able to discover the joy of a complete sexual relationship leading to fatherhood. His tragedy is that, although he knew passion, he was never able to love any woman deeply or for long: nor could he accept the boundless love that they offered him in return.

NOTES

RA SP = Stuart Papers in Royal Archives, Windsor Castle
AN = Archives Nationales, Paris
AEMD = Archives Etrangères. Mémoires et Documents, French Foreign Ministry Archives, Paris
Arsenal = Archives de la Bastille, Musée de l'Arsenal, Paris
NLS = National Library of Scotland

1. YE BONNY PRINCE

1. The Place Royale is now the Place des Vosges and Louise's house, the Hotel de Guéméné, houses the Victor Hugo Museum.
2. The undated letters which Louise, Duchesse de Montbazon, sent to the Prince and their intermediaries during their passionate affair are among the Stuart Papers at Windsor Castle. They have been published and the liaison documented for the first time by Laurence L. Bongie in his book, The Love of a Prince, published in 1986. I am indebted to the work of Professor Bongie, who has transcribed and dated the letters as closely as possible. The letters can be found in the RA SP 316/3 to 91.
3. Duc de Luynes, Mémoires du Duc de Luynes sur la Cour de Louis XV, Vol. 4, p. 296.
4. L.L. Bongie, The Love of a Prince, pp. 10 and 396.
5. David, Lord Elcho, A Short Account of the Affairs of Scotland in the Years 1744, 1745 and 1746, p. 26

6. Ibid., pp. 306–7.
7. See Chapter 5, Page 49.
8. James Lees-Milne, The Last Stuarts, p. 71.
9. Letter from Magdalen (Maddie) Pringle to her sister, Isabella (Tibbie), 18 September 1745. Henrietta Tayler, A Jacobite Miscellany, p. 39.
10. Peggy Miller, James, p. 267.
11. Baron de Pollnitz, Memoirs, Vol. 2, p. 196.
12. W.B. Blaikie, Origins of the '45, p. 243.
13. Hugh Douglas, Charles Edward Stuart, the Man, the King, the Legend, p. 245.
14. Andrew Lang. Prince Charles Edward Stuart, p. 4.
15. The date of Charles's death is usually given as 31 January 1788, but Lord Stanhope claimed that he actually died the previous day, and his brother and others suppressed the news because that was too ill-omened a day for the Stuarts, the anniversary of the execution of his great-grandfather, Charles I. The relevant pages from Henry's diary are missing.

288

2. A POISONED INHERITANCE

1. Robert Burns, letter to Edinburgh Evening Courant, 8 November 1788.
2. The spelling was changed in the sixteenth century while Mary, Queen of Scots was living in France, in order to accommodate the lack of a letter 'W' in the French alphabet and to facilitate pronunciation.
3. La race du Stuarts a mis 119 ans à s'éteindre après avoir perdu le trône qu'elle n'a jamais retrouvé. Trois prétendants se sont transmis dans l'exil à l'ombre d'une couronne: ils avaient de l'intelligence et du courage, que leur a-t-il manqué? La main du Dieu. – Chateaubriand. Quoted in Marchesa Nobili-Vitelleschi, A Court in Exile, Vol. 1, p. 1.
4. The King's Quhair (The King's Book) first published by William Tytler in 1783 from manuscript now in Bodleian Library, Oxford.
5. John Major, History of Greater Britain, 1512. (Scottish History Society edition), p. 368.
6. Gordon Donaldson, Scottish Kings, p. 159.
7. R.H. Mahon, Mary, Queen of Scots, p. 120.
8. Maurice Lee, John Maitland of Thirlestane and the Foundations of the Stewart Despotism in Scotland, p. 177.
9. Otto J. Scott, James I, p. 177.
10. James VI, Basilikon Doron. Scottish Text Society edition. Second Book, p. 131.
11. Mme de Motteville, Mémoires. Quoted in C. Oman, Henrietta Maria, p. 72.
12. Berwick, Duke of, Mémoires du Maréchal de Berwick, écrit par lui-même, p. xxiv.
13. Peggy Miller, A Wife for the Pretender, pp. 20–1.
14. Frank McLynn, The Jacobites, pp. 190–1
15. Historical Manuscripts Commission, Stuart Papers, Vol. 5, pp. 234–5.
16. Ibid.

3. JEWEL OF THE SOBIESKIS

1. Lubomirski Papers, No.2, p. 1. Quoted in Peggy Miller, A Wife for the Pretender, p. 39.
2. Otto Forst de Battaglia, Jan Sobieski, König von Polen, p. 16.
3. Ibid. p. 19
4. Ibid. p. 23
5. Ibid. p. 29
6. Ibid. p. 306
7. W.R. Morfill, Poland, p. 164.
8. Ibid. p. 172.
9. Norman Davies, God's Playground, Vol. 1, p. 489.
10. W.R. Morfill, Poland, p. 175.
11. O.F. de Battaglia, Jan Sobieski, König von Polen, p. 307
12. W.R. Morfill, Poland, p. 488.
13. Lubomirski Papers, No.2, p. 1. Quoted in P. Miller, A Wife for the Pretender, p. 39.
14. H. Tayler, Jacobite Epilogue, p. 281.
15. Sir Charles Petrie, The Jacobite Movement, pp. 308–9.
16. James to Duke of Ormonde, 11 November 1720. RA SP 50/30.
17. Duke of Berwick to James, 9 November 1720. RA SP 30/3.
18. Charles Edward's birthday was 31 December 1720, but in Scotland they celebrated it on 20 December because Britain had not yet adopted the New

Style Gregorian calendar and consequently was eleven days behind the rest of Europe: the British government did not fall into line until 1752.

19. The Cracas, 4 January 1721, quoted in Nobili-Vitelleschi, A Court in Exile, p. 115. The Cracas was a weekly diary of political news published in Rome between 1614 and 1798, when it was replaced by the Monitore della Repubblica Romana.

20. Andrew Lang, quoting the spy Baron Philip von Stosch in Prince Charles Edward Stuart, p. 13.

21. Susan MacLean Kybett, Bonnie Prince Charlie, p. 30.

22. A correspondence on Prince Charlie's health was published in The Scotsman during April 1988 (15 April, 22 April and 26 April).

23. John William O'Sullivan's Narrative. H. Tayler, 1745 and After, p. 188.

24. Mrs Fabienne Smith. Letter to The Scotsman, 22 April 1988.

25. Mrs Helen Cassels. Letter to The Scotsman, 15 April 1988.

26. Dr Rosalind K. Marshall. Letter to The Scotsman, 26 April 1988.

4. BELOVED, BETRAYED CARLUSU

1. Charles Edward to James, 4 May 1728. RA SP 115/161.

2. Clementina to James, 31 July 1722. RA SP 61/64.

3. John Hay (Earl of Inverness) to Duke of Mar, 21 April 1722. RA SP 61/29.

4. Hay to Clementina 1722, dated only Thursday evening. RA SP 64/93.

5. Complete Letters of Lady Mary Wortley Montagu, ed. Robert Halsband, Vol. 2, p. 228.

6. S.M. Kybett, Bonnie Prince Charlie, p. 32.

7. James to Prince James Sobieski, 16 November 1725. RA SP 87/81.

8. G. Lockhart of Carnwath, Memoirs Concerning the Affairs of Scotland, Vol. 2, p. 265.

9. James to Clementina, 9 November 1725. RA SP 87/94.

10. P. Miller, James, p. 281.

11. Margaret Forster, The Rash Adventurer, p. 25.

12. Hay (Lord Inverness) to Dr John Higgens, 20 May 1724. RA SP 74/84.

13. James to Francis Atterbury, 21 April 1724. RA SP 106/40.

14. Charles to James, 4 May 1728. RA SP 115/161.

15. James to Hay, 7 February 1728. RA SP 114/16.

16. H. Douglas, Charles Edward Stuart, The Man, The King, The Legend, p. 38.

17. Charles to James, 10 June 1729. RA SP 129/16. Author's italics.

18. James to Clementina, 12 June 1729. RA SP 129/29.

19. James to Hay, 12 August 1733. RA SP 164/16.

5. CARLUCCIO – 'DUTIFULL SON'

1. Charles to James, 10 June 1729. RA SP 129/16.

2. Dunbar to James, 19 June 1742. RA SP 246/139.

3. Ibid.

4. Ibid.

5. Alice Shield, Biography of Cardinal of York. Preface. p. xx.

6. James Lees-Milne, The Last Stuarts, p. 153.

7. Edgar to James, 20 November 1742. RA SP 245/146.
8. Ibid.
9. A. Lang, Prince Charles Edward Stuart, p. 39.
10. Dunbar to James, 19 June 1737. RA SP 198/29.
11. Sir Charles Petrie, The Jacobite Movement, p. 342.
12. James to Lord Sempill, 8 February 1742. RA SP 239/183.
13. Duncan C. Towey (ed.), Letters of Thomas Gray, Vol. VI, p. 74.
14. Although much has been said of the Prince's vow of chastity, I have seen no proof that Charles ever made a formal pledge to have nothing to do with women. Without doubt he put the restoration first up to the end of the '45. I am indebted to L.L. Bongie for this reference to a partly coded message from Drummond of Balhaldy to James's secretary, James Edgar, contained in RA SP 289/120.
15. Nancy Mitford, Madame de Pompadour, p. 1.
16. The duke's despicable intrigues are fully described in L.L. Bongie, The Love of a Prince, Chapters 1–5.
17. James to James Sobieski, 13 July 1737. RA SP 199/46.
18. Bouillon to James, 9 January 1743. RA SP 246/178.
19. Duc de Luynes, Mémoires du Duc de Luynes sur la Cour de Louis XV, 12 December 1742, Vol. 4, p. 296.
20. Ibid., Vol. 4, pp. 410–15.
21. Mémoires du Comte de Maurepas, Vol. III, p. 166. For this reference and its translation I am indebted to L.L. Bongie, The Love of a Prince, Appendix B, II, 1, p. 390.
22. Letter from James, dated 1 October 1742. Quoted in Sir Fitzroy Maclean, Bonnie Prince Charlie, p. 20.
23. Edgar to Earl Marischal. Quoted in H. Douglas, Charles Edward Stuart, The Man, The King, The Legend, p. 53.
24. Frank McLynn, Charles Edward Stuart, A Tragedy in Many Acts, p. 80.
25. British Museum, C115.i.362.
26. Rosalind K. Marshall, Bonnie Prince Charlie, p. 51.

6. THE GIRL HE LEFT BEHIND

1. Charles to James, 11 January 1745. RA SP 261/155.
2. A. Lang, Prince Charles Edward Stuart, p. 64.
3. Brian Fothergill, The Cardinal King, p. 40.
4. Charles to James, 10 February 1744. RA SP 255/163.
5. Ibid.
6. James to Lord Sempill, 13 February 1744. RA SP 252/82
7. Charles to James, 16 April 1744. RA SP 256/197.
8. Jon Manchip White, Marshal of France: The Life and Times of Maurice de Saxe, p. 132.
9. Charles to Lord Sempill, 15 March 1744. RA SP 256/131.
10. Rosalind K. Marshall, Bonnie Prince Charlie, p. 60.
11. Charles to James, 16 November 1744. Quoted in A. Lang, Prince Charles Edward Stuart, p. 78.
12. Charles to James, 3 January 1745. RA SP 261/109. I am indebted to L.L. Bongie for this and the next references.
13. Sir Thomas Sheridan to James Edgar, 21 December 1744. RA SP 261/12.

14. Duc de Luynes, Mémoires du Duc de Luynes sur la Cour de Louis XV (1735–1758), Vol. VI, p. 167.
15. Charles to James, 11 January 1745. RA SP 261/155.
16. Duc de Luynes, Mémoires du Duc de Luynes sur la Cour de Louis XV (1735–1758), Vol. 4, pp. 355–6.
17. Charles to James, 28 February 1745. RA SP 263/24.
18. Charles to James, 16 May 1745. RA SP 264/173.
19. Charles to Duke of Bouillon, dated 12 June 1745, but not sent until Charles Edward was ready to sail. AN 273 AP/206.

7. UNDER PETTICOAT PATRONAGE

1. The Female Rebels, pamphlet, no author, p. 6.
2. Sir Bruce Gordon Seton, Prisoners of the '45, Vol. 1, p. 212.
3. Ibid.
4. M. Forster, The Rash Adventurer, pp. 112–13.
5. R. Forbes, The Lyon in Mourning, Vol. 1, pp. 292–3.
6. James Caulfield, Remarkable Persons, p. 99. Quoted in Scottish Art and Letters, Vol. II, No. 4, 1903, p. 394.
7. Ibid.
8. Ibid.
9. Information from James Revie, East Kilbride Historical Society.
10. Ibid.
11. Lewis Spence, Prows o' Reekie, poem in collection, Plumes of Time, p. 35.

O wad this braw hie-heapit toun
Sail aff like an enchanted ship.

Drift owre the warld's seas up and doun
An' kiss wi' Venice lip to lip,
Or anchor into Naples Bay
A misty island far astray,
Or set her rock to Athens wa'.
Pillar to pillar, stane to stane,
The cruikit spell o' her backbane,
Yon shadow-smile o' spire and vane,
Wad ding them a', wad ding them a'
Cadiz wad tine the admiralty
O' yonder emrod fair sea,
Gibraltar frown for frown exchange
Wi' Nigel's Crags at elbuck range,
The rose-red banks o' Lisbon make
Mair room in Tagus for her sake.

12. Edinburgh Evening Courant, 10 September 1745.
13. W.B. Blaikie, Edinburgh at the Time of the Occupation of Prince Charles, p. 4.
14. Ibid.
15. Letter from Magdalen Pringle, 18 September 1745. H. Tayler, A Jacobite Miscellany, p. 38.
16. Ibid.
17. The Autobiography of Alexander Carlyle of Inveresk. Quoted in David Daiches, Bonnie Prince Charlie, p. 130.
18. Letter from Magdalen Pringle, 18 September 1745. H. Tayler, A Jacobite Miscellany, p. 38.
19. Letter from Magdalen Pringle, 13 October 1745. Ibid., p. 40.
20. John Home, History of the Rebellion in Scotland, pp. 71–2.
21. Diary of David, Lord Elcho. H. Tayler, A Jacobite Miscellany, p. 145.
22. The Woodhouselee Manuscript. A Narrative of Events in Edinburgh and District During the Jacobite

Occupation, September to November, 1745, p. 26.

23. James Maxwell of Kirkconnell, Narrative of Charles Prince of Wales's Visit to Scotland in the Year 1745, p. 38.

24. Magdalen Pringle to her sister, 18 September 1745. H. Tayler, A Jacobite Miscellany, p. 39.

25. Ibid.

26. Florence E. Dyer, 'The Highlanders in Edinburgh'. Article in SMT Magazine, August 1936, p. 27.

27. David, Lord Elcho, A Short Account of the Affairs of Scotland in the Years 1744, 1745 and 1746, pp. 306–7.

28. Magdalen Pringle, 18 September 1745. H. Tayler, A Jacobite Miscellany, p. 39.

29. Ibid. Note 4.

30. Woodhouselee Manuscript, p. 40. Note.

31. Threiplands of Fingask, p. 43. Quoted in W.B. Blaikie, Edinburgh at the Time of the Occupation of Prince Charles, p. 56.

32. Lord Elcho, Short Account of the Affairs of Scotland, pp. 306–7.

33. O'Sullivan's narrative. A.& H. Tayler, 1745 and After, p. 88.

34. Letter from Magdalen Pringle, 13 October 1745. H. Tayler, A Jacobite Miscellany, p. 40.

35. Ibid., pp. 40–1.

36. Andrew Lang, Prince Charles Edward Stuart, p. 3.

8. CONQUEST AT BANNOCKBURN

1. 'Mémoire rélatif à la naissance de Charlotte, fille de Charles Edouard, Prince de Galles.' Laid before King Louis in 1774. In Oeuvres Complètes de Louis de Saint Simon, p. 234. Quoted in C.L. Berry, The Young Pretender's Mistress, p. 101.

2. R. Forbes, Lyon in Mourning, Vol. 1, p. 185.

3. Ibid., title page.

4. Ibid., Vol 1. Preface, pp.xi–xxii.

5. Sir Bruce Seton, The Orderly Book of Lord Ogilvy's Regiment, pp. 17–18.

6. Sir Fitzroy Maclean, Bonnie Prince Charlie, p. 100.

7. The Female Rebels, p. 33.

8. A.F. Steuart, Scottish Art and Letters, Vol.11, No. 4, p. 395. I have been unable to trace this letter in Lang.

9. Henry Fielding, Tom Jones. Everyman edition, 1950, Vol. 2, p. 85.

10. Robert Ford (ed.), Vagabond Songs and Ballads of Scotland, With Many Old and Familiar Melodies (Paisley, 1901), pp. 12–14. I am indebted to Donald F. MacDonald for this reference.

11. Compton Mackenzie, Prince Charlie and his Ladies, p. 50.

12. O'Sullivan's Narrative. A. & H. Tayler, 1745 and After, p. 102.

13. The Female Rebels, p. 33.

14. 20 December by the Old Style calendar. 31 December, New Style.

15. Sir B. Seton, Prisoners of the '45, p. 214.

16. F. McLynn, Charles Edward Stuart, p. 204.

17. A. Lang, Prince Charles Edward Stuart, p. 238.

18. W. Drummond Norie, Life and Adventures of Prince Charles Edward Stuart, Vol. 3, pp. 15–17.

19. The fullest biography of Clementine Walkinshaw is The Young Pretender's Mistress by C. Leo Berry (Edinburgh,

1977). Mr Berry spent many years sifting through the many myths and slanders relating to the unfortunate Clementine.

20. H. Tayler, Prince Charlie's Daughter, p. 27.

21. Martin Haile, James Francis Edward, the Old Chevalier, p. 428.

22. W.D. Norie, Life and Adventures of Prince Charles Edward Stuart, Vol. 3, pp. 15–16.

23. Charlotte Stuart's Memorandum to Louis XV, 1774, printed in Oeuvres Complètes de Louis de Saint-Simon (published 1791). Quoted in C.L. Berry, The Young Pretender's Mistress, p. 28.

24. C.L. Berry, The Young Pretender's Mistress, p. 28.

25. H. Tayler, A Jacobite Miscellany, p. 154.

26. C.L. Berry, The Young Pretender's Mistress, p. 36.

27. R. Forbes, Lyon in Mourning, Vol. 2, p. 126.

28. Sir F. Maclean, Bonnie Prince Charlie, p. 168.

29. John Home, History of the Rebellion in Scotland, p. 355.

30. AEMD Angleterre. 81/94. Quoted in F. McLynn, Charles Edward Stuart, p. 416.

31. Tom Cross, A Lakeland Princess, p. 6.

32. Notes and Queries, 8th series, Vol. XI, 23 January 1897, pp. 66–7.

33. Donald Nicholas quoted by C.L. Berry, The Young Pretender's Mistress, p. 32.

34. Canon Townley's notes on his investigations into the Finsthwaite Princess are in the Abbot Hall Art Gallery, Kendal.

35. June C.F. Barnes, 'The Finsthwaite Princess'. In The Scots Magazine, April 1993.

36. Ibid.

37. H.S. Cowper, Hawkshead – its History, p. 253.

38. C.L. Berry, The Young Pretender's Mistress, Preface, p. x.

39. Robert Strange & Andrew Lumisden, Memoirs, ed. J. Dennison, Vol. 2, pp. 214–15.

9. 'COLONEL' ANNE AND HER REGIMENT

1. Alexander M. Mackintosh, The Mackintoshes and Clan Chattan, p. 335, footnote.

2. Cumberland to Newcastle, 2 February 1746. Quoted in T.E. Niven, East Kilbride, the History of the Parish and Village, p. 121.

3. W.B. Blaikie. Letter to The Scotsman, 13 July 1907.

4. Donald F. MacDonald, 'Bonnie Jean Cameron'. In The Scottish Field, February 1969.

5. F. Macdonald, 'Colonel Anne' Lady Anne MacKintosh 1723–1784, p. 3.

6. Ibid., pp. 3–4.

7. John Hill Burton and David Laing (eds), Jacobite Correspondence of the Atholl Family 1745–6, p. 95.

8. A. and H. Tayler, O'Sullivan's Narrative, 1745 and After, p. 129.

9. R. Forbes, Lyon in Mourning, Vol. 2, p. 137.

10. Ibid., pp. 135–6.

11. A. and H. Tayler, O'Sullivan's Narrative, 1745 and After, p. 130.

12. Ibid., p.129.

13. Ibid., p.131.

14. R. Forbes, Lyon in Mourning, Vol. 2, p. 269.

15. A. and H. Tayler, O'Sullivan's narrative, 1745 and After, pp. 130–1.
16. Sir F. Maclean, Bonnie Prince Charlie, p. 187.
17. F. Macdonald, 'Colonel' Anne, p. 13.
18. F. McLynn,Charles Edward Stuart, p. 233.
19. A. & H. Tayler, O'Sullivan's Narrative 1745 and After, p. 145.
20. James Ray, Complete History of the Rebellion. Quoted in Compton Mackenzie, Prince Charlie and his Ladies, p. 64.
21. R. Forbes, Lyon in Mourning, Vol. 2, pp. 113–14.
22. Ibid., Vol. 3, p. 155.
23. Ibid., Vol. 2, pp. 206–8 and p. 299.
24. Ibid., Vol. 3, p. 72.

10. THE ROMANCE THAT NEVER WAS

1. 'The Skye Boat Song' is a Victorian ballad with words by Sir Harold Boulton and music based on an old tune which Annie Campbell MacLeod heard Highland sailors singing while they rowed. It was first published in Songs of the North.
2. R. Forbes, Lyon in Mourning, Vol. 1, p. 304.
3. The first, by Flora's kinsman, Neil MacEachain, was lost in France at the time of the Revolution, but reappeared and was published in the New Monthly Magazine in 1840 and subsequently in Blaikie's Origins of the Forty-Five in 1916. Felix O'Neil's account appears in Forbes, Lyon in Mourning, Vol. 1, pp. 102–8.
4. Letter from Flora MacDonald to Sir John MacPherson, 21 October 1789. NLS ms. 2618.

5. R. Forbes, Lyon in Mourning, Vol. 1, p. 106.
6. Ibid., Vol. 2, pp. 32 and 46.
7. Ibid., Vol. 1, p. 111.
8. Ibid., Vol. 1, p. 299.
9. W.B. Blaikie, Origins of the '45, p. 264.
10. R. Forbes, Lyon in Mourning, Vol. 2, p. 25.
11. Ibid., Vol. 2, p. 31.
12. Alexander MacGregor, Life of Flora MacDonald, p. 149.
13. R. Forbes, Lyon in Mourning. Vol. 2, p. 21.
14. Ibid., Vol. 2, p. 26.
15. Ibid.

11. DEAREST COUSINS

1. Louise to Charles, undated. RA SP 316/30.
2. R. Forbes, Lyon in Mourning, Vol. 1, p. 112.
3. Letter from Captain Knowler possibly to Commodore Smith, 30 November 1746. NLS 3736/511.
4. Sir B. Seton, Prisoners of the '45, Vol. 1, p. 213.
5. Ibid., Vol. 1, p. 89.
6. R.C. Jarvis, Collected Papers on the Jacobite Risings, Vol.1, pp. 272–8.
7. Ibid. Vol. 1, pp. 278–9.
8. Sir B. Seton, Prisoners of the '45, Vol. 1, p. 214.
9. Scottish Arts and Letters, Vol. II, No. 4, p. 397.
10. W.B. Blaikie's Collection of Jacobite and Whig Mss. Scottish Arts and Letters, Vol. II, No. 4, p. 395.
11. Lieutenant-Colonel Rich, commander of Barrel's Regiment at Culloden.
12. W.B. Blaikie, Mss. Scottish Art and Letters, Vol. II, No. 4, pp. 396–7.
13. Ibid.

14. David Ure, History of Rutherglen and East Kilbride, p. 166.
15. T.E. Niven, East Kilbride, the History of the Parish and Village, p. 122.
16. D. Ure, The History of Rutherglen and East Kilbride, p. 166.
17. H. Tayler, Jacobite Epilogue, pp. 153–60.
18. R. Forbes, The Lyon in Mourning, Vol. 1, pp. 54–5.
19. E.J.F. Barbier, Journal Historique et Anecdotique du Règne de Louis XV, Vol. IV, p. 153.
20. James to Charles, 17 April 1747. RA SP 283/7.
21. Cardinal Albani to Sir Horace Mann, 23 December 1747. RA SP 98/52.
22. RASP 279/171 I am grateful to F. McLynn for this reference.
23. James to Charles, 13 June 1747. RA SP 284/103. See also Chapter 1, p. 9.
24. Charles to James, 10 July 1747. RA SP 285/104.
25. A. Lang, Prince Charles Edward Stuart, p. 344.
26. L.L. Bongie, The Love of a Prince, p. 8.
27. A. Lang, Prince Charles Edward Stuart, p. 344.
28. Marquis d'Argenson, Journal et Mémoires, Vol. 5, p. 232.
29. The fictitious tale written by Charles. Translated by L.L Bongie, The Love of a Prince, pp. 9–10.
30. Paris police official Poussot to Nicolas-René Berryer, Lieutenant-General of Paris Police, 17 November 1747. Archives of the Bastille in Musée de l'Arsenal, Mss. 11658, feuille 90. I am indebted to L.L. Bongie for this source.
31. Draft Charles to James, 30 October 1747. RA SP 287/76.
32. James to Charles, 21 November 1747. RA SP 288/74.
33. The police reports are contained in Arsenal mss. 11658, feuilles 84–120.
34. Mémoire from Rulhière, 29 October 1747. Arsenal mss. 11658, feuille 87.
35. Ibid. Mémoire from Rulhière, 8 November 1747, Mss. 11658, ff. 93–4. Mémoire from Poussot, 8 November 1747. Arsenal mss, 11658, ff. 99–100. Mémoire from Poussot, 13 November 1747, ff. 106–7.
36. Mémoire from Poussot, 17 November 1747. Ibid., ff. 109–10.
37. Rulhière to Berryer, 11 November 1747 and Poussot to Berryer, 11 November 1747. Arsenal mss. 11658, ff. 102–3 and 106–7.
38. Mémoire from Poussot, 19 November 1747. Ibid. f. 112.
39. Rulhiére to Berryer, 17 November 1747. Arsenal mss. 11658, f. 110–11.
40. Berryer to Kelly, 21 November 1747. RA SP 288/73.
41. Draft letter, Berryer to Kelly, 21 November 1747. Arsenal mss. 11658, f. 117.
42. Louise to Charles, undated. RA SP 316/19.
43. Louise to Charles, undated. RA SP 316/24.

12. A DAGGER IN MY HEART

1. Louise to Charles, undated. RA SP 316/70.
2. L.L. Bongie, The Love of a Prince, p. 193.
3. Charles to Louise, dated only 'Sunday at 4 hours after midnight'. RA SP Box 2/98.

4. Louise to Charles, undated. RA SP 316/40.

5. Anne-Françoise de Carteret to Charles. RA SP Box 4, Folder 1/114. Professor Bongie has dated this as probably written on 27 January, four days after the confrontation. L.L. Bongie, The Love of a Prince, pp. 205–7 and p. 314, n.4.

6. Louise to Charles, 28 January 1748. RA SP 316/13.

7. Louise to Charles, 23 January 1748. RA SP 316/41.

8. Louise to Charles, 28 January 1748. RA SP316/13.

9. Louise to Charles, 28 January 1748. RA SP 316/13a.

10. Anne-Françoise de Carteret to Charles. RA SP Box 4, Folder 1/114.

11. L.L. Bongie, The Love of a Prince, p. 208.

12. Louise to Chrétien, her former footman, undated. RA SP 316/3.

13. Louise to Daniel O'Brien, 29 April 1747. RA SP 316/58.

14. L.L. Bongie, The Love of a Prince, p. 223.

15. Louise to Charles, undated. RA SP 316/90.

16. Louise to Daniel O'Brien, undated. RA SP 316/71.

17. Louise to Charles, undated. RA SP 316/83.

18. Ibid.

19. Louise to Charles, undated. RA SP 316/70.

20. Le Prince Edouard s'amuse à faire l'amour. Mme de Guéméné l'a presque pris à force; ils se sont brouillés par une scène ridicule. R. d'Argenson, Journal et Mémoires, Vol. 5, p. 232.

21. L.L. Bongie, The Love of a Prince, pp. 2 & 271.

22. Ibid., p. 285.

13. *CHERCHEZ LA FEMME*

1. Horace Walpole, Correspondence, ed. W.S. Lewis, Vol. 8, p. 106.

2. L.L. Bongie, The Love of a Prince, p. 219.

3. F. McLynn, Charles Edward Stuart, p. 346.

4. H. Walpole, Correspondence with Sir Horace Mann, Vol. 8, pp. 104–6.

5. Ibid., pp. 105–6.

6. F. McLynn, Charles Edward Stuart, p. 347.

7. Charles to Frederick the Great, 4 April 1748. RA SP 290/97.

8. Charles's instructions to Sir John Graeme, 4 April 1748. RA SP 290/98.

9. Frederick the Great to Baron von Mardefeld, 25 May 1748. Frederick the Great, Politische Correspondenz, Vol. VI, p. 125.

10. Correspondence from Graeme, various dates. RA SP 291/124, 75, 114, 153.

11. Charles to Graeme, 7 June 1748. RA SP 291/33.

12. Charles to Graeme, 10 July 1748. RA SP 292/13.

13. Charles to Graeme, 11 August 1748. RA SP 292/181.

14. d'Argenson, Journal et Mémoires, Vol. 5, p. 278.

15. Duc de Luynes, Mémoires du Duc de Luynes sur la Cour de Louis XV (1735–1758), Vol. 9, p. 258 & d'Argenson, Journal et Mémoires, Vol. 5, p. 288.

16. d'Argenson, Journal et Mémoires, 26 November 1748, Vol. 5, p. 289.

17. Andrew Lang, Pickle The Spy, pp. 44–6.
18. AEMD Angleterre, 82, f. 226–44.
19. Lettre de Mme de xxx a M. de xxx, December 1748. RA SP 295/104.
20. Ibid.
21. Lettre de M. Nugeon on imprisonment of Charles, December 1748. RA SP 296/7.
22. AEMD 80, f. 80.
23. d'Argenson, Journal et Mémoires, Vol. 5, pp. 318–19.
24. Ibid., p. 321.
25. E.C. Mossner, The Life of David Hume, pp. 218–19.
26. L.L. Bongie, The Love of a Prince, p. 268.
27. d'Argenson, Journal et Mémoires, Vol. 5, pp. 316–17.
28. Ibid., Vol. 5, p. 318.
29. Ibid., Vol. 5, p. 321.
30. Ibid., Vol. 5, pp. 320–1.
31. Ibid., Vol. 5, p. 320.
32. F. McLynn, Charles Edward Stuart, pp. 374–5.
33. A. Lang, Prince Charles Edward Stuart, p. 354.
34. Maurice Tourneux, Correspondence Littéraire, Philosophique et Critique par Grimm, Diderot, Rayal, Meister, etc., Vol. 12, p. 343.
35. Charles to Bulkley, 3 June 1749. RA SP 298/106.
36. British Library, Additional Manuscripts. 32.854. f.254.
37. E. de Heeckern, Correspondence de Benoit XIV avec Tencin. Vol. 2, p. 273.
38. Talmont to Charles, undated. RA SP Box 4/Folder1/56.
39. Charles to Talmont, undated. RA SP 316/100.
40. Anonymous (Talmont to Charles), undated. Reverse of RA SP 316/103.
41. Charles to Mme Beauregar (Talmont), undated, but probably April/May 1751. RA SP 319/141.
42. Madame de Talmont to Charles, March 1751. RA SP Box 4/Folder 1/83.
43. Madame de Talmont to Goring. RA SP Box 4/Folder 1/79a.
44. H. Walpole, Correspondence with Sir Horace Mann, Vol. 8, pp. 57–9.

14. DISCARDED BY 'MRS CLEMI'

1. Clementine to Charles, 22 July 1760. Original in the West Highland Museum, Fort William.
2. Lord Elcho quoted in Charles Petrie, The Jacobite Movement p. 419.
3. RA SP 311/32.
4. Edith Cuthell, The Scottish Friend of Frederick the Great; The Last Earl Marischal, Vol. 1, p. 241.
5. F. McLynn, Charles Edward Stuart, p. 415.
6. The document, in Latin on parchment, can be seen in the Bodleian Library, Oxford.
7. C.L. Berry, The Young Pretender's Mistress, p. 39.
8. J. Douglas (Charles) to O'Sullivan, end May 1752. RA SP Box 1/345.
9. O'Sullivan to Charles, 29 May 1752. RA SP 332/51.
10. O'Sullivan to Clementine Walkinshaw, 31 May 1752. RA SP 332/65.
11. O'Sullivan to Charles, 3 June 1752. RA SP Box 1/346.
12. C.S. Terry, Life of Prince Charles Stuart the Young Pretender, p. 157.
13. Ibid.

14. Goring to Charles, 7/10 June 1752. RA SP Box 1/347.

15. Lord Elcho and Oliver MacAllester both suggested that there was a liaison between Clementine and O'Sullivan. Frank McLynn has done so recently in his biography of Charles Edward and has probably come as near to the truth of this puzzle as we are likely to get, failing the emergence of some dramatic new piece of evidence.

16. Alexander Murray to Charles, 29 September 1758. Quoted in Charles Petrie, The Jacobite Movement, p. 420.

17. H. Tayler, Prince Charlie's Daughter, p. 28. See also Susan Buchan, Lady Tweedsmuir, Funeral March of a Marionette – Charlotte of Albany, p. 17.

18. Andrew Lang, Pickle the Spy, p. 213.

19. C.L. Berry, The Young Pretender's Mistress, p. 48.

20. Compton Mackenzie, Prince Charles, p. 134.

21. Charles to J. Waters, 12 November 1753. RA SP 344/161.

22. Ibid.

23. The Castaways of Disappointment Island, a True Story abridged and adapted from the book by the Rev. H. Escott-Inman. For ages 10 to 12 years. Published by Whitcombe & Tombs. No date. pp. 82–3. I am grateful to Mrs Frances Robertson of Melbourne, Australia, for this reference.

24. C.L. Berry, The Young Pretender's Mistress, pp. 52–3.

25. A. Lang, Pickle the Spy, p. 229.

26. C.S. Terry, Life of Prince Charles Stuart The Young Pretender, p. 289.

27. O'Sullivan to Clementine, 31 May 1752. RA SP 332/65.

28. Oliver MacAllester, A Series of Letters Discovering the Scheme projected by France, in MDCCLIX, for and Intended Invasion upon England, etc. To which are prefixed the Secret Adventures of the Young Pretender, Vol 2, p. 39.

29. F. McLynn, Charles Edward Stuart, p. 424.

30. Elcho, Journal, p. 211.

31. C.L. Berry, The Young Pretender's Mistress, p. 62.

32. Waters to Charles, 11 September 1754. RA SP Box 1/388.

33. Waters to Edgar, 24 Setember 1755. RA SP 359/141.

34. A. & H. Tayler, The Stuart Papers at Windsor, p. 232.

35. James to Charles, n.d. RA SP 393/120.

36. F. McLynn, Charles Edward Stuart, p. 455.

37. Clementine: memoir to Louis XV, 1774. AN. K1303,105.

38. Clementine to Charles, 22 July 1760. Original in West Highland Museum, Fort William.

39. Charles to Abbé Gordon, 26 July 1760. RA SP 404/144.

40. Abbé Gordon to Charles, 26 July 1760. RA SP 402/143.

41. C.L. Berry, The Young Pretender's Mistress, p. 71.

42. M. le Président Thiebault de Bouillon to Maréchal de Belle-Isle, 3 July 1760. RA SP 402/153.

43. John Stewart to Charles, 31 July 1760. RA SP 402/153.

44. H. Tayler, Prince Charlie's Daughter, p. 16.

45. RA SP 403/35,52,157.

15. A WIFE OR A MISTRESS?

1. Historical Manuscripts Commission Xth report, VII, App. X. H.M. Vaughan, The Last of the Royal Stuarts, p. 170.

2. Charlotte presented a number of mémoires to Kings Louis XV and XVI between 1772 and 1774 around the time of Charles's marriage. These are in the French Foreign Office Archives (AEMD K1303) This reference was included in a mémoire dated 1774. I am indebted to C.L. Berry for this reference.

3. C.L. Berry, The Young Pretender's Mistress, p. 103.

4. F.J.A. Skeet, The Life and Letters of HRH Charlotte Stuart Duchess of Albany, p. 36.

5. Historic Manuscripts Commission Xth report, VII, App. X, H.M. Vaughan. See also Life of Thomas Coutts by E.H. Coleridge, Vol. 2, p. 50 and Memoirs of Sir Robert Strange (ed. James Dennison).

6. Louis de St Simon, Histoire des Hommes Illustre. Quoted F.J.A. Skeet, Life and Letters of HRH, Charlotte Stuart Duchess of Albany, p. 36.

7. Lumisden to Clementine, 5 January 1768. Quoted in F.J.A. Skeet, Life and Letters of HRH. Charlotte Stuart Duchess of Albany, p. 36.

8. F.J.A. Skeet, Life and Letters of HRH Charlotte Stuart Duchess of Albany, p. 37.

9. Ibid., pp. 153–4.

10. AEMD K1303,105. dated 'approximately 1766', but it must have been written after 1772 since it refers to Charles's marriage to Louise of Stolberg.

11. Louis de Saint Simon, Oeuvres Complètes, p. 154.

12. Charlotte Stuart's mémoire to the French King, dated 7 September 1774. AEMD, Angleterre, 1750–1802, K1303, 88.

13. I am greatly indebted to John Horsburgh for information on irregular marriage in Scotland.

14. H. Tayler, Prince Charlie's Daughter, p. 18.

15. Charles to Abbé Gordon, 26 July 1760. RA SP 402/144.

16. AEMD, K1303, 234.

17. Clementine to Charlotte, 23 November 1784. RA SP 508/11.

18. C. Leo Berry, The Young Pretender's Mistress. pp. 196–7.

19. Roehenstart Papers. Bodleian Library. Quoted in G. Sherburn, A Late Stuart Pretender, p. 6.

16. TRUMPING THE QUEEN OF HEARTS

1. H. Walpole, Correspondence with Sir Horace Mann, Vol. 25, p. 106.

2. Sir F. Maclean, Bonnie Prince Charlie, p. 348.

3. Lady Anne Miller, Letters from Italy, Vol. 2, p. 198.

4. H. Walpole, Correspondence with Sir Horace Mann, Vol. 25, p. 106.

5. H. Douglas, Charles Edward Stuart, p. 249.

6. Fitzjames to Charles. RA SP 458/156.

7. R. Forbes, Lyon in Mourning, Vol. 3, pp. 262–3.

8. Ibid., p. 263.

9. Charles to Henry, 17 April 1772. Quoted in Andrew Lang, Prince Charles Edward, p. 415.

10. Sir F. Maclean, Bonnie Prince Charlie, p. 353.
11. RA SP 459/67.
12. A. Theiner, Geschichte des Pontificats Clemens XIV. Vol. 2, p. 161. I am indebted to F. McLynn for this reference.
13. R. Forbes, Lyon in Mourning, Vol. 3. p. 265.
14. Ibid.
15. Ibid., p. 268.
16. Ibid.
17. Denunciation of Bernardo Rotalo by Giorgio Ghalt, undated. RA SP 470/32.
18. Mann to Seymour Conway, 18 August 1774. Quoted in James Lees-Milne, The Last Stuarts, p. 108.
19. H. Walpole, Correspondence with Sir Horace Mann, Vol. 24, p. 94.
20. Charles-Victor Bonstetten, Souvenirs, pp. 61–9.
21. Ibid.
22. J. Lees-Milne, The Last Stuarts, p. 109.
23. Ibid., p. 110.
24. British Museum, Egerton Mss. 2635, f. 232. Quoted in Brian Fothergill, Sir William Hamilton; Envoy Extraordinary, p. 124.
25. J. Lees-Milne, gives a vivid description of the building in The Last Stuarts, pp. 111–12.
26. B. Fothergill, Sir William Hamilton; Envoy Extraordinary, p. 124.
27. Dr Moore to Duchess of Argyll, 1 June 1776. Intimate Society Letters of the Eighteenth Century, ed. 8th Duke of Argyll.
28. Anonymous letter to Charles,16 May 1777. RA SP 490/57. The letter is addressed to him as Count of Albany and not as king.
29. J. Lees-Milne, commenting on Henry's self-deception in The Last Stuarts, p. 125.
30. Brian Fothergill, The Cardinal King, p. 149.
31. Charles to G. Cantini, 1 January 1788. RA SP 502/149.
32. H. Walpole, Correspondence with Sir Horace Mann, Vol. 25, p. 396.
33. A.C. Ewald, Life of Prince Charles Stuart, Vol. 2, p. 306.

17. THE WILFUL LASS OF ALBANY

1. H. Walpole, Correspondence with Sir Horace Mann, Vol. 25, p. 535.
2. H. Douglas, Charles Edward Stuart, p. 264.
3. C.L. Berry, The Young Pretender's Mistress, p. 83.
4. Charlotte to Charles, 15 August 1764. Quoted in H. Tayler, Prince Charlie's Daughter, pp. 30–1.
5. H. Tayler, Prince Charlie's Daughter, p. 31.
6. H. Tayler, Prince Charlie's Daughter, p. 31. J.J.A. Skeet, Life of HRH Charlotte Stuart Duchess of Albany, pp. 31–2.
7. Clementine to Charles, 18 December 1768. RA SP 446/63.
8. H. Tayler, Prince Charlie's Daughter, p. 33.
9. Clementine to Charles and Pouponne (Charlotte) to Charles, 8 October 1769. RA SP 448/51/52.
10. Charlotte to Charles, 8 October 1769. RA SP 458/52.
11. Lord Caryll to Abbé Gordon, 29 June 1772. RA SP 461/57.
12. C.L. Berry, The Young Pretender's Mistress, p. 110.

13. RA SP 467/73,106,118 & 468/7,71. Historical Manuscripts Commission 10, vi, p. 234.
14. Charlotte to Charles, 24 July 1773. RA SP 468/70.
15. Abbé Gordon to Caryll, 27 February 1775. RA SP 480/48.
16. H. Tayler, Prince Charlie's Daughter, p. 42.
17. F. Doran, Mann and Manners at the Court of Florence, p. 405. H. Walpole, Correspondence with Sir Horace Mann, Vol. 25, p. 513.
18. Charlotte to Charles, 16 August 1784. Letter in West Highland Museum, Fort William.
19. F. Doran, Mann and Manners at the Court of Florence, p. 405. H. Walpole, Correspondence with Sir Horace Mann, Vol. 25, p. 522.
20. F. McLynn, Charles Edward Stuart, p. 544.
21. Declaration of 11 March 1785. Brayne Mss. Historical Manuscripts Commission, Vol. X, f. 163. Translation from C.L. Berry, The Young Pretender's Daughter, p. 147.
22. Robert Burns, The Bonnie Lass of Albanie, written to mark the conferring of the title Duchess of Albany on Charlotte, 1787. Text from The Complete Works of Robert Burns, ed. James A. Mackay, p. 302.
23. Charlotte to Clementine, 22 August 1785. quoted in H. Tayler, Prince Charlie's Daughter, p. 76.
24. The Gentleman's Magazine, December 1797.
25. British Museum, Additional Mss. 34,634, ff. 79–81. I am grateful to F. McLynn for this reference.
26. Charlotte to Clementine, 11 March 1785. C.L. Berry, The Young Pretender's Mistress, p. 149.
27. Henrietta Tayler gives a fascinating resumé of Charlotte's correspondence with her mother in Prince Charlie's Daughter, pp. 55–79.
28. J. Lees-Milne, The Last Stuarts, p. 134.
29. A. Lang, Prince Charles Edward Stuart, p. 448.
30. A.C. Ewald, Life and Times of Prince Charles Edward Stuart, pp. 317–18.
31. The Gentleman's Magazine, December 1797.
32. H. Tayler, Prince Charlie's Daughter, p. 86.
33. Decline of the Last Stuarts, Roxburghe Club, p. 93.
34. H. Tayler, Prince Charlie's Daughter, p. 113.

18. LOVE LOST AND LOVE FOUND

1. L.L. Bongie, The Love of a Prince, p. 271.
2. Marquise du Deffand, Lettres à Horace Walpole, Vol. 1, pp. 46–7. I am grateful to L.L. Bongie for this reference.
3. Letter dated 1 October 1831. Published in The Edinburgh Literary Journal; or, Weekly Register of Criticism and Belles Lettres, n.d., p. 227.
4. The full story of Flora's experiences in America are told in Hugh Douglas, Flora MacDonald: The Most Loyal Rebel, Chapters 9–15.
5. Samuel Johnson, Works (12 vols, 1823), Vol. 9, pp. 391–2.
6. H. Douglas, Charles Edward Stuart, p. 270.

7. Compton Mackenzie, Prince Charlie and his Ladies, p. 261.

8. The story of the Sobieski Stuarts can be found in The Truth about the Sobieski Stuarts by Miss Mairi A. MacDonald. Transactions of the Gaelic Society of Inverness, Vol. XLV, 1967–69, pp. 232–56.

9. Margaret Forster, The Rash Adventurer, p. 330.

BIBLIOGRAPHY

Andrieux, Maurice, *Daily Life in Papal Rome in the Eighteenth Century*. London, 1968.

Argenson, René, Marquis d', *Journal et Mémoires*. ed. E.J.B. Rathery, 9 vols. Paris, 1859–67.

Argyll, 8th Duke of (ed.), *Intimate Society Letters of the Eighteenth Century*.

Ashley, Maurice, *The Stuarts in Love*. London, 1963.

Barbier, E.J.F., *Chronique de la Régence et du Règne de Louis XV*, 8 vols. Paris, 1847.

Berry, C. Leo, *The Young Pretender's Mistress*. Edinburgh, 1977.

Berwick, Duke of, *Mémoires du Maréchal de Berwick, écrit par lui-même*. Paris, 1778.

Blaikie, Walter Biggar, *Edinburgh at the Time of the Occupation of Prince Charles*. Edinburgh, 1909.

—— *Itinerary of Prince Charles Edward Stuart from his Landing in Scotland, July 1745 to his Departure in September 1746*. Edinburgh, 1897.

—— *Origins of the Forty-Five and Other Papers Relating to the Rising*. Scottish Historical Society, 1916.

Bongie, Laurence L., *The Love of a Prince, Bonnie Prince Charlie in France, 1744–48*. Vancouver, 1986.

Bonstetten, Charles-Victor, *Souvenirs*. Paris, 1832.

Buchan, Susan, Lady Tweedsmuir, *Funeral March of a Marionette – Charlotte of Albany*. London, 1935.

Burton, John Hill and Laing, David (eds), *Jacobite Correspondence of the Atholl Family 1745–6*. Edinburgh, 1840.

Cameron, Archibald, *The Life of Dr Archibald Cameron, brother to Donald Cameron of Lochiel to which is added the Life of Jenny Cameron*. London, 1753.

BIBLIOGRAPHY

Cameron, Jenny, *A Brief Account of the life of Miss Jenny Cameron, the reputed mistress of the Pretender's eldest son*. London, 1746.

Carlyle, Alexander of Inveresk, *Autobiography*. Edinburgh, 1860.

Chambers, Robert, *History of the Rebellion in 1745, 1746, etc.* Edinburgh, 1827.

Coyer, Abbé, *Histoire de Jean Sobieski, Roi de Pologne*. Warsaw and Paris, 1761.

Cross, Tom, *A Lakeland Princess*. Penrith, 1945.

Cuthell, Edith, *The Scottish Friend of Frederick the Great; The last Earl Marischal*, 2 vols. 1915.

Daiches, David, *Charles Edward Stuart,The Life and Times of Bonnie Prince Charlie*. London, 1973.

Davies, Norman, *God's Playground*, 2 vols. Oxford, 1981.

Donaldson, Gordon, *Scottish Kings*. London, 1977.

Doran, F., *Mann and Manners at the Court of Florence 1740–1786*, 2 vols. London, 1876.

Douglas, Hugh, *Charles Edward Stuart, the man, the King, the Legend*. London, 1975.

—— *Flora MacDonald, the Most Loyal Rebel*. Stroud, 1993.

Duke, Winifred, *The Rash Adventurer*. London, 1952.

Dumont-Wilden, L., *The Wandering Prince*. London, 1934.

Dupaty, Charles, *Lettres sur l'Italie en 1785*. Paris, 1796.

Dutens, Louis, *Mémoires d'un Voyageur qui se Repose*. Paris, 1806.

Dyer, Florence E., 'The Highlanders in Edinburgh'. In *SMT Magazine*, August 1937.

Edinburgh Evening Courant.

Elcho, David, Lord, 'Diary'. In Tayler, Henrietta, *Jacobite Miscellany*. Roxburghe Club, Oxford, 1946.

—— *A Short Account of the Affairs of Scotland in the Years 1744, 1745, and 1746*. Edinburgh, 1907.

Erickson, Carolly, *Bonnie Prince Charlie*. London, 1993.

Ewald, A.C., *Life and Times of Prince Charles Stuart*, 2 vols. London, 1875.

Fasso, Luigi (ed.), *Vita de Vittorio Alfieri da Asti, scritta da eso*, 2 vols. Asti, 1951.

Forbes, Duncan of Culloden, *Culloden Papers: Comprising an extensive and interesting correspondence for the years 1625 to 1748, including numerous letters from the unfortunate Lord Lovat and other distinguished persons of the time; with occasional State Papers.* London, 1815.

Forbes, Revd Robert, *The Lyon in Mourning*, 3 vols, ed. Henry Paton. Scottish Historical Society, Edinburgh, 1895–6.

Forster, Margaret, *The Rash Adventurer*. London, 1973.

Fothergill, Brian, *The Cardinal King*. London, 1958.

—— *Sir William Hamilton; Envoy Extraordinary*. London, 1969.

Fraser, Antonia, *Mary, Queen of Scots*. London, 1969.

Frederick the Great, *Politische Correspondenz*, 45 vols. Berlin, 1879–82.

Gilbert, Sir John T., *Narratives of the Detention, Liberation and Marriage of Maria Clementina Sobieska styled Queen of Great Britain & Ireland by Sir Charles Wogan and others*. Dublin, 1894.

Haile, Martin, *James Francis Edward, the Old Chevalier*. London, 1907.

Henderson, Andrew, *History of the Rebellion in 1745 and 1746*. London, 1748.

Herking, Marie-Louise, *Charles-Victor Bonstetten 1745–1832. Sa Vie, Ses Oeuvres*. Lausanne, 1921.

Home, John, *History of the Rebellion in Scotland*. Edinburgh, 1822.

James VI & I, *Basilikon Doron, 1599*. Scottish Text Society, 1944.

Jarvis, Rupert C., *Collected Papers on the Jacobite Risings*, 2 vols. Manchester, 1971.

Kelly, B.W., *Life of Cardinal York*. London, 1899.

Klose, C.L., *Memoirs of Prince Charles Stuart*. London, 1845.

Kybett, Susan Maclean, *Bonnie Prince Charlie*. London, 1988.

Lang, Andrew, *Prince Charles Edward Stuart, The Young Chevalier*. London, 1903.

—— *Pickle the Spy*. London, 1897.

Lee, Maurice, *John Maitland of Thirlestane and the Foundations of the Stewart Despotism in Scotland*. Princeton, 1959.

Lee, Vernon, *The Countess of Albany*. London, 1909.

Lees-Milne, James, *The Last Stuarts*. London, 1983.

Lewis, Lesley, *Connoisseurs and Secret Agents in 18th-Century Rome*. London, 1961.

Linklater, Eric, *The Royal House of Scotland*. London, 1970.

Lockhart of Carnwath, George, *Memoirs Concerning the Affairs of Scotland*. London, 1817.

Luynes, Duc de, *Mémoires du Duc de Luynes sur la Cour de Louis XV (1735–1758)*, vols. IV–VII. Paris, 1861.

MacAllester, Oliver, *A Series of Letters Discovering the Scheme projected by France, in MDCCLIX, for and Intended Invasion upon England, etc. To which are prefixed the Secret Adventures of the Young Pretender*, 2 vols. London, 1767.

Macdonald, F., *'Colonel Anne' Lady Anne MacKintosh 1723–1784*. Scotland's Cultural Heritage, Edinburgh, 1987.

Mackenzie, Compton, *Prince Charlie and His Ladies*. London, 1934.

—— *Prince Charlie*. London, 1938.

Maclean, Fitzroy, *Bonnie Prince Charlie*. London, 1988.

McLynn, Frank, *Charles Edward Stuart, A Tragedy in Many Acts*. London, 1988.

—— *The Jacobites*. London, 1985.

Mahon, Lord (ed.), *Decline of the Last Stuarts* (Sir Horace Mann's reports from Florence). London, 1845.

Mahon, R.H., *Mary, Queen of Scots*. Cambridge, 1924.

Major, John, *History of Greater Britain, 1512*. Scottish History Society, vol. 10. Edinburgh, 1887.

Marchant, John, *History of the Rebellion*. London, 1746.

Marshall, Rosalind K., *Bonnie Prince Charlie*. Edinburgh, 1988.

Maxwell, James, of Kirkconnel, *Narrative of Charles Prince of Wales's Visit to Scotland in the Year 1745*. Maitland Club, Edinburgh, 1841.

Miller, Lady Anne, *Letters from Italy*, 3 vols. London, 1776.

Miller, Peggy, *A Wife for the Pretender*. London, 1965.

—— *James*. London, 1971.

Mitford, Nancy, *Madame de Pompadour*. London, 1954.

Morfill, W.R., *Poland*. London, 1893.

Motteville, Madame de, *Mémoires*. London, 1902.

Murray, John, of Broughton, *Genuine Mewmors of John Murray of Broughton*. London, 1747.

Niven, T.E., *East Kilbride, the History of the Parish and Village*. Glasgow, 1965.

Nobili-Vitelleschi, Marchesa, *A Court in Exile. Charles Edward Stuart and the Romance of the Countess d'Albanie*, 2 vols. London, 1903.

Norie, W. Drummond, *Life and Adventures of Prince Charles Edward Stuart*, 3 vols. London, 1903.

Oman, Carola, *Prince Charles Edward*. London, 1935.

Pellegrini, Carlo, *La Contessa d'Albany e il Salotto del Lungarno*. Naples, 1951.

Petrie, Sir Charles, *The Jacobite Movement*. London, 1958.

Pichot, Joseph, *Histoire de Charles Edouard*. Paris, 1833.

de Polnay, Peter, *Death of a Legend*. London, 1952.

Pringle, Magdalen, 'Two Letters to her Sister, Isabella'. In H. Teyler, *A Jacobite Miscellany*. Roxburghe Club, Oxford, 1946.

Ray, James, *Complete History of the Rebellion*. York, 1746.

Saint-Simon, Louis, duc de, *Oeuvres Complètes*. Strasbourg, 1791.

de Salvandy, N.A., *Histoire du Roi Jean Sobieski et du Royaums de Pologne*, 4 vols. Paris, 1863.

The Scotsman, Edinburgh, 9 April 1988. Article, 'Charlie the Feeble'.

Scott, Otto J., *James I*. New York, 1976.

Seton, Sir Bruce Gordon, *Prisoners of the '45*, 3 vols. Edinburgh, 1928.

—— 'Orderly Book of Lord Ogilvy's Regiment'. In *Journal of the Society of Army Historical Research*, Vol. 2, 1923.

Seton, W.W., *Relations of Henry, Cardinal York with the British Government*. London, 1920.

Shield, A., *Henry Stuart, Cardinal of York*. London, 1907.

Skeet, F.J.A., *Life and Letters of HRH Charlotte Stuart, Duchess of Albany*. London, 1932.

SMT Magazine, August 1936 & August 1945.

Spence, Lewis, *Plumes of Time*. London, 1926.

Strange, Robert and Lumisden, Andrew, *Memoirs*, ed. J. Dennistoun, 2 vols. London, 1855.

Stuart, Charles Edward, *Full Collection of All the Proclamations and Orders published by Authority of Charles, Prince of Wales Since His Arrival in Edinburgh, 17th September, 1745*.

—— *Copy of a Letter from a French Lady in Paris giving Particular account of ther manner in which Prince Edward was arrested, 1749*.

Stuart Papers in the Royal Archives, Windsor Castle. 541 bound volumes of letters and manuscript material acquired from Cardinal York and his estate by the Prince Regent in 1804, 1805 and 1816.

Stuarts, *Decline of the Last Stuarts. Extracts from the Despatches of British Envoys to the Secretary of State*. Roxburghe Club, London, 1843.

Tayler, Alistair and Henrietta, *The Stuart Papers at Windsor*. London, 1939.

Tayler, Henrietta, *A Jacobite Miscellany*. Roxburghe Club, Oxford, 1946.

—— Henrietta, *Jacobite Epilogue*. London, 1941.

—— Henrietta, *Prince Charlie's Daughter, being the Life and Letters of Charlotte of Albany*. London, 1950.

Terry, C.S., *Life of Prince Charles Stuart the Young Pretender*. London, 1903.

Theiner, A., *Geschichte des Pontificats Clemens XIV*, 2 vols. Leipzig, 1853.

Thomson, Mrs, *Memoirs of the Jacobites*. London, 1846.

Threiplands of Fingask, *The Threiplands of Fingask*. Edinburgh, 1880.

Tourneux, Maurice, *Correspondence Littéraire, Philosophique et Critique par Grimm, Diderot, Rayal, Meister, etc.*, 16 vols. Paris, 1880.

Ure, David, *The History of Rutherglen and East Kilbride*. Glasgow, 1793.

Vaughan, H.M., *The Last Stuart Queen*. London, 1910.

—— *The Last of the Royal Stuarts*. London, 1906.

Waliszewski, K., *Marysienka, Marie de las Grange d'Arquien, Queen of Poland, and wife of Sobieski*. London, 1898.

Walpole, Horace, *Correspondence*, ed. W.S. Lewis, 45 vols. London, 1960.

White, Jon Manchip, *Marshal of France: The Life and Times of Maurice de Saxe*. London, 1962.

Wilkinson, Clennell, *Bonnie Prince Charlie*. London, 1932.

Woodhouselee Manuscript, *A Narrative of Events in Edinburgh and District During the Jacobite Occupation, September to November, 1745*. Edinburgh, 1907.

INDEX

INDEX